THE WRITERS' WAR

About the Author

Felicity Trotman was born in Belfast, moving to Wiltshire as a child. Having studied graphic design, and taken a History degree, she worked in publishing. She was a fiction editor at Puffin and at Macmillan Children's Books. Eventually turning freelance, she added history and military history to her children's speciality – though she admits that she prefers firing guns to writing about them. She is a churchwarden and school governor, and has spent many happy years as a member of the English Civil War Society.

THE WRITERS' WAR

The Great War in the Words of Great Writers Who Experienced It

EDITED BY FELICITY TROTMAN

AMBERLEY

ACKNOWLEDGEMENTS

The compiler and publisher would like to thank the following for permission to include copyright material: 'My First English Victim' from *The Red Baron* by Manfred von Richthofen, published by Pen & Sword Books.

First published 2014
This edition published 2016

Amberley Publishing
The Hill, Stroud
Gloucestershire, GL5 4EP

www.amberley-books.com

British Library Cataloguing in Publication Data.
A catalogue record for this book is available from the British Library.

ISBN 978-1-4456-5535-2 (paperback)
ISBN 978-1-4456-3825-6 (e-book)

Typesetting and Origination by Amberley Publishing.
Printed in the UK.

CONTENTS

Contents

Before 1914

The Theory
From *The Riddle of the Sands*, Erskine Childers

Davies leaned back and gave a deep sigh, as though he still felt the relief from some tension. I did the same, and felt the same relief. The chart, freed from the pressure of our fingers, rolled up with a flip, as though to say, 'What do you think of that?' I have straightened out his sentences a little, for in the excitement of his story they had grown more and more jerky and elliptical.

'What about Dollmann?' I asked.

'Of course,' said Davies, 'what about him? I didn't get at much that night. It was all so sudden. The only thing I could have sworn to from the first was that he had purposely left me in the lurch that day. I pieced out the rest in the next few days, which I'll just finish with as shortly as I can. Bartels came aboard next morning, and though it was blowing hard still we managed to shift the *Dulcibella* to a place where she dried safely at the mid-day low water, and we could get at her rudder. The lower screw-plate on the stern post had wrenched out, and we botched it up roughly as a makeshift. There were other little breakages, but nothing to matter, and the loss of the jib was nothing, as I had two spare ones. The dinghy was past repair just then, and I lashed it on deck.

'It turned out that Bartels was carrying apples from Bremen to Kappeln (in this fiord), and had run into that channel in the sands for shelter from the weather. Today he was bound for the Eider River, whence, as I told you, you can get through (by river and canal) into the Baltic. Of course the Elbe route, by the new Kaiser Wilhelm Ship Canal, is the shortest. The Eider route is the old one, but he hoped to get rid of some of his apples at Tönning, the town at its mouth. Both routes touch the Baltic at Kiel. As you know, I had been running for the Elbe, but yesterday's muck-up put me off, and I changed my mind – I'll tell you why presently – and decided to sail to the Eider along with the *Johannes* and get through that way. It cleared from the east next day, and I raced him there, winning hands down, left him at Tönning, and in three days was in the Baltic. It was just a week after I ran ashore that I wired to you. You see, I had come to the conclusion that *that chap was a spy*.

In the end it came out quite quietly and suddenly, and left me in profound amazement. 'I wired to you – that chap was a spy.' It was the close association of these two ideas that hit me hardest at the moment. For a second I was back in the dreary splendour of the London club-room, spelling out that crabbed scrawl from Davies, and fastidiously criticizing its proposal in the light of a holiday. Holiday! What was to be its issue? Chilling and opaque as the fog that filtered through the skylight there flooded my imagination a mist of doubt and fear.

'A spy!' I repeated blankly. 'What do you mean? Why did you wire to me? A spy of what – of whom?'

'I'll tell you how I worked it out,' said Davies. 'I don't think "spy" is the right word; but I mean something pretty bad.

'He purposely put me ashore. I don't think I'm suspicious by nature, but I know something about boats and the sea. I know he could have kept close to me if he had chosen, and I saw the whole place at low water when we left those sands on the second day. Look at the chart again. Here's the Hohenhörn bank that I showed you as blocking the road. It's in two pieces – first the west and then the east. You see the Telte channel dividing into two branches and curving round it. Both branches are broad and deep, as channels go in those waters. Now, in sailing in I was nowhere near either of them. When I last saw Dollmann he must have been steering straight for the bank itself, at a point somewhere *here*, quite a mile from the northern arm of the channel, and two from the southern. I followed by compass, as you know, and found nothing but breakers ahead. How did I get through? That's where the luck came in. I spoke of only two channels, that is, *round* the bank – one to the north, the other to the south. But look closely and you'll see that right through the centre of the West Hohenhörn runs another, a very narrow and winding one, so small that I hadn't even noticed it the night before, when I was going over the chart. That was the one I stumbled into in that tailor's fashion, as I was groping along the edge of the surf in a desperate effort to gain time. I bolted down it blindly, came out into this strip of open water, crossed that aimlessly, and brought up on the edge of the *East* Hohenhörn, *here*. It was more than I deserved. I can see now that it was a hundred to one in favour of my striking on a bad place outside, where I should have gone to pieces in three minutes.'

'And how did Dollmann go?' I asked.

'It's as clear as possible,' Davies answered. 'He doubled back into the northern channel when he had misled me enough. Do you remember my saying that when I last saw him I *thought* he had luffed and showed his broadside? I had another bit of luck in that. He was luffing towards the north – so it struck me through the blur – and when I in my turn came up to the bank, and had to turn one way or the other to avoid it, I think I should naturally have turned north too, as he had done. In that case I should have been done for, for I should have had a mile of the bank to skirt before reaching the North Channel, and should have driven ashore long before I got there. But as a matter of fact I turned south.'

'Why?'

'Couldn't help it. I was running on the starboard tack – boom over to port; to turn north would have meant a jibe, and as things were I couldn't risk one. It was blowing like fits; if anything had carried away I should have been on shore in a jiffy. I scarcely thought about it at all, but put the helm down and turned her south. Though I knew nothing about it, that little central channel was now on my port hand, distant about two cables. The whole thing was luck from beginning to end.'

Helped by pluck, I thought to myself, as I tried with my landsman's fancy to conjure up that perilous scene. As to the truth of the affair, the chart and Davies's version were easy enough to follow, but I felt only half convinced. The 'spy', as Davies strangely called his pilot, might have honestly mistaken the course himself, outstripped his convoy inadvertently, and escaped disaster as narrowly as she did. I suggested this on the spur of the moment, but Davies was impatient.

'Wait till you hear the whole thing,' he said. 'I must go back to when I first met him. I told you that on that first evening he began by being as rude as a bear and as cold as stone, and then became suddenly friendly. I can see now that in the talk that followed he was pumping me hard. It was an easy game to play, for I hadn't seen a gentleman since Morrison left me, I was tremendously keen about my voyage, and I thought the chap was a good sportsman, even if he was a bit dark about the ducks. I talked quite freely – at least, as freely as I could with my bad German – about my last fortnight's sailing; how I had been smelling out all the channels in and out of the islands, how interested I had been in the whole business, puzzling out the effect of the winds on the tides, the set of the currents, and so on. I talked about my difficulties, too; the changes in the buoys, the prehistoric rottenness of the English charts. He drew me out as much as he could, and in the light of what followed I can see the point of scores of his questions.

'The next day and the next I saw a good deal of him, and the same thing went on. And then there were my plans for the future. My idea was, as I told you, to go on exploring the German coast just as I had the Dutch. His idea – Heavens, how plainly I see it now! – was to choke me off, get me to clear out altogether from that part of the coast. That was why he said there were no ducks. That was why he cracked up the Baltic as a cruising-ground and shooting-ground. And that was why he broached and stuck to that plan of sailing in company direct to the Elbe. It was to *see* me clear.

'He improved on that.'

'Yes, but after that, it's guess-work. I mean that I can't tell when he first decided to go one better and drown me. He couldn't count for certain on bad weather, though he held my nose to it when it came. But, granted that he wanted to get rid of me altogether, he got a magnificent chance on that trip to the Elbe lightship. I expect it struck him suddenly, and he acted on the impulse. Left to myself I was all right; but the short cut was a grand idea of his. Everything was in its favour – wind, sea, sand, tide. He thinks I'm dead.'

'But the crew?' I said; 'what about the crew?'

'That's another thing. When he first hove to, waiting for me, of course they were on deck (two of them, I think) hauling at sheets. But by the time I had drawn tip level the *Medusa* had worn round again on her course, and no one was on deck but Dollmann at the wheel. No one overheard what he said.'

'Wouldn't they have *seen* you again?'

'Very likely not; the weather was very thick, and the *Dulce* is very small.'

The incongruity of the whole business was striking me. Why should anyone want to kill Davies, and why should Davies, the soul of modesty and simplicity, imagine that anyone wanted to kill him? He must have cogent reasons, for he was the last man to give way to a morbid fancy.

'Go on,' I said. 'What was his motive? A German finds an Englishman exploring a bit of German coast, determines to stop him, and even to get rid of him. It looks so far as if you were thought to be the spy.'

Davies winced. '*But he's not a German*,' he said, hotly. 'He's an Englishman.'

'An Englishman?'

'Yes, I'm sure of it. Not that I've much to go on. He professed to know very little English, and never spoke it, except a word or two now and then to help me out of a sentence; and as to his German, he seemed to me to speak it like a native; but, of course, I'm no judge.' Davies sighed. 'That's where I wanted someone like you. You would have spotted him at once, if he wasn't German. I go more by a – what do you call it? – a –'

'General impression,' I suggested.

'Yes, that's what I mean. It was something in his looks and manner; you know how different we are from foreigners. And it wasn't only himself, it was the way he talked – I mean about cruising and the sea, especially. It's true he let me do most of the talking; but, all the same – how can I explain it? I felt we understood one another, in a way that two foreigners wouldn't.'

'He pretended to think me a bit crazy for coming so far in a small boat, but I could swear he knew as much about the game as I did; for lots of little questions he asked had the right ring in them. Mind you, all this is an afterthought. I should never have bothered about it – I'm not cut out for a Sherlock Holmes – if it hadn't been for what followed.'

'It's rather vague,' I said. 'Have you no more definite reason for thinking him English?'

'There were one or two things rather more definite,' said Davies, slowly. 'You know when he hove to and hailed me, proposing the short cut, I told you roughly what he said. I forget the exact words, but "abschneiden" came in – "durch Watten" and "abschneiden" (they call the banks "watts", you know); they were simple words, and he shouted them loud, so as to carry through the wind. I understood what he meant, but, as I told you, I hesitated before consenting. I suppose he thought I didn't understand, for just as he was drawing ahead again he pointed to the suth'ard, and then shouted through his hands as a trumpet "Verstehen Sie? shortcut through sands; follow me!" the last two sentences in downright English. I can hear those words now, and I'll swear they were in his native tongue. Of course I thought nothing of it at the time. I was quite aware that he knew a few English words, though he had always mispronounced them; an easy trick when your hearer suspects nothing. But I needn't say that just then I was observant of trifles. I don't pretend to be able to unravel a plot and steer a small boat before a heavy sea at the same moment.'

'And if he was piloting you into the next world he could afford to commit himself before you parted! Was there anything else? By the way, how did the daughter strike you? Did she look English too?'

Two men cannot discuss a woman freely without a deep foundation of intimacy, and, until this day, the subject had never arisen between us in any form. It was the last that was likely to, for I could have divined that Davies would have met it with an armour of reserve. He was busy putting on this armour now; yet I could not help feeling a little brutal as I saw how badly he jointed his clumsy suit of mail. Our ages were the same, but I laugh now to think how old and *blasé* I felt as the flush warmed his brown skin, and he slowly propounded the verdict, 'Yes, I think she did.'

'She *talked* nothing but German, I suppose?'

'Oh, of course.'

'Did you see much of her?'

'A good deal.'

'Was she –' (how frame it?) 'Did she want you to sail to the Elbe with them?'

'She seemed to,' admitted Davies, reluctantly, clutching at his ally, the match-box. 'But, hang it, don't dream that she knew what was coming,' he added, with sudden fire.

I pondered and wondered, shrinking from further inquisition, easy as it would have been with so truthful a victim, and banishing all thought of ill-timed chaff. There was a cross-current in this strange affair, whose depth and strength I was beginning to gauge with increasing seriousness. I did not know my man yet, and I did not know myself. A conviction that events in the near future would force us into complete mutual confidence withheld me from pressing him too far. I returned to the main question; who was Dollmann, and what was his motive? Davies struggled out of his armour.

'I'm convinced,' he said, 'that he's an Englishman in German service. He must be in German service, for he had evidently been in those waters a long time, and knew every inch of them; of course, it's a very lonely part of the world, but he has a house on Norderney Island; and he, and all about him, must be well known to a certain number of people. One of his friends I happened to meet; what do you think he was? A naval officer. It was on the afternoon of the third day, and we were having coffee on the deck of the *Medusa*, and talking about next day's trip, when a little launch came buzzing up from seaward, drew alongside, and this chap I'm speaking of came on board, shook hands with Dollmann, and stared hard at me. Dollmann introduced us, calling him Commander von Brüning, in command of the torpedo gunboat *Blitz*. He pointed towards Norderney, and I saw her – a low, grey rat of a vessel – anchored in the Roads about two miles away. It turned out that she was doing the work of fishery guardship on that part of the coast.

'I must say I took to him at once. He looked a real good sort, and a splendid officer, too – just the sort of chap I should have liked to be. You know I always wanted – but that's an old story, and can wait. I had some talk with him, and we got on capitally as far as we went, but that wasn't far, for I left pretty soon, guessing that they wanted to be alone.'

'*Were* they alone then?' I asked, innocently.

'Oh, Fräulein Dollmann was there, of course,' explained Davies, feeling for his armour again.

'Did he seem to know them well?' I pursued, inconsequently.

'Oh, yes, very well.'

Scenting a faint clue, I felt the need of feminine weapons for my sensitive antagonist. But the opportunity passed.

'That was the last I saw of him,' he said. 'We sailed, as I told you, at daybreak next morning. Now, have you got any idea what I'm driving at?'

'A rough idea,' I answered. 'Go ahead.'

Davies sat up to the table, unrolled the chart with a vigorous sweep of his two hands, and took up his parable with new zest.

'I start with two certainties,' he said. 'One is that I was "moved on" from that coast, because I was too inquisitive. The other is that Dollmann is at some devil's work there which is worth finding out. Now'– he paused in a gasping effort to be logical and articulate. 'Now – well, look at the chart. No, better still, look first at this map

of Germany. It's on a small scale, and you can see the whole thing.'
He snatched down a pocket-map from the shelf and unfolded it.
'Here's this huge empire, stretching half over central Europe – an
empire growing like wildfire, I believe, in people, and wealth, and
everything. They've licked the French, and the Austrians, and are the
greatest military power in Europe. I wish I knew more about all that,
but what I'm concerned with is their sea-power. It's a new thing with
them, but it's going strong, and that Emperor of theirs is running
it for all it's worth. He's a splendid chap, and anyone can see he's
right. They've got no colonies to speak of, and *must* have them, like
us. They can't get them and keep them, and they can't protect their
huge commerce without naval strength. The command of the sea
is *the* thing nowadays, isn't it? I say, don't think these are my ideas,'
he added, naively. 'It's all out of Mahan and those fellows. Well, the
Germans have got a small fleet at present, but it's a thundering good
one, and they're building hard. There's the – and the –.' He broke
off into a digression on armaments and speeds in which I could not
follow him. He seemed to know every ship by heart. I had to recall
him to the point. 'Well, think of Germany as a new sea-power,' he
resumed. 'The next thing is, what is her coastline? It's a very queer
one, as you know, split clean in two by Denmark, most of it lying
east of that and looking on the Baltic, which is practically an inland
sea, with its entrance blocked by Danish islands. It was to evade that
block that William built the ship canal from Kiel to the Elbe, but
that could be easily smashed in war-time. Far the most important
bit of coastline is that which lies *west* of Denmark and looks on the
North Sea. It's there that Germany gets her head out into the open,
so to speak. It's there that she fronts us and France, the two great sea
powers of Western Europe, and it's there that her greatest ports are
and her richest commerce.

'Now it must strike you at once that it's ridiculously short compared
with the huge country behind it. From Borkum to the Elbe, as the crow
flies, is only seventy miles. Add to that the west coast of Schleswig, say
120 miles. Total, say, two hundred. Compare that with the seaboard of
France and England. Doesn't it stand to reason that every inch of it is

important? Now what *sort* of coast is it? Even on this small map you can see at once, by all those wavy lines, shoals and sand everywhere, blocking nine-tenths of the land altogether, and doing their best to block the other tenth where the great rivers run in. Now let's take it bit by bit. You see it divides itself into three. Beginning from the west the *first piece* is from Borkum to Wangeroog – 50 odd miles. What's that like? A string of sandy islands backed by sand; the Ems River at the western end, on the Dutch border, leading to Emden – not much of a place. Otherwise, no coast towns at all. *Second piece:* a deep sort of bay consisting of the three great estuaries – the Jade, the Weser, and the Elbe – leading to Wilhelmshaven (their North Sea naval base), Bremen, and Hamburg. Total breadth of bay twenty odd miles only; sandbanks littered about all through it. *Third piece:* the Schleswig coast, hopelessly fenced in behind a 6 to 8 mile fringe of sand. No big towns; one moderate river, the Eider. Let's leave that third piece aside. I may be wrong, but, in thinking this business out, I've pegged away chiefly at the other two, the 70-mile stretch from Borkum to the Elbe – half of it estuaries, and half islands. It was there that I found the *Medusa*, and it's that stretch that, thanks to him, I missed exploring.'

I made an obvious conjecture. 'I suppose there are forts and coast defences? Perhaps he thought you would see too much. By the way, he saw your naval books, of course?'

'Exactly. Of course that was my first idea; but it can't be that. It doesn't explain things in the least. To begin with, there *are* no forts and can be none in that first division, where the islands are. There might be something on Borkum to defend the Ems; but it's very unlikely, and, anyway, I had passed Borkum and was at Norderney. There's nothing else to defend. Of course it's different in the second division, where the big rivers are. There are probably hosts of forts and mines round Wilhelmshaven and Bremerhaven, and at Cuxhaven just at the mouth of the Elbe. Not that I should ever dream of bothering about them; every steamer that goes in would see as much as me. Personally, I much prefer to stay on board, and don't often go on shore. And, good Heavens!' (Davies leant back and laughed joyously) 'do I *look* like that kind of spy?'

I figured to myself one of those romantic gentlemen that one reads of in sixpenny magazines, with a Kodak in his tie-pin, a sketch-book in the lining of his coat, and a selection of disguises in his hand luggage. Little disposed for merriment as I was, I could not help smiling, too.

'About this coast,' resumed Davies. 'In the event of war it seems to me that every inch of it would be important, *sand and all.* Take the big estuaries first, which, of course, might be attacked or blockaded by an enemy. At first sight you would say that their main channels were the only things that mattered. Now, in time of peace there's no secrecy about the navigation of these. They're buoyed and lighted like streets, open to the whole world, and taking an immense traffic; well charted, too, as millions of pounds in commerce depend on them. But now look at the sands they run through, intersected, as I showed you, by threads of channels, tidal for the most part, and probably only known to smacks and shallow coasters, like that galliot of Bartels.

'It strikes me that in a war a lot might depend on these, both in defence and attack, for there's plenty of water in them at the right tide for patrol-boats and small torpedo craft, though I can see they take a lot of knowing. Now, say *we* were at war with Germany – both sides could use them as lines between the three estuaries; and to take our own case, a small torpedo-boat (not a destroyer, mind you) could on a dark night cut clean through from the Jade to the Elbe and play the deuce with the shipping there. But the trouble is that I doubt if there's a soul in our fleet who knows those channels. *We* haven't coasters there; and, as to yachts, it's a most unlikely game for an English yacht to play at; but it does so happen that I have a fancy for that sort of thing and would have explored those channels in the ordinary course.' I began to see his drift.

'Now for the islands. I was rather stumped there at first, I grant, because, though there are lashings of sand behind them, and the same sort of intersecting channels, yet there seems nothing important to guard or attack.

'Why shouldn't a stranger ramble as he pleases through them? Still Dollmann had his headquarters there, and I was sure that had some meaning. Then it struck me that the same point held good, for that strip of Frisian coast adjoins the estuaries, and would also form a splendid base for raiding midgets, which could travel unseen right through from the Ems to the Jade, and so to the Elbe, as by a covered way between a line of forts.

'Now here again it's an unknown land to us. Plenty of local galliots travel it, but strangers never, I should say. Perhaps at the most an occasional foreign yacht gropes in at one of the gaps between the islands for shelter from bad weather, and is precious lucky to get in safe. Once again, it was my fad to like such places, and Dollmann cleared me out. He's not a German, but he's in with Germans, and naval Germans too. He's established on that coast, and knows it by heart. And he tried to drown me. Now what do you think?' He gazed at me long and anxiously.

Herr von Kwarl
From *When William Came,* Saki (H. H. Munro)

Herr von Kwarl sat at his favourite table in the Brandenburg Café, the new building that made such an imposing show (and did such thriving business) at the lower end of what most of its patrons called the Regentstrasse. Though the establishment was new it had already achieved its unwritten code of customs, and the sanctity of Herr von Kwarl's specially reserved table had acquired the authority of a tradition. A set of chess-men, a copy of the *Kreuz Zeitung* and *The Times,* and a slim-necked bottle of Rhenish wine, ice-cool from the cellar, were always to be found there early in the forenoon, and the honoured guest for whom these preparations were made usually arrived on the scene shortly after eleven o'clock. For an hour or so he would read and silently digest the contents of his two newspapers, and then at the first sign of flagging interest on his part, another of the café's regular customers would march across the floor, exchange a word or two on the affairs of the day, and be bidden with a wave of the hand into the opposite seat. A waiter would instantly place the chess-board with its marshalled ranks of combatants in the required position, and the contest would begin.

Herr von Kwarl was a heavily built man of mature middle age, of the blond North-German type, with a facial aspect that suggested stupidity and brutality. The stupidity of his mien masked an ability and shrewdness that was distinctly above the average and the suggestion of brutality was belied by the fact that von Kwarl was as kind-hearted a man as one could meet with in a day's journey. Early in life, almost before he was in his teens, Fritz von Kwarl had made up his mind to accept the world as it was, and to that philosophical resolution, steadfastly adhered to, he attributed his excellent digestion and his unruffled happiness. Perhaps he confused cause and effect; the excellent digestion may have been responsible for at least some of the philosophical serenity.

He was a bachelor of the type that is called confirmed, and which might better be labelled consecrated; from his early youth onward to his present age he had never had the faintest flickering intention of marriage. Children and animals he adored, women and plants he accounted somewhat of a nuisance. A world without women and roses and asparagus would, he admitted, be robbed of much of its charm, but with all their charm these things were tiresome and thorny and capricious, always wanting to climb or creep in places where they were not wanted, and resolutely drooping and fading away when they were desired to flourish. Animals, on the other hand, accepted the world as it was and made the best of it, and children, at least nice children, uncontaminated by grown-up influences, lived in worlds of their own making.

Von Kwarl held no acknowledged official position in the country of his residence, but it was an open secret that those responsible for the real direction of affairs sought his counsel on nearly every step that they meditated, and that his counsel was very rarely disregarded. Some of the shrewdest and most successful enactments of the ruling power were believed to have originated in the brain cells of the bovine-fronted *Stammgast* of the Brandenburg Café.

Around the wood-panelled walls of the Café were set at intervals well-mounted heads of boar, elk, stag, roebuck, and other game-beasts of a northern forest, while in between were carved armorial escutcheons of the principal cities of the lately expanded realm, Magdeburg, Manchester, Hamburg, Bremen, Bristol and so forth. Below these came shelves on which stood a wonderful array of stone beer-mugs, each decorated with some fantastic device or motto, and most of them pertaining individually and sacredly to some regular and unfailing customer. In one particular corner of the highest shelf, greatly at his ease and in nowise to be disturbed, slept Wotan, the huge grey housecat, dreaming doubtless of certain nimble and audacious mice down in the cellar three floors below, whose nimbleness and audacity were as precious to him as the forwardness of the birds is to a skilled gun on a grouse moor. Once every day Wotan came marching in stately fashion across the polished floor, halted midway to resume an unfinished toilet operation, and then proceeded to pay his leisurely respects to his friend von Kwarl. The latter was said to be prouder of this daily demonstration of esteem than of his many coveted orders of merit. Several of his friends and acquaintances shared with him the distinction of having achieved the Black Eagle, but not one of them had ever succeeded in obtaining the slightest recognition of their existence from Wotan.

The daily greeting had been exchanged and the proud grey beast had marched away to the music of a slumberous purr. The *Kreuz Zeitung* and the *Times* underwent a final scrutiny and were pushed aside, and von Kwarl glanced aimlessly out at the July sunshine bathing the walls and windows of the Piccadilly Hotel. Herr Rebinok, the plump little Pomeranian banker, stepped across the floor, almost as noiselessly as Wotan had done, though with considerably less grace, and some half-minute later was engaged in sliding pawns and knights and bishops to and fro on the chessboard in a series of lightning moves bewildering to look on. Neither he nor his opponent played with the skill that they severally brought to bear on banking and statecraft, nor did they conduct their game with the politeness that they punctiliously observed in other affairs of life. A running fire of contemptuous remarks and aggressive satire accompanied each move, and the mere record of the conversation would have given an uninitiated onlooker the puzzling impression that an easy and crushing victory was assured to both the players.

'Aha, he is puzzled. Poor man, he doesn't know what to do ... Oho, he thinks he will move there, does he? Much good that will do him ... Never have I seen such a mess as he is in ... He cannot do anything, he is absolutely helpless, helpless.'

'Ah, you take my Bishop, do you? Much I care for that. Nothing. See, I give you check. Ah, now he is in a fright! He doesn't know where to go. What a mess he is in ...'

So the game proceeded, with a brisk exchange of pieces and incivilities and fluctuation of fortunes, till the little banker lost his queen as the result of an incautious move, and, after several woebegone contortions of his shoulders and hands, declined further contest. A sleek-headed piccolo rushed forward to remove the board, and the erstwhile combatants resumed the courteous dignity that they discarded in their chess-playing moments.

'Have you seen the *Germania* today?' asked Herr Rebinok, as soon as the boy had receded to a respectful distance.

'No,' said von Kwarl, 'I never see the *Germania*. I count on you to tell me if there is anything noteworthy in it.'

'It has an article today headed, "Occupation or Assimilation",' said the banker. 'It is of some importance, and well written. It is very pessimistic.'

'Catholic papers are always pessimistic about the things of this world,' said von Kwarl, 'just as they are unduly optimistic about the things of the next world. What line does it take?'

'It ways that our conquest of Britain can only result in a temporary occupation, with a "notice to quit" always hanging over our heads; that we can never hope to assimilate the people of these islands in our Empire as a sort of maritime Saxony or Bavaria, all the teaching of history is against it; Saxony and Bavaria are part of the Empire because of their past history. England is being bound into the Empire in spite of her past history; and so forth.'

'The writer of the article has not studied history very deeply,' said von Kwarl. 'The impossible thing that he speaks of has been done before, and done in these very islands, too. The Norman Conquest became an assimilation in comparatively few generations.'

'Ah, in those days, yes,' said the banker, 'but the conditions were altogether different. There was not the rapid transmission of news and the means of keeping the public mind instructed in what was happening; in fact, one can scarcely say that the public mind was there to instruct. There was not the same strong bond of brotherhood between men of the same nation that exists now. Northumberland was almost as foreign to Devon or Kent as Normandy was. And the Church in those days was a great international factor, and the Crusades bound men together fighting under one leader for a common cause. Also there was not a great national past to be forgotten as there is in this case.'

'There are many factors, certainly, that are against us,' conceded the statesman, 'but you must also take into account those that will help us. In most cases in recent history where the conquered have stood out against all attempts at assimilation, there has been a religious difference to add to the racial one – take Poland, for instance, and the Catholic parts of Ireland. If the Bretons ever seriously begin to assert their nationality as against the French, it will be because they have remained more Catholic in practice and sentiment than their neighbours. Here there is no such complication; we are in the bulk a Protestant nation with a Catholic minority, and the same may be said of the British. Then in modern days there is the alchemy of Sport and the Drama to bring men of different races amicably together. One or two sportsmanlike Germans in a London football team will do more to break down racial antagonism than anything that governments or councils can effect. As for the Stage, it has long been international in its tendencies. You can see that every day.'

The banker nodded his head.

'London is not our greatest difficulty,' continued von Kwarl. 'You must remember the steady influx of Germans since the war; whole districts are changing the complexion of their inhabitants, and in some streets you might almost fancy yourself in a German town. We can scarcely hope to make much impression on the country districts and the provincial towns at present, but you must remember that thousands and thousands of the more virile and restless-souled men have emigrated, and thousands more will follow their example. We shall fill up their places with our own surplus population, as the Teuton races colonised England in the old pre-Christian days. That is better, is it not, to people the fat meadows of the Thames valley and the healthy downs and uplands of Sussex and Berkshire than to go hunting for elbow-room among the flies and fevers of the tropics? We have somewhere to go to, now, better than the scrub and the veldt and the thorn-jungles.'

'Of course, of course,' assented Herr Rebinok, 'but while this desirable process of infiltration and assimilation goes on, how are you going to provide against the hostility of the conquered nation? A people with a great tradition behind them and the ruling instinct strongly developed, won't sit with their eyes closed and their hands folded while you carry on the process of Germanisation. What will keep them quiet?'

'The hopelessness of the situation. For centuries Britain has ruled the seas, and been able to dictate to half the world in consequence; then she let slip the mastery of the seas, as something too costly and onerous to keep up, something which aroused too much jealousy and uneasiness in others, and now the seas rule her. Every wave that breaks on her shore rattles the keys of her prison. I am no fire-eater, Herr Rebinok, but I confess that when I am at Dover, say, or Southampton, and see those dark blots on the sea and those grey specks in the sky, our battleships and cruisers and aircraft, and realise what they mean to us, my heart beats just a little quicker. If every German was flung out of England tomorrow, in three weeks' time we should be coming in again on our own terms. With our sea scouts and air scouts spread in organised network around, not a shipload of food-stuff could reach the country. They know that; they can calculate how many days of independence and starvation they could endure, and they will make no attempt to bring about such a certain fiasco. Brave men fight for a forlorn hope, but the bravest do not fight for an issue they know to be hopeless.'

'That is so,' said Herr Rebinok. 'As things are at present they can do nothing from within, absolutely nothing. We have weighed all that beforehand. But, as the *Germania* points out, there is another Britain beyond the seas. Supposing the Court at Delhi were to engineer a league – '

'A league? A league with whom?' interrupted the statesman. 'Russia we can watch and hold. We are rather nearer to its western frontier than Delhi is, and we could throttle its Baltic trade at five hours' notice. France and Holland are not inclined to provoke our hostility; they would have everything to lose by such a course.'

'There are other forces in the world that might be arrayed against us,' argued the banker. 'The United States, Japan, Italy, they all have navies.'

'Does the teaching of history show you that it is the strong Power, armed and ready, that has to suffer from the hostility of the world?' asked von Kwarl. 'As far as sentiment goes, perhaps, but not in practice. The danger has always been for the weak, dismembered nation. Think you a moment, has the enfeebled, scattered British Empire overseas no undefended territories that are a temptation to her neighbours? Has Japan nothing to glean where we have harvested? Are there no North American possessions which might slip into other keeping? Has Russia herself no traditional temptations beyond the Oxus? Mind you, we are not making the mistake Napoleon made, when he forced all Europe to be for him or against him. We threaten no world aggressions, we are satiated where he was insatiable. We have cast down one overshadowing Power from the face of the world, because it stood in our way, but we have made no attempt to spread our branches over all the space that it covered. We have not tried to set up a tributary Canadian republic or to partition South Africa; we have dreamed no dream of making ourselves Lords of Hindostan. On the contrary, we have given proof of our friendly intentions towards our neighbours. We backed France up the other day in her squabble with Spain over the Moroccan boundaries, and proclaimed our opinion that the Republic had as indisputable a mission on the North Africa coast as we have in the North Sea. That is not the action or the language of aggression. No,' continued von Kwarl, after a moment's silence, 'the world may fear us and dislike us, but, for the present at any rate, there will be no leagues against us. No, there is one rock on which our attempt at assimilation will founder or find firm anchorage.'

'And that is –'

'The youth of the country, the generation that is at the threshold now. It is them that we must capture. We must teach them to learn, and coax them to forget. In course of time Anglo-Saxon may blend with German, as the Elbe Saxons and the Bavarians and Swabians have blended with the Prussians into a loyal united people under the sceptre of the Hohenzollerns. Then we should be doubly strong, Rome and Carthage rolled into one, an Empire of the West greater than Charlemagne ever knew. Then we could look Slav and Latin and Asiatic in the face and keep our place as the central dominant force of the civilised world.'

The speaker paused for a moment and drank a deep draught of wine, as though he were invoking the prosperity of that future world-power. Then he resumed in a more level tone:

'On the other hand, the younger generation of Britons may grow up in hereditary hatred, repulsing all our overtures, forgetting nothing and forgiving nothing, waiting and watching for the time when some weakness assails us, when some crisis entangles us, when we cannot be everywhere at once. Then our work will be imperilled, perhaps undone. There lies the danger, there lies the hope, the younger generation.'

'There is another danger,' said the banker, after he had pondered over von Kwarl's remarks for a moment or two amid the incense-clouds of a fat cigar, 'a danger that I foresee in the immediate future; perhaps not so much a danger as an element of exasperation which may ultimately defeat your plans. The law as to military service will have to be promulgated shortly, and that cannot fail to be bitterly unpopular. The people of these islands will have to be brought into line with the rest of the Empire in the matter of military training and military service, and how will they like that? Will not the enforcing of such a measure infuriate them against us? Remember, they have made great sacrifices to avoid the burden of military service.'

'Dear God,' exclaimed Herr von Kwarl, 'as you say, they have made sacrifices on that altar!'

Arrested For Spying
From *The Secrets of the German War Office*,
Dr Armgaard Karl Graves

About a week after, I received information that William Beardmore & Co., of Glasgow, were constructing some new fourteen-inch guns for the British government. That meant a change of base.

I at once made it my business to go to Glasgow and get particulars. I installed myself in the Central Station Hotel, and in a few weeks gained all the information I wanted. It would take too long to detail how this was done, but you have a very expressive saying, 'money talks.' I had the plans, firing systems, everything of interest about the new fourteen-inch turret guns. While in Glasgow I received letters addressed to me as James Stafford. I received two such letters, and upon my calling at a General Post Office for a third, I was informed that there was a letter for A. Stafford.

'Oh yes, that is my letter,' I said.

The clerk demurred and replied:

'You asked for James Stafford. Under those circumstances I cannot hand you this letter. It is against the postal law.'

Not being in a position to raise a question I let it go at that, never for a moment thinking that my employers would be so culpably careless as to put any incriminating evidence in the mail. Events proved that that is just what they did. Moreover, I later came to know why that particular letter was addressed not to James but to A. Stafford. All my previous letters were addressed to me as Dr A. K. Graves and were enclosed in the business envelope of the well-known chemical firm of Burroughs & Wellcome, Snowhills, London, E. C. – which paper had been fabricated for the purpose.

Of course the letters were sent from the Continent to London and there reposted. The stationery of this chemical firm was fabricated so as to disarm any possible suspicion, for European post offices are taught to be suspicious. It would be perfectly natural for me, a physician in Edinburgh, to receive a letter from a very well-known chemical concern.

When I left Edinburgh to find out about the fourteen-inch guns, I gave our people in London instructions to use plain envelopes and to address them to James Stafford, G. P. O., Glasgow. The first two letters were addressed correctly and plain envelopes were used. The third was not only misaddressed but was enclosed in one of the B. & W. envelopes – this, as I later learned, for a reason.

No one having called for it, the letter was returned to the chemical company. At their office it was opened and found to contain a typewritten letter in the German language and five ten-pound notes of the Bank of England. The contents of the letter, was such as to lead the firm to call in the police.

On the evening of April 10, I had just put on my evening clothes and gone to the upstairs writing room. I was awaiting a party of gentlemen who were coming to dine with me in the hotel. There came a 'buttons' who announced:

'There's a gentleman downstairs to see you, Doctor.'

A premonition stole over me. I realised that if I was going to be caught there was no avoiding it. Secret Service makes a man a fatalist. I took the precaution, however, to slip inside my dinner coat just under the arm, my little bag of chemicals, so often handy in an emergency. Then I went downstairs, one hand was thrust in my pocket, the other folded across my breast so that I could snatch the little bag of chemicals in an emergency.

I had hardly reached the last step of the grand stairway when four big plain-clothes men, pounced upon me. I had to do some swift thinking. I could have flung the chemicals in their faces and escaped, but I knew I could never get outside of the British Isles without being caught, or outside of Glasgow for that matter. Such resistance would only incriminate matters still more, so I let my hand fall down to my side. More for the fun of it than anything else, I guess, I got on my horse and demanded to know what was the matter.

'You'll soon know,' Inspector French declared.

He then ordered his men to search me and seemed amazed when they couldn't find any six shooters, daggers or bombs. I was taken back to my room and there he began going through my effects, and bundling them up. I knew I was up against it; but I wasn't going to make it any easier for them. I requested Mr Morris, then manager of the hotel, and another witness to be called into my room. These gentlemen were kind enough to put down on paper a description of all my effects that were being taken away by the police. I was extremely careful to see that they noted and described all papers and written matters of any kind. There are often produced in court documents that are not found on a Secret Service agent at the time of his arrest. Inspector French was preparing to ride over me roughshod. I insisted that he read the warrant for my arrest and with much grumbling he finally did so. It had been issued under the Official Secret Act that had been rushed through the House of Commons. I was charged with endangering the safeguards of the British Empire.

I spent the night in the Glasgow City Prison, and was taken the next day before a magistrate and formally committed to a sheriff's court.

On 12 July my case came up before the sheriff's court. I was committed for trial to the Edinburgh High Court. It is significant that the extreme length of a committal without trial under British law is 105 calendar days, which hundred and five days up to the last minute I certainly waited. They were trying to find out my antecedents but they did not succeed.

A letter from the Lord Provost informed me that all material for my defence should be in his hands a day before the trial. I had no defence. I neither denied nor admitted anything. I replied to his Lordship that as I was unaware of any offence there was no need of any defence. My attitude was a profound puzzle, which was as I wanted.

If you care to look over the back files of the English and Scottish newspapers of the time you will read that my trial was 'the most sensational court procedure ever held in a Scottish court of justice.'

Now I shall reveal every circumstance of it. For the first time I shall explain how, why and by whom I was secretly released. Until I revealed myself in the United States, even the German Foreign Office thought me in jail.

Against me the Crown had summoned forty-five witnesses. They included admirals, colonels, captains, military and naval experts, Post Office officials, I cannot recall all. The press from all parts of Europe was represented. My memory shows me again the crowds that packed the big Supreme Court building at Edinburgh on the first day of the proceedings. The imposing names connected with the trial, the strange circumstances, a spy, moreover a German! These things brought the excitement to fever heat.

Presiding was the Lord Justice of Scotland, himself no mean expert in military matters. The Solicitor General of Scotland, A. M. Anderson, who prosecuted for the crown, was supported by G. Morton, Advocate Deputy. The government had indeed an imposing array of bewigged, black-gowned, legal notables marshalled against me.

Those familiar with English court procedure know the impressive manner with which justice is dispensed. Punctually at ten on the morning of 22 July 1912, my trial opened. Clad in his royal red robe with the ermine collar of supreme justice, the Lord Justice entered the court. Before him walked a mace bearer, intoning 'Gentlemen, the Lord Justice! Gentlemen, the Court!' After the impressive ceremonies had been observed, the jury was quickly empanelled, I making several challenges. Twelve years in the Secret Service naturally has made me know something of men. I knew that those twelve hard-headed, cautious Scottish jurymen would demand pretty substantial proof before convicting.

Expressing astonishment at my refusal to accept counsel, which was subsequently forced on me, His Lordship promised to guard my interest on legal points; and guard it he did. Repeatedly he ruled against the Solicitor General and challenged him on more than one point. I am frank in my admiration of British justice. My trial was a model of fairness.

On the first day I waived examination on all witnesses but the naval and military experts. I directed my fire against Rear Admiral T. B. Stratton Adair, who superintended the ordnance factories of the Beardmore Gun Works in Glasgow. The Admiral, a typical English gentleman of the naval officer type, long, lank with a rather ascetic, clear-cut Roman head, not unlike Chamberlain in general appearance, even to the single eye-glass, did not make much of a showing as an expert witness for the prosecution. The Admiral was called in on testimony concerning the new fourteen-inch gun. The point they were trying to establish was that it was impossible for a man to have my knowledge of these guns unless he had obtained it first-hand from the works in Glasgow. Of course that brought the testimony into technicalities. I managed to involve the Admiral in a heated altercation on the trajectory and penetrating power of the so-much disputed fourteen-inch gun. One word led to another and notwithstanding that he ranked at that time as a rear admiral of the British Navy, the Admiral showed that he did not know as much about his own guns as I. Backed into this corner he was about to divulge things in support of his knowledge when he recovered himself, pulled up suddenly and appealed to the Court:

> Your Lordship, it is against the British Government to have any more questions on this point in open court.

I maintained that my knowledge of guns was such that I did not need to spy at Beardmore to obtain the things I knew. Subsequently after being cross-examined by me another of the government's naval experts told the court:

> It is quite possible for one with a ballistic knowledge such as the defendant's to be able with very little data to arrive at accurate conclusions regarding our new fourteen-inch guns.

A word of advice to the Admiral. Do not talk so much when you go motor boating with pretty young musical comedy girls. You see,

Admiral, I made it my business to see those young ladies in Glasgow. What an interest they took in you, a great Admiral! It is you, Admiral, whom I thank for aiding me in securing the right persons from whom the secrets of your new fourteen-inch guns could be obtained.

A note they found in my effects was introduced as evidence. It read as follows:

The firm of William Beardmore and Co., Parkhead, Glasgow. B first orders F new 13.5 guns F, Navy. Length 51 feet, weight 73 tons. One foot longer than 12-inch, but 12 tons heavier. Weight of shot, 1,250 lb., 400 lb. more than the 12-inch gun.

The upshot of it was that the first day of the trial ended with everybody positive that I would not be found guilty on the charge of obtaining secret information about their guns. Of course all this information I had obtained.

The second day of the trial brought the Burroughs & Wellcome letter into the testimony – the letter that had been refused me and had in turn gone back to the Chemical Company. Very gravely Sir Anderson, Crown Prosecutor, read the contents of this letter aloud. As I recall the exact wording it was:

Dear Sir:

We are pleased to learn of your successful negotiation of the business at hand. Be pleased to send us an early sample. As regards the other matter in hand I do not know how useful it will be to us: In any case my firm is not willing to pay you more than 100 in this case.

It was unsigned.

While reading, Sir Anderson held the five ten-pound notes in his hand. Upon finishing he began a vigorous indictment, which in substance he declaimed in this way:

On the face of it, this letter does not seem suspicious. But if you gentlemen will recall the times of Prince Charles' insurrections, periods whenever intrigues were going on, you will remember that in communications of this sort a government was always referred to as a 'firm.' If this was an honest business letter why was it enclosed in the envelope stationery of a company that knew nothing about it? Why was this letter unsigned? Why was cash enclosed, with it? What was his firm willing to pay 100 pounds for? Gentlemen, the reasons for all these things are obvious.

But the letter puzzled not only the court, the jury, the newspapers, but all England. For the first time I shall now explain it:

It was from the German government. By the 'business at hand' they meant a new explosive and slow-burning powder that was to be used in the new type of fourteen-inch turret guns being made in Glasgow. Some of that explosive was in my possession. The fact that it was not discovered in my effects, nor was anything else incriminating found on me is because the Secret Agent who knows his business leaves nothing about; but he 'plants' things, that is to say, leaves them in a safe deposit vault with the key in the hands of a person with power of attorney.

By the 'sample' in the letter was meant a sample of the explosive. The 'other business at hand' was spoken of as of tremendous importance, more vital to the safeguards of Britain than the other points mentioned in the letter.

There were sub-agents working at Cromarty. I did not know who they were; they simply made their reports to me, signing their German Secret Service number. I took up their points with Berlin. Well, the 'other business in hand' was to put a certain British army officer under a monthly retaining fee of £100 for which in the event of war he was to commit an act of unspeakable treason and treachery on a certain harbour defence.

I had judged my jurymen right, for they were very little impressed by this letter. It was all too vague and even the fluent language of a Crown Prosecutor does not impress a hard-headed Scotchman. I was feeling in high spirits indeed, when I saw one of the attendants approach Sir

Anderson and deliver a document that had been handed into court. I at once recognised it and my heart dropped into my shoes.

The Solicitor General read the document and smiled. I knew they had me.

In addressing the court, the Solicitor General produced two pieces of thin paper the same that had been brought in on the previous afternoon.

'I have got to show the court,' he said impressively, 'the most deadly code ever prepared against the safeguards of Great Britain.'

And it certainly was. It contained the name of every vessel in the British Navy, every naval base, fortification and strategic point, in Great Britain. There were over ten thousand names and opposite each was written a number. For example, the battle cruiser *Queen Mary* was number 813.

As I have confessed, I am superstitious. And have I not reason to be?

It was the Burroughs & Wellcome letter that got me caught in the first place. And my secret code was written in a book issued for the use of physicians by Burroughs & Wellcome! Both times the B. & W. mark was upon me.

Using a magnifying glass, I had written in tiny characters my code. There were so many names it was impossible to memorise them all. Two opposite sheets of the little memoranda book were used, then the edges of the pages were pasted together. Whenever I learned the British warships were going to put to sea, I slipped the book in my pocket, went to a position of vantage where I could make out the silhouettes of the warships, classified them in my mind, and then writing out a cable put down the code numbers, say in this way:

214, 69, 700, 910, 21 (Necessary words were filled in by the A. B. C. code).

This message was sent by way of Brussels or Paris to the Intelligence Department of the German Admiralty in Berlin and told them what warships were putting to sea or arriving at Rossyth. The code contained such phrases as this: 'Current rumours.' 'Incoming.' 'Outgoing.' 'Clearing for action.' 'Have lowered defending nets.' 'Land fortifications are manned.' 'Protective manoeuvers are being carried out at sea.' 'Coal being carried by rail.' 'Remarkable influx of Reservists.' 'Mine fields being laid.' 'All is quiet; nothing important to report.' 'Liners are appearing.'

The accidental finding of this code of course settled all further argument. I called no witness for the defence except two or three personal acquaintances to each of whom I put this question:

'What is your knowledge of my attitude as regards England?'

They all declared that even if I was a spy in the pay of any foreign government I certainly had never shown any personal feeling or animosity toward Great Britain.

All of which I figured might aid the cause of clemency. The jury was not out more than half an hour. I was found guilty of endangering the safeguards of the British Empire and under the new law that had been aimed against German spies I was liable to seven years' penal servitude. Even then my spirits were not down. I had what Americans call 'a hunch.'

Just before his Lordship the Chief Justice summed up, an aristocratic, grey-clad Englishman, who never had been in the court room before, appeared and was courteously, almost impressively, conducted to the bench. I noticed that the Chief Justice bowed to him with unction and they had about two minutes' whispered conversation. His Lordship was nodding repeatedly. This worried me. I felt I was going to get it good.

But, in substance, his Lordship's verdict was:

'Taking all the circumstances into consideration, the court pronounces a sentence of eighteen months' imprisonment.'

I smiled and said:

'Exit Armgaard Karl Graves.'

A murmur of astonishment was audible. Everybody in court was surprised. I heard gasps all around me, especially among the foreign newspaper reporters. With everybody expecting seven years of penal servitude, eighteen months of plain imprisonment was a bombshell. Why?

I was taken first to Carlton Hill Jail, Edinburgh, and transferred after two weeks to Barlinney Prison near Glasgow. Considering the circumstances, I was treated with surprising consideration. The conditions that had characterised my trial prevailed in the prison. I soon perceived that the Barlinney prison officials were trying to sound me in a canny Scotch way with no result.

'You're foolish to stay in here. You must have something worthwhile. Why don't you get out?'

That was the gist of their talks with me from the warders up. I kept my mouth shut.

On the fifth week of my imprisonment I was taken to the office of the Governor of the prison. As I entered I saw a slight, soldierly looking English gentleman of the cavalry type (a cavalry officer has certain mannerisms that invariably give him away to one who knows). The Governor spoke first:

'Graves, here is a gentleman who wishes to see you.'

The stranger nodded to the Governor and said:

'I may be quite a while. You have your instructions.'

'That's all right, sir,' replied the Governor.

The Governor left and we were alone. The stranger rose.

'My name is Robinson, Doctor. Please take a seat.'

Of course, being a prisoner, I had remained standing. Robinson began some casual conversation.

'How are they treating you?'

'I have no complaints to make.'

'Is the confinement irksome to you?'

'Naturally.' I looked him straight in the face. 'I am a philosopher. Kismet, Captain.'

He laughed for some time. Then suddenly he changed front. Point blank he asked me:

'Now, old chap, we know that you worked for Germany against us. We also know that you are not a German. Is there any reason why you should not work for us? Any private reason?'

'Captain,' I said, 'you of all men ought to know that the betrayal of your employers for a monetary or a liberty reason alone is never entertained by a man who has been in my work. We go into it with our eyes open, well knowing the consequences if we are caught. We do not squeal if we are hurt.'

For a time he looked at me very earnestly.

'H-m,' he said. 'That just bears out what we have been able to ascertain about you. It puzzled us how a man of your known ability acted the way you did. From the moment you landed in England, all the time you were doing your work, even after your arrest, in prison and in court you show a sort of listless, almost an indifferent attitude. If I may put it this way, you seemed in no way keen to go to extremes in any possible missions you might have had,' he paused. 'We think you could have done more than you did... The mildness of your sentence, has it surprised you?'

I grinned.

'Nothing surprises me, Captain.'

1914

Channel Firing
Thomas Hardy

That night your great guns, unawares,
Shook all our coffins as we lay,
And broke the chancel window-squares,
We thought it was the Judgment-day

And sat upright. While drearisome
Arose the howl of wakened hounds:
The mouse let fall the altar-crumb,
The worms drew back into the mounds,

The glebe cow drooled. Till God called, 'No;
It's gunnery practice out at sea
Just as before you went below;
The world is as it used to be:

'All nations striving strong to make
Red war yet redder. Mad as hatters
They do no more for Christ's sake
Than you who are helpless in such matters.

'That this is not the judgment-hour
For some of them's a blessed thing,
For if it were they'd have to scour
Hell's floor for so much threatening...

'Ha, ha. It will be warmer when
I blow the trumpet (if indeed
I ever do; for you are men,
And rest eternal sorely need).

So down we lay again. 'I wonder,
Will the world ever saner be,'
Said one, 'than when He sent us under
In our indifferent century!'

And many a skeleton shook his head.
'Instead of preaching forty year,'
My neighbour Parson Thirdly said,
'I wish I had stuck to pipes and beer.'

Again the guns disturbed the hour,
Roaring their readiness to avenge,
As far inland as Stourton Tower,
And Camelot, and starlit Stonehenge.

April 1914

The Contemptible Little Army
From *The German War*, Sir Arthur Conan Doyle

Early last year, in the course of some comments which I made upon the slighting remarks about our Army by General von Bernhardi, I observed, 'It may be noted that General von Bernhardi has a poor opinion of our troops. This need not trouble us. We are what we are, and words will not alter it. From very early days our soldiers have left their mark upon Continental warfare, and we have no reason to think that we have declined from the manhood of our forefathers.' Since then he has returned to the attack. With that curious power of coming after deep study to the absolutely diametrically wrong conclusion which the German expert, political or military, appears to possess, he says in his *War of Today*, 'The English Army, trained more for purposes of show than for modern war,' adding in the same sentence a sneer at our 'inferior Colonial levies.' He will have an opportunity of reconsidering his views presently upon the fighting value of our over-sea troops, and surely so far as our own are concerned he must already be making some interesting notes for his next edition, or rather for the learned volume upon *Germany and the Last War*, which will no doubt come from his pen. He is a man to whom we might well raise a statue, for I am convinced that his cynical confession of German policy has been worth at least an army corps to this country. We may address to him John Davidson's lines to his enemy:

> Unwilling friend, let not your spite abate,
> Spur us with scorn, and strengthen us with hate.

There is another German gentleman who must be thinking rather furiously. He is a certain Colonel Gadke, who appeared officially at Aldershot some years ago, was hospitably entreated, being shown all that he desired to see, and on his return to Berlin published a most depreciatory description of our forces. He found no good thing in them. I have some recollection that General French alluded in a public speech to this critic's remarks, and expressed a modest hope that he and his men would someday have the opportunity of showing how far they were deserved. Well, he has had his opportunity, and Colonel Gadke, like so many other Germans, seems to have made a miscalculation.

An army which has preserved the absurd *Paradeschritt*, an exercise which is painful to the bystander, as he feels that it is making fools of brave men, must have a tendency to throw back to earlier types. These Germans have been trained in peace and upon the theory of books. In all that vast host there is hardly a man who has previously stood at the wrong end of a loaded gun. They live on traditions of close formations, vast cavalry charges, and other things which will not fit into modern warfare. Braver men do not exist, but it is the bravery of men who have been taught to lean upon each other, and not the cold, self-contained, resourceful bravery of the man who has learned to fight for his own hand. The British have had the teachings of two recent campaigns fought with modern weapons – that of the Tirah and of South Africa. Now that the reserves have joined the colours there are few regiments which have not a fair sprinkling of veterans from these wars in their ranks. The Pathan and the Boer have been their instructors in something more practical than those Imperial Grand Manoeuvres where the all-highest played with his puppets in such a fashion that one of his generals remarked that the chief practical difficulty of a campaign so conducted would be the disposal of the dead.

Boers and Pathans have been hard masters, and have given many a slap to their admiring pupils, but the lesson has been learned. It was not show troops, General, who, with two corps, held five of your best day after day from Mons to Compiègne. It is no reproach to your valour: but you were up against men who were equally brave and knew a great deal more of the game. This must begin to break upon you, and will surely grow clearer as the days go by. We shall often in the future take the knock as well as give it, but you will not say that we have a show army if you live to chronicle this war, nor will your Imperial master be proud of the adjective which he has demeaned himself in using before his troops had learned their lesson.

The fact is that the German army, with all its great traditions, has been petrifying for many years back. They never learned the lesson of South Africa. It was not for want of having it expounded to them, for their military attaché – 'im with the spatchcock on 'is 'elmet,' as I heard him described by a British orderly – missed nothing of what occurred, as is evident from their official history of the war. And yet they missed it, and with it all those ideas of individual efficiency and elastic independent formations, which are the essence of modern soldiering. Their own more liberal thinkers were aware of it. Here are the words which were put into the mouth of Güntz, the representative of the younger school, in Beyerlein's famous novel:

> The organisation of the German army rested upon foundations which had been laid a hundred years ago. Since the Great War they had never seriously been put to the proof, and during the last three decades they had only been altered in the most trifling details. In three long decades! And in one of those decades the world at large had advanced as much as in the previous century.
>
> Instead of turning this highly developed intelligence to good account, they bound it hand and foot on the rack of an everlasting drill which could not have been more soullessly mechanical in the days of Frederick. It held them together as an iron hoop holds together a cask the dry staves which would fall asunder at the first kick.

Lord Roberts has said that if ten points represent the complete soldier, eight should stand for his efficiency as a shot. The German maxim has rather been that eight should stand for his efficiency as a drilled marionette. It has been reckoned that about 200 books a year appear in Germany upon military affairs, against about twenty in Britain. And yet after all this expert debate the essential point of all seems to have been missed – that in the end everything depends upon the man behind the gun, upon his hitting his opponent and upon his taking cover so as to avoid being hit himself.

After all the efforts of the General Staff the result when shown upon the field of battle has filled our men with a mixture of admiration and contempt – contempt for the absurd tactics, admiration for the poor devils who struggle on in spite of them. Listen to the voices of the men who are the real experts. Says a Lincolnshire sergeant, 'They were in solid square blocks, and we couldn't help hitting them.' Says Private Tait (2nd Essex), 'Their rifle shooting is rotten. I don't believe they could hit a haystack at 100 yards.' 'They are rotten shots with their rifles,' says an Oldham private. 'They advance in close column, and you simply can't help hitting them,' writes a Gordon Highlander.

'You would have thought it was a big crowd streaming out from a Cup-tie,' says Private Whitaker of the Guards. 'It was like a farmer's machine cutting grass,' so it seemed to Private Hawkins of the Coldstreams. 'No damned good as riflemen,' says a Connemara boy. As to their rifle fire, it was useless. They shoot from the hip, and don't seem to aim at anything in particular.'

These are the opinions of the practical men upon the field of battle. Surely a poor result from the 200 volumes a year, and all the weighty labours of the General Staff! 'Artillery nearly as good as our own, rifle fire beneath contempt,' that is the verdict. How will the well-taught *Paradeschritt* avail them when it comes to a stricken field?

But let it not seem as if this were meant for disparagement. We should be sinking to the Kaiser's level if we answered his 'contemptible little army' by pretending that his own troops are anything but a very formidable and big army. They are formidable in numbers, formidable, too, in their patriotic devotion, in their native courage, and in the possession of such material, such great cannon, aircraft, machine guns, and armoured cars, as none of the Allies can match. They have every advantage which a nation would be expected to have when it has known that war was a certainty, while others have only treated it as a possibility. There is a minuteness and earnestness of preparation which are only possible for an assured event. But the fact remains, and it will only be brought out more clearly by the Emperor's unchivalrous phrase, that in every arm the British have already shown themselves to be the better troops. Had he the Froissart spirit within him he would rather have said, 'You have today a task which is worthy of you. You are faced by an army which has a high repute and a great history. There is real glory to be won today.' Had he said this, then, win or lose, he would not have needed to be ashamed of his own words – the words of an ungenerous spirit.

It is a very strange thing how German critics have taken for granted that the British Army had deteriorated, while the opinion of all those who were in close touch with it was that it was never so good. Even some of the French experts made the same mistake, and General Bonnat counselled his countrymen not to rely upon it, since 'it would take refuge amid its islands at the first reverse.' One would think that the causes which make for its predominance were obvious. Apart from any question of national spirit or energy, there is the all-important fact that the men are there of their own free will, an advantage which I trust that we shall never be compelled to surrender. Again, the men are of longer service in every arm, and they have far more opportunities of actual fighting than come to any other force. Finally, they are divided into regiments, with centuries of military glory streaming from their banners, which carry on a mighty tradition. The very words the Guards, the Rifles, the Connaught Rangers, the Buffs, the Scots Greys, the Gordons, sound like bugle calls. How could an army be anything but dangerous which had such units in its line of battle?

And yet there remains the fact that both enemies and friends are surprised at our efficiency. This is no new phenomenon. Again and again in the course of history the British Armies have had to win once more the reputation, which had been forgotten. Continentals have always begun by refusing to take them seriously. Napoleon, who had never met them in battle, imagined that their unbroken success was due to some weakness in his marshals rather than to any excellence of the troops. 'At last I have them, these English,' he exclaimed, as he gazed at the thin red line at Waterloo. 'At last they have me, these English,' may have been his thought that evening as he spurred his horse out of the debacle. Foy warned him of the truth. 'The British infantry is the devil,' said he. 'You think so because you were beaten by them,' cried Napoleon. Like von Kluck or von Kluck's master, he had something to learn.

Why this continual depreciation? It may be that the world pays so much attention to our excellent right arm that it cannot give us credit for having a very serviceable left as well. Or it may be that they take seriously those jeremiads over our decay which are characteristic of our people, and very especially of many of our military thinkers. I have never been able to understand why they should be of so pessimistic a turn of mind, unless it be a sort of exaltation of that grumbling which has always been the privilege of the old soldier. Croker narrates how he met Wellington in his latter years, and how the Iron Duke told him that he was glad that he was so old, as he would not live to see the dreadful military misfortunes which were about to come to his country. Looking back we can see no reasons for such pessimism as this. Above all, the old soldier can never make any allowance for the latent powers which lie in civilian patriotism and valour. Only a year ago I had a long conversation with a well-known British General, in which he asserted with great warmth that in case of an Anglo-German war with France involved, the British public would never allow a trained soldier to leave these islands. He is at the Front himself and doing such good work that he has little time for reminiscence, but when he has he must admit that he underrated the nerve of his countrymen.

And yet under the pessimism of such men as he, there is a curious contradictory assurance that there are no troops like our own. The late Lord Goschen used to tell a story of a letter that he had from a captain in the Navy at the time when he was First Lord. This captain's ship was lying alongside a foreign cruiser in some port, and he compared in his report the powers of the two vessels. Lord Goschen said that his heart sank as he read the long catalogue of points in which the British ship was inferior – guns, armour, speed – until he came to the postscript, which was: 'I think I could take her in twenty minutes.'

With all the grumbling of our old soldiers there is always some reservation of the sort at the end of it. Of course those who are familiar with our ways of getting things done would understand that a good deal of the croaking is a means of getting our little army increased, or at least preventing its being diminished. But whatever the cause, the result has been the impression abroad of a 'contemptible little army.' Whatever surprise in the shape of 17-inch howitzers or 900-foot Zeppelins the Kaiser may have for us, it is a safe prophecy that it will be a small matter compared to that which Sir John French and his men will be to him.

But above all I look forward to the development of our mounted riflemen. This I say in no disparagement of our cavalry, who have done so magnificently. But the mounted rifleman is a peculiarly British product – British and American – with a fresh edge upon it from South Africa. I am most curious to see what a division of these fellows will make of the Uhlans. It is good to see that already the old banners are in the wind – Lovat's Horse, Scottish Horse, King Edward's Horse, and the rest. All that cavalry can do will surely be done by our cavalry. But I have always held, and I still very strongly hold, that the mounted rifleman has it in him to alter our whole conception of warfare, as the mounted archer did in his day; and now in this very war will be his first great chance upon a large scale. Ten thousand well-mounted, well-trained riflemen, young officers to lead them, all broad Germany with its towns, its railways, and its magazines before them – there lies one more surprise for the doctrinaires of Berlin.

Alliterativism
G. K. Chesterton

('French airmen have been flying over Baden and Bavaria, violating Belgian neutrality' – stated on German authority in the *Westminster Gazette*)

See the flying French depart
Like the bees of Bonaparte,
Swarming up with a most venomous vitality.
Over Baden and Bavaria,
And Brighton and Bulgaria,
Thus violating Belgian neutrality.

And the injured Prussian may
Not unreasonably say
'Why, it cannot be so small a nationality!

Since Brixton and Batavia,
Bolivia and Belgravia,
Are bursting with the Belgian neutrality.

By pure Alliteration
You may trace this curious nation,
And respect this somewhat scattered principality;
When you see a B in Both
You may take your Bible oath
You are violating Belgian neutrality.

Paris Mobilises
From *Fighting France: Dunkerque to Belfort*,
Edith Wharton

On the 30 July 1914, motoring north from Poitiers, we had lunched somewhere by the roadside under apple trees on the edge of a field. Other fields stretched away on our right and left to a border of woodland and a village steeple. All around was noonday quiet, and the sober, disciplined landscape which the traveller's memory is apt to evoke as distinctively French. Sometimes, even to accustomed eyes, these ruled-off fields and compact grey villages seem merely flat and tame; at other moments the sensitive imagination sees in every thrifty sod and even furrow the ceaseless vigilant attachment of generations faithful to the soil. The particular bit of landscape before us spoke in all its lines of that attachment. The air seemed full of the long murmur of human effort, the rhythm of oft-repeated tasks, the serenity of the scene smiled away the war rumours which had hung on us since morning.

All day the sky had been banked with thunderclouds, but by the time we reached Chartres, toward four o'clock, they had rolled away under the horizon, and the town was so saturated with sunlight that to pass into the cathedral was like entering the dense obscurity of a church in Spain. At first all detail was imperceptible; we were in a hollow night. Then, as the shadows gradually thinned and gathered themselves up into pier and vault and ribbing, there burst out of them great sheets and showers of colour. Framed by such depths of darkness, and steeped in a blaze of mid-summer sun, the familiar windows seemed singularly remote and yet overpoweringly vivid. Now they widened into dark-shored pools splashed with sunset, now glittered and menaced like the shields of fighting angels. Some were cataracts of sapphires, others roses dropped from a saint's tunic, others great carven platters strewn with heavenly regalia, others the sails of galleons bound for the Purple Islands; and in the western wall the scattered fires of the rose-window hung like a constellation in an African night. When one dropped one's eyes from these ethereal harmonies, the dark masses of masonry below them, all veiled and muffled in a mist pricked by a few altar lights, seemed to symbolise the life on earth, with its shadows, its heavy distances and its little islands of illusion. All that a great cathedral can be, all the meanings it can express, all the tranquilising power it can breathe upon the soul, all the richness of detail it can fuse into a large utterance of strength and beauty, the cathedral of Chartres gave us in that perfect hour.

It was sunset when we reached the gates of Paris. Under the heights of St Cloud and Suresnes, the reaches of the Seine trembled with the blue-pink lustre of an early Monet. The Bois lay about us in the stillness of a holiday evening, and the lawns of Bagatelle were as fresh as June. Below the Arc de Triomphe, the Champs Elysées sloped downward in a sun-powdered haze to the mist of fountains and the ethereal obelisk; and the currents of summer life ebbed and flowed with a normal beat under the trees of the radiating avenues. The great city, so made for peace and art and all humanest graces, seemed to lie by her riverside like a princess guarded by the watchful giant of the Eiffel Tower.

The next day, the air was thundery with rumours. Nobody believed them, everybody repeated them. War? Of course there couldn't be war! The Cabinets, like naughty children, were again dangling their feet over the edge; but the whole incalculable weight of things-as-they-were, of the daily necessary business of living, continued calmly and convincingly to assert itself against the bandying of diplomatic words. Paris went on steadily about her mid-summer business of feeding, dressing, and amusing the great army of tourists who were the only invaders she had seen for nearly half a century.

All the while, everyone knew that other work was going on also. The whole fabric of the country's seemingly undisturbed routine was threaded with noiseless invisible currents of preparation, the sense of them was in the calm air as the sense of changing weather is in the balminess of a perfect afternoon. Paris counted the minutes till the evening papers came.

They said little or nothing except what everyone was already declaring all over the country. 'We don't want war – *mais il faut que cela finisse!*' 'This kind of thing has got to stop': that was the only phase one heard. If diplomacy could still arrest the war, so much the better: no one in France wanted it. All who spent the first days of August in Paris will testify to the agreement of feeling on that point. But if war had to come, the country, and every heart in it, was ready.

At the dressmaker's, the next morning, the tired fitters were preparing to leave for their usual holiday. They looked pale and anxious – decidedly, there was a new weight of apprehension in the air. And in the Rue Royale, at the corner of the Place de la Concorde, a few people had stopped to look at a little strip of white paper against the wall of the Ministère de la Marine. 'General mobilisation' they read – and an armed nation knows what that means.

But the group about the paper was small and quiet. Passersby read the notice and went on. There were no cheers, no gesticulations: the dramatic sense of the race had already told them that the event was too great to be dramatised. Like a monstrous landslide it had fallen across the path of an orderly laborious nation, disrupting its routine, annihilating its industries, rending families apart, and burying under a heap of senseless ruin the patiently and painfully wrought machinery of civilisation ...

That evening, in a restaurant of the Rue Royale, we sat at a table in one of the open windows, abreast with the street, and saw the strange new crowds stream by. In an instant we were being shown what mobilisation was – a huge break in the normal flow of traffic, like the sudden rupture of a dyke. The street was flooded by the torrent of people sweeping past us to the various railway stations. All were on foot, and carrying their luggage; for since dawn every cab and taxi and motor-omnibus had disappeared. The War Office had thrown out its drag-net and caught them all in. The crowd that passed our window was chiefly composed of conscripts, the *mobilisables* of the first day, who were on the way to the station accompanied by their families and friends; but among them were little clusters of bewildered tourists, labouring along with bags and bundles, and watching their luggage pushed before them on handcarts – puzzled inarticulate waifs caught in the cross tides racing to a maelstrom.

In the restaurant, the befrogged and red-coated band poured out patriotic music, and the intervals between the courses that so few waiters were left to serve were broken by the ever-recurring obligation to stand up for the 'Marseillaise', to stand up for 'God Save the King', to stand up for the Russian National Anthem, to stand up again for the 'Marseillaise'. '*Et dire que ce sont des Hongrois qui jouent tout cela!*', a humourist remarked from the pavement.

As the evening wore on and the crowd about our window thickened, the loiterers outside began to join in the war songs. '*Allons, debout!*', and the loyal round begins again. '*La chanson du depart*' is a frequent demand; and the chorus of spectators chimes in roundly. A sort of quiet humour was the note of the street. Down the Rue Royale, toward the Madeleine, the bands of other restaurants were attracting other throngs, and martial refrains were strung along the boulevard like its garlands of arc-lights. It was a night of singing and acclamations, not boisterous, but gallant and determined. It was Paris *badauderie* at its best.

Meanwhile, beyond the fringe of idlers, the steady stream of conscripts still poured along. Wives and families trudged beside them, carrying all kinds of odd improvised bags and bundles. The impression disengaging itself from all this superficial confusion was that of a cheerful steadiness of spirit. The faces ceaselessly streaming

by were serious but not sad; nor was there any air of bewilderment
– the stare of driven cattle. All these lads and young men seemed
to know what they were about and why they were about it. The
youngest of them looked suddenly grown up and responsible; they
understood their stake in the job, and accepted it.

The next day, the army of mid-summer travel was immobilised
to let the other army move. No more wild rushes to the station, no
more bribing of concierges, vain quests for invisible cabs, haggard
hours of waiting in the queue at Cook's. No train stirred except to
carry soldiers, and the civilians who had not bribed and jammed their
way into a cranny of the thronged carriages leaving the first night
could only creep back through the hot streets to their hotel and wait.
Back they went, disappointed yet half-relieved, to the resounding
emptiness of porterless halls, waiterless restaurants, motionless lifts:
to the queer disjointed life of fashionable hotels suddenly reduced to
the intimacies and make-shift of a Latin Quarter pension. Meanwhile
it was strange to watch the gradual paralysis of the city. As the
motors, taxis, cabs and vans had vanished from the streets, so the
lively little steamers had left the Seine. The canalboats too were gone,
or lay motionless: loading and unloading had ceased. Every great
architectural opening framed an emptiness; all the endless avenues
stretched away to desert distances. In the parks and gardens no one
raked the paths or trimmed the borders. The fountains slept in their
basins, the worried sparrows fluttered unfed, and vague dogs, shaken
out of their daily habits, roamed unquietly, looking for familiar eyes.
Paris, so intensely conscious yet so strangely entranced, seemed to
have had curare injected into all her veins.

The next day – 2 August – from the terrace of the Hotel de Crillon
one looked down on a first faint stir of returning life. Now and then a
taxi-cab or a private motor crossed the Place de la Concorde, carrying
soldiers to the stations. Other conscripts, in detachments, tramped
by on foot with bags and banners. One detachment stopped before
the black-veiled statue of Strasbourg and laid a garland at her feet.
In ordinary times this demonstration would at once have attracted
a crowd; but at the very moment when it might have been expected

to provoke a patriotic outburst it excited no more attention than if one of the soldiers had turned aside to give a penny to a beggar. The people crossing the square did not even stop to look. The meaning of this apparent indifference was obvious. When an armed nation mobilises, everybody is busy, and busy in a definite and pressing way. It is not only the fighters that mobilise: those who stay behind must do the same. For each French household, for each individual man or woman in France, war means a complete reorganisation of life. The detachment of conscripts, unnoticed, paid their tribute to the Cause and passed on...

Looked back on from these sterner months those early days in Paris, in their setting of grave architecture and summer skies, wear the light of the ideal and the abstract. The sudden flaming up of national life, the abeyance of every small and mean preoccupation, cleared the moral air as the streets had been cleared, and made the spectator feel as though he were reading a great poem on war rather than facing its realities.

Something of this sense of exaltation seemed to penetrate the throngs who streamed up and down the boulevards till late into the night. All wheeled traffic had ceased, except that of the rare taxi-cabs impressed to carry conscripts to the stations; and the middle of the boulevards was as thronged with foot-passengers as an Italian market place on a Sunday morning. The vast tide swayed up and down at a slow pace, breaking now and then to make room for one of the volunteer 'legions' which were forming at every corner: Italian, Romanian, South American, North American, each headed by its national flag and hailed with cheering as it passed. But even the cheers were sober: Paris was not to be shaken out of her self-imposed serenity. One felt something nobly conscious and voluntary in the mood of this quiet multitude. Yet it was a mixed throng, made up of every class, from the scum of the Exterior Boulevards to the cream of the fashionable restaurants. These people, only two days ago, had been leading a thousand different lives, in indifference or in antagonism to each other, as alien as enemies across a frontier: now workers and idlers, thieves, beggars, saints, poets, drabs and sharpers, genuine people and showy shams, were all bumping up against each other in an instinctive community of emotion. The 'people,' luckily, predominated; the faces of workers look best in such a crowd, and there were thousands of them, each illuminated and singled out by its magnesium-flash of passion.

I remember especially the steady-browed faces of the women; and also the small but significant fact that every one of them had remembered to bring her dog. The biggest of these amiable companions had to take their chance of seeing what they could through the forest of human legs; but every one that was portable was snugly lodged in the bend of an elbow, and from this safe perch scores and scores of small serious muzzles, blunt or sharp, smooth or woolly, brown or grey or white or black or brindled, looked out on the scene with the quiet awareness of the Paris dog. It was certainly a good sign that they had not been forgotten that night.

The Send-Off
Wilfred Owen

Down the close, darkening lanes they sang their way
To the siding-shed,
And lined the train with faces grimly gay.

Their breasts were stuck all white with wreath and spray
As men's are, dead.

Dull porters watched them, and a casual tramp
Stood staring hard,
Sorry to miss them from the upland camp.

Then, unmoved, signals nodded, and a lamp
Winked to the guard.

So secretly, like wrongs hushed-up, they went.
They were not ours:
We never heard to which front these were sent.

Nor there if they yet mock what women meant
Who gave them flowers.

Shall they return to beatings of great bells
In wild trainloads?
A few, a few, too few for drums and yells,
May creep back, silent, to still village wells
Up half-known roads.

Jem Blythe Goes to War
From *Rilla of Ingleside*, L. M. Montgomery

Jem Blythe and Jerry Meredith left next morning. It was a dull day, threatening rain, and the clouds lay in heavy grey rolls over the sky; but almost everybody in the Glen and Four Winds and Harbour Head and Upper Glen and over-harbour – except Whiskers-on-the-moon – was there to see them off. The Blythe family and the Meredith family were all smiling. Even Susan, as Providence did ordain, wore a smile, though the effect was somewhat more painful than tears would have been. Faith and Nan were very pale and very gallant. Rilla thought she would get on very well if something in her throat didn't choke her, and if her lips didn't take such spells of trembling. Dog Monday was there, too. Jem had tried to say good-bye to him at Ingleside but Monday implored so eloquently that Jem relented and let him go to the station. He kept close to Jem's legs and watched every movement of his beloved master.

'I can't bear that dog's eyes,' said Mrs Meredith.

'The beast has more sense than most humans,' said Mary Vance. Well, did we any of us ever think we'd live to see this day? I bawled all night to think of Jem and Jerry going like this. I think they're plumb deranged. Miller got a maggot in his head about going but I soon talked him out of it – likewise his aunt said a few touching things. For once in our lives Kitty Alec and I agree. It's a miracle that isn't likely to happen again.

'There's Ken, Rilla.' Rilla knew Kenneth was there. She had been acutely conscious of it from the moment he had sprung from Leo West's buggy. Now he came up to her smiling.

'Doing the brave-smiling-sister-stunt, I see. What a crowd for the Glen to muster! Well, I'm off home in a few days myself.'

A queer little wind of desolation that even Jem's going had not caused blew over Rilla's spirit.

'Why? You have another month of vacation.'

'Yes – but I can't hang around Four Winds and enjoy myself when the world's on fire like this. It's me for little old Toronto where I'll find some way of helping in spite of this bally ankle.' I'm not looking at Jem and Jerry – makes me too sick with envy. 'You girls are great – no crying, no grim endurance. The boys'll go off with a good taste in their mouths. I hope Persis and mother will be as game when my turn comes.'

'Oh, Kenneth the war will be over before your turn cometh.'

There – the train was coming – mother was holding Jem's hand – Dog Monday was licking it – everybody was saying goodbye – the train was in! Jem kissed Faith before everybody – old Mrs Drew whooped hysterically – the men, led by Kenneth, cheered – Rilla felt Jem seize her hand – 'Good-bye, Spider' – somebody kissed her cheek – she believed it was Jerry but never was sure – they were off – the train was pulling out – Jem and Jerry were waving to everybody – everybody was waving back – mother and Nan were smiling still, but as if they had just forgotten to take the smile off – Monday was howling dismally and being forcibly restrained by the Methodist minister from tearing after the train – Susan was waving her best bonnet and hurrahing like a man – had she gone crazy? – the train rounded a curve. They had gone.

Rilla came to herself with a gasp. There was a sudden quiet. Nothing to do now but to go home – and wait. The doctor and Mrs

Blythe walked off together – so did Nan and Faith – so did John Meredith and Rosemary. Walter and Una and Shirley and Di and Carl and Rilla went in a group. Susan had put her bonnet back on her head, hindside foremost, and stalked grimly off alone. Nobody missed Dog Monday at first. When they did Shirley went back for him. He found Dog Monday curled up in one of the shipping-sheds near the station and tried to coax him home. Dog Monday would not move. He wagged his tail to show he had no hard feelings but no blandishments availed to budge him.

'Guess Monday has made up his mind to wait there till Jem comes back,' said Shirley, trying to laugh as he rejoined the rest. This was exactly what Dog Monday had done. His dear master had gone – he, Monday, had been deliberately and of malice aforethought prevented from going with him by a demon disguised in the garb of a Methodist minister. Wherefore, he, Monday, would wait there until the smoking, snorting monster, which had carried his hero off, carried him back.

Ay, wait there, little faithful dog with the soft, wistful, puzzled eyes. But it will be many a long bitter day before your boyish comrade comes back to you.

Airmen From Overseas
Laurence Binyon

Who are these that come from the ends of the oceans,
Coming as the swallows come out of the South
In the glory of Spring? They are come among us
With purpose in the eyes, with a smile on the mouth.

These are they who have left the familiar faces,
Sights, sounds and scents of familiar land,
Taking no care for security promised aforetime,
Sweetness of home and the future hope had planned.

A lode-star drew them: Britain, standing alone
Clear in the darkness, not to be overcome,
Though the huge masses of hate are hurled against her –
Wherever the spirit of freedom breathes, is Home.

Soon are they joined with incomparable comrades,
Britain's flower, Britain's pride,
Against all odds despising the boastful Terror;
On joyous wings in the ways of the wind they ride.

From afar they battle for our ancient island,
Soaring and pouncing, masters of the skies,
They are heard in the night by the lands betrayed and captive
And a throbbing of hope to their thunder-throb replies.

To dare incredible things, from the ends of ocean
They are coming and coming over the perilous seas.
How shall we hail them? Truly there are no words
And no song worthy of these.

Attack from the Sea
From *The Crowded Street*, Winifred Holtby

Because Aunt Rose was not yet well, breakfast at 199 The Esplanade, Scarborough, was postponed until nine o'clock. Uncle George, of course, kept to his usual punctuality of half past eight. Muriel at half past seven that morning could hear him whistling cheerily as he trotted along to the bathroom.

She lay between linen sheets that felt chill and smooth. Her hot-water bottle had grown cold as a dead fish. Drowsily she moved it to the edge of the bed with her feet. She seemed to have lain like this all night, waiting for the maid to bring her water, and thinking sleepily of Godfrey Neale.

It had been such a funny evening. She and her mother and Uncle George had met him at the Princess Royal Hotel, and had dined together. A queer self-possession alien to her nature had seized upon Muriel. She remembered looking at her slim figure in the long glass of the corridor and thinking that she ought all her life to have worn that vivid cherry colour instead of blues and greys. It gave her a strange courage and merriment, so that she had laughed and talked, conscious of the flame of her bright dress, and feeling like a princess in a fairytale suddenly released from her enchantment.

She had seen things about Godfrey too that she had never seen before. Most clearly she remembered how, when they were sitting in the lounge after dinner, his lean brown fingers had pressed the charred end of his cigarette into the saucer of his coffee-cup, and she had thought, 'He is like that. When he has finished with a thing, he crushes it like that without thinking. He is not cruel, nor ungrateful, only a little stupid and lacking in imagination.' She remembered the stories that Marshington told of his flirtations with Gladys Seton, and the Honourable Lucy Leyton, and then Phyllis Marshall Gurney. He had meant nothing. He simply had never given a thought to what they might have dreamed to be his meaning. She had felt old and very wise and disillusioned.

Then the orchestra played, and he had looked up suddenly, twisting his head and frowning and beating time against the arm of his chair. He said to Muriel:

'What is this tune? I seem to know it?'

'It's Mignon's song, *Kennst du das Land*. Have you heard Mignon?'

'No,' he said. A shadow of discomfort crossed his face. He struggled to remember something. Muriel, knowing what he sought, remembered the day in spring when he had driven her home from the Vicarage. 'No. I can't say I have. Yet I heard that tune...'

'At our house,' said Muriel. 'The first time that you ever came. Had you forgotten?'

He looked at her then, and seeing that she offered him simple friendliness he said, speaking deliberately:

'No. I have not forgotten. I think, whatever happens, that I shall never forget.'

And she had nodded, understanding him. And for the first time she had been aware that someday he might ask her to marry him simply because she would not ask him to forget.

As they walked home, wrapped in furs, along the Esplanade, Mrs Hammond had murmured happily:

'Well, dear, did Godfrey suggest meeting us again?'

'Yes, he wants me to go to the pictures with him on Monday afternoon. We could have tea at the new Pavilion place first.'

The wind blew from the darkness against them. It lashed Muriel's hair against her eyes, and rushed against her, as though it were forcing her back along the road to Godfrey.

Mrs Hammond seemed to be quite sure now. Muriel lay wondering. Until that night, she had never believed it to be possible, but now she saw that it was almost likely, for nobody else would ask from him so little, and he, she realised it at last, had not been proud but humble, aware how little there was for him to give. She had never liked him so well as now when she knew that he had been true to his idea of Clare. He was conceited. He was sure of himself. He was terribly limited and arrogant and complacent, but he was wistful, too, for something quite beyond his comprehension, and just because of that he might ask Muriel to marry him. There were, of course, other reasons, and to Godfrey they would be important, for nine-tenths of him was just the practical country squire, devoted to his estate and his position. The Hammonds had money. In spite of her father's recklessness, he was himself too able, and Old Dickie Hammond had been too cautious, to allow the business once built up to crumble. With the Hammond money Godfrey could keep hunters. He would not upset Mrs Neale, who wanted to have a grandson, and who cared little for the smart young women from the county families. Arthur Hammond's daughter would present to her no insurmountable obstacle, because Muriel was also Rachel Bennet's daughter, and the Bennets had once been as good a stock as any in the East Riding. Muriel, too, was all Bennet and no Hammond. She was not like Connie, with the coarse strain that gave her vitality hardly curbed by Bennet gentleness.

If he asked her to marry him, she would, of course, accept. It would be a splendid triumph, the end of her long years of waiting and feeling that she was a complete failure. It would be the consummation of her duty to her mother, of her success as a woman. She would be the mistress of the Weare Grange, the mother of its heir. She would be mistress then of Marshington, and of her own rich destiny.

Strange, it seemed to her, that her body lay limp and unresponsive between the cold sheets, that the word marriage conveyed to her, not a picture of Godfrey but of the Weare Grange, that she shrank from the thought of further intimacy with his bodily perfection and his limited mind. He was nice, far nicer than she had thought. There was even that little unexpected strain of the romantic in him. She was sure that she could love him. 'I *have* loved him all my life,' said Muriel, and lay, waiting to feel the glow of love warming her coldness.

'This is not as it should be,' she felt. But nothing ever was as it should be in a world where the best conclusion was a compromise. She turned her face into the pillow and thought of Martin Elliott, and the happiness that glowed about Delia's swift mind. 'Well, if Godfrey had been like Martin Elliott,' she thought.

Crash!

As though the fury of a thousand thunderbolts had hurled, crashing against the house, the noise shattered the morning and then ceased.

So swiftly the quietness closed in again, it seemed as though the sound were but a jagged rent across the silence, letting into the world for a moment the roaring of the spheres. Yet, though this one blow crashed and then was still, Muriel felt as though such violence must last for ever, and silence became the incredible thing.

She lay quite still, her limbs relaxed in the flat darkness of the bed, her arms lying beside her, heavy with sleep. She did not believe that the sound had really happened. Her thoughts returned to their path. If Godfrey had been a man like Martin Elliott, someone in whom one could seek companionship of mind, with whom one could feel as much at home as with one's own thoughts...

Crash! Crash! Crash!

It really had happened then.

It was not an illusion. She drew one hand across her forehead that felt damp and cold.

Of course this was what Uncle George had said would happen. The noise was the noise of guns, big guns firing. This was what the little pamphlets had told them to prepare for. This was the War. Only it had no business to happen so early in the morning before they were properly awake.

Crash! Crash!

Huge sounds, flat and ugly, dropped into the silence of the room. Slowly she turned and sat up in bed. Her curtains were drawn aside, but she could see nothing through her window. The panes looked as though they had been painted grey. Solid and opaque, the fog blotted out the sea.

It seemed absurd that this blinding, shattering immensity of sound should yet convey no impression to the eye.

She lay back in bed, her mind completely calm and rather listless, but she could feel the perspiration from her armpits soaking her nainsook nightgown. That was curious.

'Muriel! Muriel!'

In an interval of silence her mother's voice called to her. The door opened. Mrs Hammond in her dressing-gown of padded lilac silk stood by the bed.

'Muriel, are you there? Are you all right?'

'Yes. Of course I am all right. What is it?'

She wished that her mother would go away and let her lie there quietly.

'Get up, get up. Come to my room. You mustn't lie there, facing the sea.' There was a sharp note of anxiety in her mother's voice.

Facing the sea. Why shouldn't she face the sea? Slowly Muriel thrust her feet out of bed, her toes twitching in the cold air as she felt for her slippers along the carpet.

'Quick, quick, never mind your slippers. Ah!'

Another sound broke about them, sharper than any before, as though the whole world had splintered into fragments round them. Muriel still fumbled below the bed.

'I can't find my slippers,' she said stupidly.

'Look!' gasped Mrs Hammond.

Muriel looked at the window. The shattered edges of the panes still shivered in their wooden frame. On the floor below broken glass lay scattered. The noise had become visible at last.

After that, a series of odd and ridiculous things all happened very quickly. Uncle George appeared in his shirt-sleeves, with one side of his face lathered for shaving.

'I'm going to the Garbutts'. Their car must take Rose. Get her ready.'

Mrs Hammond and Muriel hurried to Aunt Rose's room. Muriel always remembered afterwards kneeling by her aunt's bed and drawing cashmere stockings, two pairs, over those fat legs, where blue veins ran criss-cross below the tight-stretched skin. It seemed to her a fantastic sort of nightmare that could bring her to such close contemplation of her aunt's legs. Then Uncle George returned, and they all bundled Aunt Rose's shawls downstairs into the car, hoping that she was still inside them, for they could see nothing of her.

As the door opened, and Muriel saw the blank wall of fog along the Esplanade, she felt as though she were standing on the world's edge, staring into the din of chaos. All the time the vast noise pounded on above them.

Then they were all running, Uncle George, her mother and herself, down a grey funnel with tall looming sides. They stumbled in a little tripping run as one runs in a dream. Muriel tried to tell herself, 'This is an immense adventure. The Germans are landing at Cayton Bay under cover of the fog. Or they are on the foreshore. This noise is a bombardment from battleships to cover the landing, and we are running for our lives to Seamer Valley. This grey funnel is a street leading to Mount Road. I am running for my life and I am not afraid.'

The noise crashed above them through the fog, as though a grey curtain of sound had shut out the light. Little knots of people in peculiar attire appeared from the grey mists, and blew like wandering smoke along the alley, only to vanish again into vapour.

'In another moment,' Muriel told herself, 'we may all be dead.' But she could not make herself feel really interested in anything except her stockings, which were sliding to her ankles, and felt most uncomfortable. She would have liked to stop and fasten them, but she felt that it would somehow not be etiquette, to stop to fasten one's stockings in the middle of a race for life. 'I was not brought up to adventures,' she told herself. 'I don't yet know the way to manage them.'

Then her mother stopped. 'I–I can't–run–any–more,' she panted. Her small, fat figure in its fur coat had been bouncing along in little hops, like an India-rubber ball. Now she stumbled and clung on to a railing for support. 'You–go–on. I'll come.'

'Draw a deep breath, Rachel, and count three,' said Uncle George solemnly. He performed Sandow's exercises every morning before breakfast and was therefore an athletic authority.

Muriel watched them, while the running figures stumbled past, quiet beneath a canopy of sound.

' You–go–on,' Mrs Hammond repeated.

'Now, Rachel, go steady. Breathe as I count. One, two.'

They were not afraid, any of them. They had a strange, courageous dignity, these two comical little people, standing beneath the desolation of deafening clamour and breathing deeply. 'Mother,' thought Muriel, 'is thinking of Father.' Uncle George was thinking of Aunt Rose. Muriel was thinking about herself, and the strangeness of it all, and how she was not afraid. For there was something that made each one of them feel stronger than the fear of death.

A woman rushing along the pavement with her perambulator pushed it into Muriel and nearly knocked her over. She sobbed as she ran and the two babies in the perambulator were crying.

'This is real,' said Muriel to herself. 'This is a really great adventure, and none of us know this minute where we shall be tomorrow and nothing matters like success or failure now, but only courage. This must be why the soldiers sing when they go to the trenches. It's all so beautifully simple.' She wanted to die then, when life was simple, rather than face Marshington again and the artificial complications that entangled her life there.

An elation possessed her. She could have sung and shouted. She stumbled down the rough road again, holding her mother's arm and talking to her foolishly about what they would have for breakfast when they awoke from this strange dream. She remembered saying that she would have kippers, although she knew that she really hated them and rarely ate more than toast and marmalade. But then she didn't run for her life every morning before breakfast. She saw Seamer as some goal of human endeavour, very far away in the distance. It did not seem to be an ordinary place at all.

Suddenly from their feet, the Mere stretched, flat and lifeless beyond tall reeds, clouded like a looking-glass on which somebody has breathed. The noise grew louder. Somebody called, 'Turn to your right. Your right. They're firing straight in front.'

And even then, Muriel was not frightened. They wandered in a vague, irrelevant place among heaps of garbage, and cabbage stalks, and teapot lids, and torn magazine covers. Just to their left rose a little hovel, the crazy sort of shelter that allotment holders erect to hold their tools. She looked at it, blinking through the mist and noise, and then, suddenly, it was not there. It just collapsed and sank quietly down in a little cloud of smoke, hardly denser than the fog. It seemed appropriate to the absurd nightmare of the whole affair that a board on a post should grin to them out of the mist, saying, 'Rubbish may be shot here.'

'Ha, ha!' laughed Uncle George. 'They're shooting rubbish, and no mistake.'

And Mrs Hammond pushed back her hair feebly with one free hand and laughed too.

Then they were all leaning over a gate, unable for the moment to run further. As though for their amusement, a grotesque and unending procession passed before them on the road to Seamer. There was a small child, leading a great collie dog that limped forlornly on three legs; an old man, leading two pretty young girls with greatcoats above their nightgowns, who giggled and shivered as they ran. There were little boys pushing wheelbarrows, and waggons holding school children, and motor cars, and bicycles, and ladies in fur coats and lacy caps. Then a girls' school came trotting, two and two, in an orderly procession, laughing and chattering as they ran. Then more cars and cycles and donkey carts.

Nothing was quite normal except the girls' school. Everyone else was a little fantastic, a little distorted, like people in a dream.

All the time on the other side of the road, the soldiers were passing into Scarborough, some marching, some swinging their legs from the back of motor-lorries, some flashing past on motorcycles. As they passed, some of them cheered the procession leaving the town and called, 'Are we downhearted?' And the refugees shouted 'No!' And some cried and sobbed as they ran, and some shouted back and some said nothing, but plodded on silently looking neither to the left nor right.

A cheerful, round-faced man in pyjamas and a woman's flannel dressing-jacket nodded at Uncle George.

'Heard the news?' he shouted. 'They've got into the town. That's why the firing has stopped. Our chaps are giving 'em hell. I'll give 'em half an hour until the fleet comes up.'

Everybody talked to everybody else. And Scarborough was said to be in flames, and our men were fighting all along the foreshore, where the little cheap booths stood in summer. While they talked, the mist seemed to break, and the steep hills of Seamer shouldered up from the tattered cloaks of fog.

It was just then that a lorry swung by down the road, and stopped for a moment, blocked by the crowd. The officer in charge stood up to see what had happened, and Muriel saw standing very tall and clear against the hills of Seamer, her lord and master, Godfrey Neale. He had seen Muriel.

Their eyes met, and for a moment they became conscious of nothing but each other. He smiled at her and stooped down from the lorry.

'You are all right?'

'Quite. We're going to Seamer. We shall be all right.'

She thought that he was going to his death, and then the thought came to her that she loved him. Here at last she had found all that she had been seeking. The fullness of life was hers, here on the threshold of death. She knew that it must always be so; and she lifted her head to meet love, unafraid.

'Good luck to you!' she called, and smiled to him across the road.

'Good luck!' he said.

The words came back to her, 'Good luck have thou with thine honour. Ride on because of the word of truth of meekness and righteousness, and thy right hand shall teach thee terrible things.'

The lorry swept him away along the road.

Retreat
Charles T. Foxcroft

It was a nightmare week of thirst and dust –
With fairly heavy scraps at the beginning –
And disappointment, mixed with a queer trust
That we were winning.

They say one German rush stopped strangely short –
The Boches fell back; their horses couldn't face
Something! when we were in a tightish place –
Somewhere near Agincourt.

I wasn't there – and of that whole crammed week
Only two little things stick in my mind;
Our battery – we were rearmost, so to speak –
Had left me miles behind.

In a great field of roots – there crouching tight
Across those turnips casting backwards glances –
Less than a mile behind on a low height
I caught a gleam of lances!

(I'd felt that thrill in my small boy existence
When Porsena of Clusium in his pride

Marched upon Rome – and the 'wan burghers spied'
His vanguard in the distance!)

Behind that hill was hid a host too vast
To count – much too tremendous to alarm me!
These were *their* first – and I the very last
Of French's little army!

– Oh yes, we'd lots of shelling, heaps of scraps –
They all but had us once – and shot my stallion
From Fez – but funked a dozen Highland chaps
Who tricked a whole Battalion!

One other thing – I'd halted fairly beat –
A baking road – some poplars over-arching –
Men simply tumbling down with thirst and heat,
And crumpled up with marching.

There was a weedy 'Sub', who used to shy
At work and drill and such – like useless trifles!
Just then he passed me, limping, *whistling,* by
Hung stiff with Tommies' rifles!

* * *

Though of that week I never want to talk –
I'll think of Mons, whenever I remember
The valse tune that he whistled – or I walk
Through turnips in September

The Wounded from the Aisne
From *Diary of A Nursing Sister on the Western Front,* Anon.

Le Mans, Saturday, September 19th. It seems that we five who came
up last Monday are being kept to staff another Stationary Hospital

farther up, when it is ready; at least that is what it looks like from sundry rumours – if so – good enough.

We have been all day in caps and aprons at L'Evêché, marking linen and waiting for orders on the big staircase. I've also been over both hospitals. The bad cases all seem to be dropped here off the trains; there are some awful mouth, jaw, head, leg, and spine cases, who can't recover, or will only be crippled wrecks. You can't realise that it has all been done on purpose, and that none of them are accidents or surgical diseases. And they seem all to take it as a matter of course; the bad ones who are conscious don't speak, and the better ones are all jolly and smiling, and ready 'to have another smack.' One little room had two wounded German prisoners, with an armed guard. One who was shot through the spine died while I was there – his orderly and the Sister were with him. The other is a spy – nearly well – who has to be very carefully watched.

They are all a long time between the field and the Hospital. One told me he was wounded on Tuesday, was one day in a hospital, and then travelling till today, Saturday. No wonder their wounds are full of straw and grass. (Haven't heard of any more tetanus.) Most haven't had their clothes off, or washed, for three weeks, except face and hands.

No war news today, except that the Germans are well fortified and entrenched in their positions N. of Rheims.

Sunday, September 20th. Began with early service at the Jesuit School Hospital at 6.30, and the rest of the day one will never forget. The fighting for these concrete entrenched positions of the Germans behind Rheims has been so terrific since last Sunday that the number of casualties has been enormous. Three trains full of wounded, numbering altogether 1,175 cases, have been dressed at the station today; we were sent down at 11 this morning. The train I was put to had 510 cases. You boarded a cattle-truck, armed with a tray of dressings and a pail; the men were lying on straw; had been in trains for several days; most had only been dressed once, and many were gangrenous. If you found one urgently needed amputation or operation, or was likely to die, you called an M.O. to have him taken off the train for Hospital. No one grumbled or made any fuss. Then you joined the throng in the dressing-station, and for hours doctors of all ranks, Sisters and orderlies, grappled with the stream of stretchers, and limping, staggering, bearded, dirty, fagged men, and ticketed them off for the motor ambulances to the Hospitals, or back to the train, after dressing them. The platform was soon packed with stretchers with all the bad cases waiting patiently to be taken to Hospital. We cut off the silk vest of a dirty, brigandish-looking officer, nearly finished with a wound through his lung. The Black Watch and Camerons were almost unrecognisable in their rags. The staple dressing is tincture of iodine; you don't attempt anything but swabbing with lysol, and then gauze dipped in iodine. They were nearly all shrapnel shell wounds more ghastly than anything I have ever seen or smelt; the Mauser wounds of the Boer War were pin-pricks compared with them. There was also a huge train of French wounded being dressed on the other side of the station, including lots of weird, gaily-bedecked Zouaves.

There was no real confusion about the whole day, owing to the good organising of the No.– Clearing Hospital people who run it. Every man was fed, and dressed and sorted.

They'll have a heavy time at the two hospitals tonight with the cases sent up from the trains.

M. and I are now – 9 p.m. – in charge of a train of 141 (with an M.O. and two orderlies) for St Nazaire; we jump out at the stations and see to them, and the orderlies and the people on the stations feed them: we have the worst cases next to us. We may get there some time tomorrow morning, and when they are taken off, we train back, arriving probably on Wednesday at Le Mans. The lot on this train are the best leavings of today's trains, a marvellously cheery lot, munching bread and jam and their small share of hot tea, and blankets have just been issued. We ourselves have a rug, and a ration of bread, tea, and jam; we had dinner on the station.

When I think of your Red Cross practices on boy scouts, and the grim reality, it makes one wonder. And the biggest wonder of it all is the grit there is in them, and the price they are individually and unquestioningly paying for doing their bit in this War.

Monday, September 21st. In train on way back to Le Mans from St Nazaire. We did the journey in twelve hours, and arrived at 9 this morning, which was very good, considering the congestion on the line. In the middle of the night we pulled up alongside an immense troop train, taking a whole Brigade of D. of Cornwall's L.I. up to the Front, such a contrast to our load coming away from the Front. Our lot will be a long time getting to bed; the Medical Officers at St N. told us there were already two trains in, and no beds left on hospitals or ships, and 1,300 more expected today; four died in one of the trains; ours were pretty well, after the indescribable filth and fug of the train all night; it was not an ambulance train, but trucks and ordinary carriages. The men say there are hardly any officers left in many regiments. There has never been this kind of rush to be coped with anywhere, but the Germans must be having worse. We had thirteen German prisoners tacked on to us with a guard of the London Scottish, the first Territorials to come out, bursting with health and pride and keenness. They are not in the fighting line yet, but are used as escorts for the G.P. among other jobs. One of the men on our train had had his shoulder laid open for six inches by a shell, where he couldn't see the wound. He asked me if it was a bullet wound! He himself thought it was too large for that, and might be shrapnel! He hadn't mentioned it all night.

We had some dressings to be done again this morning, and then left them in charge of the M.O. and two orderlies, and went to report ourselves to the A.D.M.S. and get a warrant for the return journey. We shall get in to Le Mans somewhere about midnight. I'm not a bit tired, strange to say; we got a few rests in the night, but couldn't sleep.

Tuesday, September 22nd. Got back to Le Mans at 2 a.m. – motor-ambulanced up to the hospital, where an orderly made lovely beds for us on stretchers, with brown blankets and pillows, in the theatre, and labelled the door 'Operation,' in case anyone should disturb us. At 6 we went to our respective diggings for a wash and breakfast, and reported to Matron at 8. We have been two days and two nights in our clothes; food where, when, and what one could get; one wash only on a station platform at a tap which a sergeant kindly pressed for me while I washed! One cleaning of teeth in the dark on the line between trucks. They have no water on trains or at stations, except on the engine, which makes tea in cans for you for the men when it stops.

We are to rest today, to be ready for another train tonight if necessary. The line from the Front to Rouen – where there are two General Hospitals – is cut; hence this appalling overcrowding at our base. When we got back this morning, nine of those we took off the trains on Sunday afternoon had died here, and one before he reached the hospital – three of tetanus. I haven't heard how many at the other hospital at the Jesuit school – tetanus there too. Some of the amputations die of septic absorption and shock, and you wouldn't wonder if you saw them. I went to the nine o'clock Choral High Mass this morning at that glorious and beautiful Cathedral – all gorgeous old glass and white and grey stone, slender Gothic and fat Norman. It was very fine and comforting.

The sick officers are frightfully pleased to see *The Times*, no matter how old; so are we. I've asked M. to collect their ½d. picture daily papers once a week for the men.

Wednesday, September 23rd. Have been helping in the wards at No.– today. The Sisters and orderlies there have all about twice what they can get through – the big dressings are so appalling and new cases have been coming in – all stretcher cases. As soon as they begin to recover at all they are sent down to the base to make room for worse ones off the trains. Tomorrow I am on station duty again – possibly for another train.

There is a rumour that three British cruisers have been sunk by a submarine – it can't be true.

I don't see why this battle along the French frontier should ever come to an end, at any rate till both armies are exhausted, and decide to go to bed. The men say we can't spot their guns – they are too well hidden in these concrete entrenchments.

The weather is absolutely glorious all day, and the stars all night. Orion, with his shining bodyguard, from Sirius to Capella, is blazing every morning at 4.

Thursday, September 24th, 3 p.m. Taking 480 sick and wounded down to St Nazaire, with a junior staff nurse, one M.O., and two orderlies. Just been feeding them all at Angers; it is a stupendous business. The train is miles long – no corridor or ambulance; they have straw to lie on the floors and stretchers. The M.O. has been two nights in the train already on his way down from the Front (four miles from the guns), and we joined on to him with a lot of hospital cases sent down to the base. I've been collecting the worst ones into carriages near ours all the way down when we stop; but of course you miss a good many. Got my haversack lined with *jaconet* and filled with cut-dressings, very convenient, as you have both hands free. We continually stop at little stations, so you can get to a good many of them, and we get quite expert at clawing along the footboards; some of the men, with their eyes, noses, or jaws shattered, are so extraordinarily good and uncomplaining. Got hold of a spout-feeder and some tubing at Angers for a boy in the Grenadier Guards, with a gaping hole through his mouth to his chin, who can't eat, and cannot otherwise drink. The French people bring coffee, fruit, and all sorts of things to them when we stop.

We shall have to wait at St Nazaire all day, and come back by night tomorrow.

One swanky Ambulance Train carries four permanent Sisters to the Front to fetch cases to Le Mans and the base. They go to Villeneuve. They say the country is deserted, crops left to waste, houses empty, and when you get there no one smiles or speaks, but listens to the guns. The men seem to think the Germans have got our range, but we haven't found theirs. The number of casualties must be nearly into five figures this last battle alone; and when you think of the Russians, the Germans, the French, the Austrians, and the Belgians all like that, the whole convulsion seems more meaningless than ever for civilised nations.

This is in scraps, owing to the calls of duty. The beggars simply swarm out of the train at every stop – if they can limp or pull up by one arm – to get the fruit and things from the French.

Friday, September 25th. In train back to Le Mans, 9 p.m. We landed our tired, stiff, painful convoy at St Nazaire at 8.45 yesterday evening. The M.O.s there told us our lot made 1,800 that had come down since early morning; one load of bad cases took eight hours to unload. The officers all seemed depressed and overworked, and they were having a very tight fit to get beds for them at the various hospitals at St Nazaire. At about 10 p.m. the last were taken off by the motor ambulances, and we got some dinner on the station with our Civil Surgeon, who was looking forward to a night in a tent out of a train.

The R.T.O. found us an empty first class carriage in the station to sleep in, and the sergeant found us a candle and matches and put us to bed, after a sketchy wash provided by the buffet lady.

The din was continuous all night, so one didn't sleep much, but had a decent rest (and a flea). The sergeant called us at 6.30, and we had another sketchy wash, and coffee and rolls and jam at the buffet. Then we found our way to the hospital ship, *Carisbrook Castle*. The Army Sister in charge was most awfully kind, showed us over, made the steward turn on hot baths for us, provided notepaper, kept us to lunch – the nicest meal we've seen for weeks! The ship had 500 cases on board, and was taking 200 more – many wounded officers.

A captain of the — told me all his adventures from the moment he was hit till now. His regiment had nine officers killed and twenty-seven wounded. He said they knew things weren't going well in that retreat, but they never knew how critical it was at the time.

After lunch, we took our grateful leave and went to the A.D.M.S.'s office for our return warrants for the R.T.O. (I have just had to sign it for fourteen, as senior officer of our two selves and twelve A.S.C. men taking two trucks of stores, who have no officer with them!) There we heard that ten of our Sisters were ordered to Nantes for

duty by the 4.28, so we headed back to the station to meet them and
see them off. They were all frightfully glad to be on the move at last,
and we had a great meeting. The rest are still bathing at La Baule and
cursing their luck.

While we were getting some coffee in the only patisserie in the
dirty little town, seven burly officer boys of the Black Watch came
in to buy cakes for the train, they said, tonight. They were nearly
all second lieutenants, one captain, and were so excited at going up
to the Front they couldn't keep still. They asked us eagerly if we'd
had many of 'our regiment' wounded, and how many casualties
were there, and how was the fighting going, and how long would
the journey take. (The nearer you get to the Front the longer it
takes, as trains are always having to shunt and go round loops
to make room for supply trains.) They didn't seem to have the
dimmest idea what they're in for, bless them. They are on this train
in the next carriage.

The Padre told me he was the only one at St Nazaire for all the
hospitals and all the troops in camp (15,000 in one camp alone).

He had commandeered the Bishop of Khartoum to help him, and
another bishop, who both happen to be here.

We are now going to turn out the light, and hope for the best till
they come to look at the warrant or turn us out to change.

6 a.m. At Sablé at 4 a.m. we were turned out for two hours; a wee
open station. Mr_ and our Civil Surgeon were most awfully decent
to us: turned a sleepy official out of a room for us, and at 5 came and
dug us out to have coffee and brioches with them. Then we went for
a sunrise walk round the village, and were finally dragged into their
carriage, as they thought it was more comfortable than ours. Just
passed a big French ambulance train full from Compiègne.

At Le Mans the train broke up again, and everybody got out. We
motor-ambulanced up to the Hospital with the three night Sisters
coming off station duty. Matron wanted us to go to bed for the day;
but we asked to come on after lunch, as they were busy and we
weren't overtired. I'm realising tonight that I have been on the train
four nights out of six, and bed is bliss at this moment.

I was sent to No._ Stationary at the Jesuits' College to take over the officers at one o'clock.

One was an angelic gunner boy with a septic leg and an undaunted smile, except when I dressed his leg and he said 'Oh, damn!' The other bad one was wounded in the shoulder. They kept me busy till Sister — came back, and then I went to my beloved Cathedral (and vergered some Highland Tommies round it, they had fits of awe and joy over it, and grieved over 'Reems'). It is awfully hard to make these sick officers comfortable, with no sheets or pillowcases, no air ring-cushions, pricky shirts, thick cups without saucers, &c. One longs for the medical comforts of —.

I hear tonight that Miss — the Principal Matron on the Lines of Communication (on the War Establishment Staff) is here again, and may have a new destination for some of us details.

The heading in *Le Matin* tonight is:

UNE LUTTE ACHARNÉE DE LA SOMME A LA MEUSE LA BATAILLE REDOUBLE DE VIOLENCE

If it redoubles *de violence* much longer who will be left?

To Stretcher Bearers
G. A. Studdert Kennedy

Easy does it – bit o' trench 'ere,
Mind that blinkin' bit o' wire,
There's a shell 'ole on your left there,
Lift 'im up a little 'igher.
Stick it, lad, ye'll soon be there now,
Want to rest 'ere for a while?
Let 'im dahn then – gently – gently,
There ye are, lad. That's the style.
Want a drink, mate? 'Ere's my bottle,
Lift 'is 'ead up for 'im, Jack,

Put my tunic underneath 'im,
'Ow's that, chummy? That's the tack!
Guess we'd better make a start now,
Ready for another spell?
Best be goin', we won't 'urt ye,
But 'e might just start to shell.
Are ye right, mate? Off we goes then.
That's well over on the right,
Gawd Almighty, that's a near 'un!
'Old your end up good and tight,
Never mind, lad, you're for Blighty,
Mind this rotten bit o' board.
We'll soon 'ave ye tucked in bed, lad,
'Opes ye gets to my old ward.
No more war for you, my 'earty,
This'll get ye well away,
Twelve good months in dear old Blighty,
Twelve good months if you're a day,
M.O.'s got a bit o' something
What'll stop that blarsted pain.
'Ere's a rotten bit o' ground, mate,
Lift up 'igher – up again,
Wish 'e'd stop 'is blarsted shellin'
Makes it rotten for the lad.
When a feller's been and got it,
It affec's 'im twice as bad.
'Ow's it goin' now then, sonny?
'Ere's that narrow bit o' trench,
Careful, mate, there's some dead Jerries,
Lawd Almighty, what a stench!
'Ere we are now, stretcher-case, boys,
Bring him aht a cup o' tea!
Inasmuch as ye have done it
Ye have done it unto Me.

A Comment on a Russian General
From *The War in Eastern Europe*, John Reed

A new-found but already intimate friend named Captain Martinev
was criticising the army with true Russian candidness.

'Horrible waste,' said he. 'Let me tell you a story. In October I was with
my regiment in Tilsit when the German drive on Warsaw began, and we
received urgent orders to hurry to Poland. Well, from Tilsit to the nearest
railroad station, Mittau, is a hundred versts. We did it in three days'
forced marches, arriving in bad shape. Something had gone wrong – we
had to wait twenty-four hours on the platform, without sleep, for it was
very cold. By train we travelled two days to Warsaw, almost starving;
no one had made arrangements for feeding us. When we arrived, Lodz
had already fallen. We got in at night and were marched across the city
to another train bound for Teresa, where they were fighting. A little way
out the tracks had been smashed by a shell; we detrained in the rain at
two o'clock in the morning, and marched five hours to Teresa.

'At eight o'clock we reached the headquarters of the division
commanded by General M_, who made such frightful mistakes
in Manchuria. Our men's feet were in terrible condition; they had
had practically no sleep for three nights, and hardly any food at all
for two days. Half an hour after we had thrown ourselves down
exhausted in the rain, the general came out with his chief of staff.

'How many men have I here?' he asked surlily.

'Eight thousand.'

'Good. Send them to relieve the trenches.'

Our colonel protested. 'But my men cannot go into the trenches.
They must have rest and food. For five days.'

'Never mind!' snapped the general. 'I don't want your opinion.
March!'

'The general went back to bed. We coaxed, pleaded, threatened,
flogged – it was terrible to hear them beg for food and sleep – and
the column staggered off to the forward trenches...

'We went in at ten in the morning and stood particularly heavy
fire all day – so heavy that the cook-wagons couldn't reach us until

midnight, so there was nothing to eat. The Germans attacked twice in the night, so there was no sleep. Next morning heavy artillery bombarded us. The men reeled as if they were drunk, forgot to take any precautions, and went to sleep while they were shooting. The officers, with blazing eyes, muttering things like men walking in their sleep, went up and down beating the soldiers with the flat of their swords. I forgot what I was doing, and so did everybody, I think; indeed, I can't remember what followed at all – but we were in there for four days and four nights. Once a night the cook-wagons brought soup and bread. At least three times a night the Germans attacked at the point of the bayonet. We retired from trench to trench, turning like beasts at bay – though we were all out of our heads...

'Finally on the fifth morning they relieved us. Out of eight thousand men two thousand came back, and twelve hundred of those went to the hospital.

'But the amusing thing about it was that all the time we were being butchered out there, there were six fresh regiments held in reserve two miles away! What on earth do you suppose General M_ was thinking of?'

A Source of Irritation
From *Extremely Entertaining Short Stories*,
Stacy Aumonier

To look at old Sam Gates you would never suspect him of having nerves. His sixty-nine years of close application to the needs of the soil had given him a certain earthy stolidity. To observe him hoeing, or thinning out a broad field of swede turnips, hardly attracted one's attention, he seemed so much part and parcel of the whole scheme. He blended into the soil like a glorified swede. Nevertheless, the half-dozen people who claimed his acquaintance knew him to be a man who suffered from little moods of irritability.

And on this glorious morning a little incident annoyed him unreasonably. It concerned his niece Aggie. She was a plump girl with clear blue eyes and a face as round and inexpressive as the dumplings for which the county was famous. She came slowly across the long sweep of the downland and, putting down the bundle wrapped up in a red handkerchief which contained his breakfast and dinner, she said:

'Well, Uncle, is there any noos?'

Now this may not appear to the casual reader to be a remark likely to cause irritation, but it affected old Sam Gates as a very silly and unnecessary question. It was moreover the constant repetition of it which was beginning to anger him. He met his niece twice a day. In the morning she brought his bundle of food at seven, and when he passed his sister's cottage on the way home to tea at five she was invariably hanging about the gate. And on each occasion she always said, in exactly the same voice:

'Well, Uncle, is there any noos?'

Noos! What noos should there be? For sixty-nine years he had never lived farther than five miles from Halvesham. For nearly sixty of those years he had bent his back above the soil. There were indeed historic occasions: once, for instance, when he had married Annie Hachet. And there was the birth of his daughter. There was also a famous occasion when he had visited London. Once he had been to a flower show at Market Roughborough. He either went or didn't go to church on Sundays. He had had many interesting chats with Mr James at The Cowman, and three years ago had sold a pig to Mrs Waig. But he couldn't always have interesting 'noos' of this sort up his sleeve. Didn't the silly gaffir know that for the last three weeks he had been thinning out turnips for Mr Dodge on this very same field? What 'noos' could there be?

He blinked at his niece, and didn't answer. She undid the parcel, and said:

'Mrs Goping's fowl got out again last night.'

He replied, 'Ah!' in a non-committal manner, and began to munch his bread and bacon. His niece picked up the handkerchief, and humming to herself, walked back across the field.

It was a glorious morning, and a white sea mist added to the promise of a hot day. He sat there munching, thinking of nothing in particular, but gradually subsiding into a mood of placid content. He noticed the back of Aggie disappear in the distance. It was a mile to the cottage, and a mile and a half to Halvesham. Silly things, girls! They were all alike. One had to make allowances. He dismissed her from his thoughts, and took a long swig of tea out of a bottle. Insects buzzed lazily. He tapped his pocket to assure himself that his pouch of shag was there, and then he continued munching. When he had finished, he lighted his pipe and stretched himself comfortably. He looked along the line of turnips he had thinned, and then across the adjoining field of swedes. Silver streaks appeared on the sea below the mist. In some dim way he felt happy in his solitude amidst this sweeping immensity of earth and sea and sky.

And then something else came to irritate him. It was one of 'these dratted airyplanes'. 'Airyplanes' were his pet aversion. He could find nothing to be said in their favour. Nasty, noisy, vile-smelling things that seared the heavens, and made the earth dangerous. And every day there seemed to be more and more of them. Of course 'this old war' was responsible for a lot of them, he knew. The war was a 'plaguey noosance'. They were short-handed on the farm. Beer and tobacco were dear, and Mrs Stevens' nephew had been and got wounded in the foot.

He turned his attention once more to the turnips. But an 'airyplane' has an annoying genius for gripping one's attention. When it appears on the scene, however much we dislike it, it has a way of taking stage-centre; we cannot help constantly looking at it. And so it was with old Sam Gates. He spat on his hands, and blinked up at the sky. And suddenly the aeroplane behaved in a very extraordinary manner. It was well over the sea when it seemed to lurch in a drunken manner, and skimmed the water. Then it shot up at a dangerous angle and zigzagged. It started to go farther out, and then turned and made for the land. The engines were making a curious grating noise. It rose once more, and then suddenly dived downward, and came plump down right in the middle of Mr Dodge's field of swedes!

Finally, as if not content with this desecration, it ran along the ground, ripping and tearing up twenty-five yards of good swedes, and then came to a stop. Old Sam Gates was in a terrible state. The aeroplane was more than a hundred yards away, but he waved his arms, and called out:

'Hi! you there, you mustn't land in they swedes! They're Mister Dodge's.'

The instant the aeroplane stopped, a man leaped out and gazed quickly round. He glanced at Sam Gates, and seemed uncertain whether to address him or whether to concentrate his attention on the flying machine. The latter arrangement appeared to be his ultimate decision. He dived under the engine, and became frantically busy. Sam had never seen anyone work with such furious energy. But all the same, it was not to be tolerated. It was disgraceful. Sam started out across the field, almost hurrying in his indignation. When he appeared within earshot of the aviator, he cried out again:

'Hi! you mustn't rest your old airyplane here. You've kicked up all Mr Dodge's swedes. A nice thing you've done!'

He was within five yards when suddenly the aviator turned and covered him with a revolver! And, speaking in a sharp, staccato voice, he said:

'Old grandfather, you must sit down. I am very much occupied. If you interfere or attempt to go away, I shoot you. So!'

Sam gazed at the horrid glittering little barrel, and gasped. Well he never! To be threatened with murder when you're doing your duty in your employer's private property! But, still, perhaps the man was mad. A man must be more or less mad to go up in one of those crazy things. And life was very sweet on that summer morning, in spite of sixty-nine years. He sat down among the swedes.

The aviator was so busy with his cranks and machinery that he hardly deigned to pay him any attention except to keep the revolver handy. He worked feverishly, and Sam sat watching him. At the end of ten minutes he appeared to have solved his troubles with the machine, but he still seemed very scared. He kept on glancing round and out to sea. When his repairs were completed, he straightened his back and wiped the perspiration from us brow. He was apparently on the point of springing back into the machine and going off, when a sudden mood of facetiousness, caused by relief from the strain he had endured, came to him. He turned to old Sam and smiled, at the same time remarking:

'Well, old grandfather, and now we shall be all right, isn't it?'

He came close up to Sam, and suddenly started back.

'Gott!' he cried, 'Paul Jouperts!'

Sam gazed at him, bewildered, and the madman started talking to him in some foreign tongue. Sam shook his head.

'You no right,' he remarked, 'to come bargin' through they swedes of Mr Dodge's.'

And then the aviator behaved in a most peculiar manner. He came up and examined his face very closely, and gave a gentle tug at his beard and hair, as if to see whether it was real or false.

'What is your name, old man?' he said.

'Sam Gates.'

The aviator muttered some words that sounded something like 'mare vudish!' and then turned to his machine. He appeared to be dazed and in a great state of doubt. He fumbled with some cranks, but kept glancing at old Sam. At last he got into the car and started the engine. Then he stopped, and sat there deep in thought. At last he suddenly sprang out again, and, approaching Sam, he said very deliberately:

'Old Grandfather, I shall require you to accompany me.'

Sam gasped.

'Eh?' he said. 'What be talkin' about? 'company? I got these here lines o' tarnips – I be already behoind.'

The disgusting little revolver once more flashed before his eyes.

'There must be no discussion,' came the voice. 'It is necessary that you mount the seat of the car without delay. Otherwise I shoot you like the dog you are. So!'

Old Sam was hale and hearty. He had no desire to die so ignominiously. The pleasant smell of the downland was in his nostrils. His foot was on his native heath. He mounted the seat of the car, contenting himself with a mutter:

'Well, that be a noice thing, I must say! Flyin' about the country with all they tarnips on'y half thinned–'

He found himself strapped in. The aviator was in a fever of anxiety to get away. The engines made a ghastly splutter and noise. The thing started running along the ground. Suddenly it shot upward, giving the swedes a last contemptuous kick. At twenty minutes to eight that morning old Sam found himself being borne right up above his fields and out to sea! His breath came quickly. He was a little frightened.

'God forgive me!' he murmured.

The thing was so fantastic and sudden, his mind could not grasp it. He only felt in some vague way that he was going to die, and he struggled to attune his mind to the change. He offered up a mild prayer to God, Who, he felt, must be very near, somewhere up in these clouds. Automatically he thought of the vicar at Halvesham, and a certain sense of comfort came to him at the reflection that on the previous day he had taken a 'cooking of runner beans' to God's representative in that village. He felt calmer after that, but the horrid machine seemed to go higher and higher. He could not turn in his seat and he could see nothing but sea and sky. Of course the man was mad, mad as a March hare. Of what earthly use could he be to any one? Besides, he had talked pure gibberish, and called him Paul Something, when he had already told him that his name was Sam. The thing would fall down into the sea soon, and they would both be drowned. Well, well! He had reached three-score years and ten.

He was protected by a screen, but it seemed very cold. What on earth would Mr Dodge say? There was no one left to work the land but a fool of a boy named Billy Whitehead at Deric's Cross. On, on, on they went at a furious pace. His thoughts danced disconnectedly from incidents of his youth, conversations with the vicar, hearty meals in the open, a frock his sister wore on the day of the postman's wedding, the drone of a psalm, the illness of some ewes belonging to Mr Dodge. Everything seemed to be moving very rapidly, upsetting his sense of time. He felt outraged and yet at moments there was something entrancing in the wild experience. He seemed to be living at an incredible pace. Perhaps he was really dead, and on his way to the Kingdom of God? Perhaps this was the way they took people?

After some indefinite period he suddenly caught sight of a long strip of land. Was this a foreign country? Or were they returning? He had by this time lost all feeling of fear. He became interested and almost disappointed. The 'airyplane' was not such a fool as it looked. It was very wonderful to be right up in the sky like this. His dreams were suddenly disturbed by a fearful noise. He thought the machine was blown to pieces. It dived and ducked through the air, and things were bursting all round it and making an awful din; and then it went up higher and higher. After a while these noises ceased, and he felt the machine gliding downwards. They were really right above solid land, trees, and fields, and streams, and white villages. Down, down, down they glided. This was a foreign country. There were straight avenues of poplars and canals. This was not Halvesham. He felt the thing glide gently and bump into a field. Some men ran forward and approached them, and the mad aviator called out to them. They were mostly fat men in grey uniforms, and they all spoke this foreign gibberish. Someone came and unstrapped him. He was very stiff and could hardly move. An exceptionally gross-looking man punched him in the ribs, and roared with laughter. They all stood round and laughed at him, while the mad aviator talked to them and kept pointing at him. Then he said:

'Old grandfather, you must come with me.'

He was led to a zinc-roofed building, and shut in a little room. There were guards outside with fixed bayonets. After a while the mad aviator appeared again, accompanied by two soldiers. He beckoned him to follow. They marched through a quadrangle and entered another building. They went straight into an office where a very important-looking man, covered with medals, sat in an easy chair. There was a lot of saluting and clicking of heels.

The aviator pointed at Sam and said something, and the man with the medals started at sight of him, and then came up and spoke to him in English.

'What is your name? Where do you come from? Your age? The name and birthplace of your parents?'

He seemed intensely interested, and also pulled his hair and beard to see if they came off. So well and naturally did he and the aviator speak English that after a voluble cross-examination they drew apart, and continued the conversation in that language. And the extraordinary conversation was of this nature:

'It is a most remarkable resemblance,' said the man with medals. '*Unglaublich!* But what do you want me to do with him, Hausemann?'

'The idea came to me suddenly, excellency,' replied the aviator, 'and you may consider it worthless. It is just this. The resemblance is so amazing. Paul Jouperts has given us more valuable information than any one at present in our service. And the English know that. There is an award of twenty-five thousand francs on his head. Twice they have captured him, and each time he escaped. All the company commanders and their staff have his photograph. He is a serious thorn in their flesh.'

'Well?' replied the man with the medals.

The aviator whispered confidentially:

'Suppose, your excellency, that they found the dead body of Paul Jouperts?'

'Well?' replied the big man.

'My suggestion is this. Tomorrow, as you know, the English are attacking Hill 701, which we have for tactical reasons decided to evacuate. If after the attack they find the dead body of Paul Jouperts in, say, the second lines, they will take no further trouble in the matter. You know their lack of thoroughness. Pardon me, I was two years at Oxford University. And consequently Paul Jouperts will be able to prosecute his labours undisturbed.'

The man with the medals twirled his moustache and looked thoughtfully at his colleague.

'Where is Paul at the moment?' he asked.

'He is acting as a gardener at the Convent of St Eloise, at Mailleton-en-Haut, which, as you know, is one hundred metres from the headquarters of the British central army staff.'

The man with the medals took two or three rapid turns up and down the room. Then he said:

'Your plan is excellent, Hausemann. The only point of difficulty is that the attack started this morning.'

'This morning?' exclaimed the other.

'Yes. The English attacked unexpectedly at dawn. We have already evacuated the first line. We shall evacuate the second line at eleven-fifty. It is now ten-fifteen. There may be just time.'

He looked suddenly at old Sam in the way that a butcher might look at a prize heifer at an agricultural show and remarked casually:

'Yes, it is a remarkable resemblance. It seems a pity not to ... do something with it.'

Then, speaking in German, he added:

'It is worth trying, and if it succeeds, the higher authorities shall hear of your lucky accident and inspiration, Herr Hausemann. Instruct Oberleutnant Schutz to send the old fool by two orderlies to the east extremity of trench 38. Keep him there till the order of evacuation is given. Then shoot him, but don't disfigure him, and lay him out face upwards.'

The aviator saluted and withdrew, accompanied by his victim. Old Sam had not understood the latter part of the conversation, and he did not catch quite all that was said in English, but he felt that somehow things were not becoming too promising, and it was time to assert himself. So he remarked when they got outside:

'Now, look'ee here, mister, when be I goin' back to my tarnips?'

And the aviator replied with a pleasant smile:

'Do not be disturbed, old grandfather; you shall ... get back to the soil quite soon.'

In a few moments he found himself in a large grey car, accompanied by four soldiers. The aviator left him. The country was barren and horrible, full of great pits and rents, and he could hear the roar of artillery and the shriek of shells. Overhead, aeroplanes were buzzing angrily. He seemed to be suddenly transported from the Kingdom of God to the Pit of Darkness. He wondered whether the vicar had enjoyed the runner beans. He could not imagine runner beans growing here, runner beans, ay! or anything else. If this was a foreign country, give him dear old England.

Gr-r-r-r–Bang! Something exploded just at the rear of the car. The soldiers ducked, and one of them pushed him in the stomach and swore.

'An ugly-looking lout,' he thought. 'If I was twenty years younger I'd give him a punch in the eye that 'ud make him sit up.'

The car came to a halt by a broken wall. The party hurried out and dived behind a mound. He was pulled down a kind of shaft and found himself in a room buried right underground, where three officers were drinking and smoking. The soldiers saluted and handed a typewritten dispatch. The officers looked at him drunkedly, and one came up and pulled his beard and spat in his face, and called him 'an old English swine'. He then shouted out some instructions to the soldiers, and they led him out into the narrow trench. One walked behind him, and occasionally prodded him with the butt-end of a gun. The trenches were half-full of water, and reeked of gases, powder, and decaying matter. Shells were constantly bursting overhead, and in places the trenches had crumbled and were nearly blocked up. They stumbled on, sometimes falling, sometimes dodging moving masses, and occasionally crawling over the dead bodies of men. At last they reached a deserted-looking trench, and one of the soldiers pushed him into the corner of it and growled something, and then disappeared round the angle. Old Sam was exhausted. He lay panting against the mud wall expecting every minute to be blown to pieces by one of those infernal things that seemed to be getting more and more insistent. The din went on for nearly twenty minutes and he was alone in the trench. He fancied he heard a whistle amidst the din. Suddenly one of the soldiers who had accompanied him came stealthily round the corner. And there was a look in his eye old Sam did not like. When he was within five yards the soldier raised his rifle and pointed it at Sam's body. Some instinct impelled the old man at that instant to throw himself forward on his face. As he did so, he was conscious of a terrible explosion and he had just time to observe the soldier falling in a heap near him, when he lost consciousness.

His consciousness appeared to return to him with a snap. He was lying on a plank in a building, and he heard someone say:

'I believe the old boy's English.'

He looked round. There were a lot of men lying there and others in khaki and white overalls were busy amongst them. He sat up, rubbed his head, and said:

'Hi, mister, where be I now?'

Someone laughed, and a young man came up and said:

'Well, old thing, you were very nearly in hell. Who the devil are you?'

Someone else came up, and two of them were discussing him. One of them said:

'He's quite all right. He was only knocked out. Better take him to the colonel. He may be a spy.'

The other came up, and touched his shoulder, and remarked:

'Can you walk, uncle?'

He replied:

'Ay, I can walk all right.'

'That's an old sport!'

The young man took his arm and helped him out of the room, into a courtyard. They entered another room, where an elderly, kind-faced officer was seated at a desk. The officer looked up and exclaimed:

'Good God! Bradshaw, do you know who you've got there?'

The younger one said:

'No, who, sir?'

'By God! It's Paul Jouperts!' exclaimed the colonel.

'Paul Jouperts! Great Scott!'

The older officer addressed himself to Sam. He said:

'Well, we've got you once more, Paul. We shall have to be a little more careful this time.'

The young officer said: 'Shall I detail a squad, sir?'

'We can't shoot him without a court-martial,' replied the kind-faced senior.

Then Sam interpolated:

'Look'ee, here, sir. I'm fair sick of all this. My name bean't Paul. My name's Sam. I was a-thinnin' a line of turnips –'

Both officers burst out laughing, and the younger one said:

'Good! Damn good! Isn't it amazing, sir, the way they not only learn the language, but even take the trouble to learn a dialect?'

The older man busied himself with some papers.

'Well, Sam,' he remarked, 'you shall be given a chance to prove your identity. Our methods are less drastic than those of your Boche masters. What part of England are you supposed to come from? Let's see how much you can bluff us with your topographical knowledge.'

'Oi was a-thinnin' a loine o' tarnips this morning at 'alf-past seven on Mr Dodge's farm at Halvesham, when one o' these 'ere airyplanes come roight down among the swedes. I tells 'e to get clear o' that, when the feller what gets owt o' the car, 'e drahs a revowlver and 'e says, "You must 'company – I –" '

'Yes, yes,' interrupted the senior officer; 'that's all very good. Now tell me – where is Halvesham? What is the name of the local vicar? I'm sure you'd know that.'

Old Sam rubbed his chin.

'I sits under the Reverend David Pryce, mister, and a good, God-fearin' man he be. I took him a cookin' o' runner beans on'y yesterday. I works for Mr Dodge what owns Greenway Manor and 'as a stud-farm at Newmarket they say.'

'Charles Dodge?' asked the young officer.

'Ay, Charlie Dodge. You write and ask 'un if he knows old Sam Gates.'

The two officers looked at each other, and the older one looked at Sam more closely.

'It's very extraordinary,' he remarked.

'Everybody knows Charlie Dodge,' added the younger officer.

It was at that moment that a wave of genius swept over old Sam. He put his hand to his head, and suddenly jerked out:

'What's more, I can tell 'ee where this yere Paul is. He's acting a gardener in a convent at –' He puckered up his brow and fumbled with his hat, and then got out:

'Mighteno.'

The older officer gasped.

'Mailleton-en-Haut! Good God! What makes you say that, old man?'

Sam tried to give an account of his experience, and the things he had heard said by the German officers. But he was getting tired, and he broke off in the middle to say:

'Ye haven't a bite o' somethin' to eat, I suppose, mister, and a glass o' beer? I usually 'as my dinner at twelve o'clock.'

Both the officers laughed, and the older said:

'Get him some food, Bradshaw, and a bottle of beer from the mess. We'll keep this old man here. He interests me.'

While the younger man was doing this, the chief pressed a button and summoned another junior officer.

'Gateshead,' he remarked, 'ring up G.H.Q. and instruct them to arrest the gardener in that convent at the top of the hill, and then to report.'

The officer saluted and went out, and in a few minutes a tray of hot food and a large bottle of beer were brought to the old man, and he was left alone in the corner of the room to negotiate this welcome compensation. And in the execution he did himself and his county credit. In the meanwhile the officers were very busy. People were coming and going and examining maps, and telephone-bells were ringing furiously. They did not disturb old Sam's gastronomic operations. He cleaned up the mess tins and finished the last drop of beer. The senior officer found time to offer him a cigarette, but he replied:

'Thankee kindly, but I'd rather smoke my pipe.'

The colonel smiled, and said:

'Oh, all right. Smoke away.'

He lighted up, and the fumes of the shag permeated the room. Someone opened another window, and the young officer who had addressed him at first suddenly looked at him and exclaimed:

'Innocent, by God! You couldn't get shag like that anywhere but in Norfolk.'

It must have been over an hour later when another officer entered and saluted.

'Message from G.H.Q., sir,' he said.

'Well?'

'They have arrested the gardener at the convent of St Eloise, and they have every reason to believe that he is the notorious Paul Jouperts.'

The colonel stood up, and his eyes beamed. He came over to old Sam and shook his hand.

'Mr Gates,' he said, 'you are an old brick. You will probably hear more of this. You have probably been the means of delivering something very useful into our hands. Your own honour is vindicated. A loving government will probably award you five shillings or a Victoria Cross, or something of that sort. In the meantime, what can I do for you?'

Old Sam scratched his chin.

'Oi want to get back 'ome,' he said.

'Well, even that might be arranged.'

'Oi want to get back 'ome in toime for tea.'

'What time do you have tea?'

'Foive o'clock or thereabouts.'

'I see.'

A kindly smile came into the eyes of the colonel. He turned to another officer standing by the table and said:

'Raikes, is anyone going across this afternoon with dispatches?'

'Yes, sir,' replied the other officer. 'Commander Jennings is leaving at three o'clock.'

'You might ask him to come and see me.'

Within ten minutes a young man in a flight commander's uniform entered.

'Ah, Jennings,' said the colonel, 'there is a little affair which concerns the honour of the British Army. My friend here, Sam Gates has come over from Halvesham in Norfolk in order to give us valuable information. I have promised him that he shall get home to tea at five o'clock. Can you take a passenger?'

The young man threw back his head and laughed.

'Lord!' he exclaimed. 'What an old sport! Yes, I expect I could just manage it. Where is the God-forsaken place?'

A large ordnance-map of Norfolk (which had been captured from a German officer) was produced, and the young man studied it closely.

At three o'clock precisely, old Sam, finding himself something of a hero and quite glad to escape from the embarrassment which this position entailed, once more sped skywards in an 'airyplane'.

At twenty minutes to five he landed once more amongst Mr Dodge's swedes. The breezy young airman shook hands with him and departed inland. Old Sam sat down and surveyed the field.

'A noice thing, I must say,' he muttered to himself as he looked along the lines of unthinned turnips. He still had twenty minutes, and so he went slowly along and completed a line which he had commenced in the morning. He then deliberately packed up his dinner-things and his tools, and started out for home.

As he came round the corner of Stillway's Meadow, and the cottage came in view, his niece stepped out of the copse with a basket on her arm.

'Well, Uncle, she said, 'is there any noos?'

It was then that old Sam became really irritated.

'Noos!' he said. 'Noos! Drat the girl! What noos should there be? Sixty-nine year I live in these here parts, hoein' and weedin' and thinnin' and mindin' Charlie Dodge's sheep. Am I one o' these here storybook folk havin' noos 'appen to me all the time? Ain't it enough, ye silly, dab-faced zany, to earn enough to buy a bite o' someat to eat, and a glass o' beer, and a place to rest a's head o'night, without always wantin' noos, noos, noos! I tell 'ee, it's this that leads 'ee to 'alf the troubles in the world. Devil take the noos!'

And turning his back on her, he went fuming up the hill.

The Owl
Edward Thomas

Downhill I came, hungry, and yet not starved,
Cold, yet had heat within me that was proof

Against the north wind; tired, yet so that rest
Had seemed the sweetest thing under a roof.

Then at the inn I had food, fire, and rest,
Knowing how hungry, cold, and tired was I.
All of the night was quite barred out except
An owl's cry, a most melancholy cry.

Shaken out long and clear upon the hill
No merry note, nor cause of merriment,
But one telling me plain what I escaped
And others could not, that night, as in I went.

And salted was my food, and my repose,
Salted and sobered too, by the bird's voice
Speaking for all who lay under the stars,
Soldiers and poor, unable to rejoice.

Serbia's Victory
From *The War in Eastern Europe*, John Reed

That night we heard the dramatic story of the great Serbian victory of
December. Twice the Austrians invaded the country, and twice were
hurled back, and the streets of Valievo groaned with wounded lying
in the rain. But the second time the enemy held Shabatz, Losnitza, and
the two rich provinces of Machva and Podrigna, and the heights of
Gouchevo. The Serbians could not dislodge them from their strongly
intrenched positions. And then, in the bitter weather of December,
the Austrians began the third invasion with five hundred thousand
men against two hundred and fifty thousand. Pouring across the
frontier at three widely separated points, they broke the Serbian
lines and rolled the little army back among its mountains. Belgrade
was abandoned to the enemy. Twice the Serbians made a desperate
stand, and twice they were forced to fall back. Ammunition began

to fail – the cannon had less than twenty shells apiece. The enemy passed Krupaign and Valievo and was within forty-five miles of Kraguijevatz, headquarters of the Serbian general staff.

And then, at the last minute, something happened. New supplies of ammunition arrived from Salonika, and the younger officers revolted against their more cautious elders, shouting that it was as well to die attacking as to be slaughtered in the trenches. General Michitch ordered an offensive. The beaten Serbians, rushing from their trenches, fell upon the leisurely Austrian columns coming along narrow mountain defiles to attack. Caught on the march, burdened with big guns and heavy baggage-trains on roads almost impassable from mud, the Austrians resisted furiously, but were forced to recoil. The line was broken. Their centre, smashed by Michitch and the first army, broke and fled in panic across the country, abandoning baggage, ammunition, and guns, and leaving behind thousands of dead and wounded, and hospitals crammed with men raving with typhus. This is how the typhus, beginning somewhere up in the plains of Hungary, entered Serbia with the Austrian army. For a time the left wing tried to hold Belgrade, but the exultant, ragged Serbians drove them literally into the River Save and shot them as they swam across.

This great battle, which Voyvoda Michitch reported laconically with the proud telegram, 'There remain no Austrian soldiers on Serbian soil except prisoners,' has been given no name. Some call it the Battle of Kolubara River and others the Battle of Valievo. But it is, perhaps, the most wonderful feat of arms in all the great World War.

An Appeal to America on Behalf of the Belgian Destitute
Thomas Hardy

Seven millions stand
Emaciate, in that ancient Delta-land: –
We here, full-charged with our own maimed and dead

And coiled in throbbing conflicts slow and sore,
Can poorly soothe these ails unmerited
Of souls forlorn upon the facing shore! –
Where naked, gaunt, in endless band on band
Seven millions stand.

   No man can say
To your great country that, with scant delay,
You must, perforce, ease them in their loud need:
We know that nearer first your duty lies;
But – is it much to ask that you let plead
Your loving-kindness with you – wooing-wise –
Albeit that aught you owe, and must repay,
No man can say?

December 1914

1915

Refugees
From *Fighting France: From Dunkerque to Belfort*,
Edith Wharton

FEBRUARY 1915

For a while, in September and October, the streets were made picturesque by the coming and going of English soldiery, and the aggressive flourish of British military motors. Then the fresh faces and smart uniforms disappeared, and now the nearest approach to 'militarism' which Paris offers to the casual sightseer is the occasional drilling of a handful of *piou-pious* on the muddy reaches of the Place des Invalides. But there is another army in Paris. Its first detachments came months ago, in the dark September days – lamentable rearguard of the Allies' retreat on Paris. Since then its numbers have grown and grown, its dingy streams have percolated through all the currents of Paris life, so that wherever one goes, in every quarter and at every hour, among the busy confident strongly-stepping Parisians one sees these other people, dazed and slowly moving – men and women with sordid bundles on their backs, shuffling along hesitatingly in their tattered shoes, children dragging at their hands and tired-out babies pressed against their shoulders: the great army of the Refugees. Their faces are unmistakable and unforgettable. No one who has ever caught that stare of dumb bewilderment – or that other look of concentrated horror, full of the reflection of flames and ruins – can shake off the obsession of the Refugees. The look in their eyes is part of the look of Paris. It is the dark shadow on the brightness of the face she turns to the enemy. These poor people cannot look across the borders to eventual triumph. They belong mostly to a class whose knowledge of the world's affairs is measured by the shadow of their village steeple. They are no more curious of the laws of causation than the thousands overwhelmed at Avezzano. They were ploughing and sowing, spinning and weaving and minding their business, when suddenly a great darkness full of fire and blood came down on them. And now they are here, in a strange country, among unfamiliar faces and new ways, with nothing left to them in the world but the memory of burning homes and massacred children and young men dragged to slavery, of infants torn from their mothers, old men trampled by drunken heels and priests slain while they prayed beside the dying. These are the people who stand in hundreds every day outside the doors of the shelters improvised to rescue them, and who receive, in return for the loss of everything that makes life sweet, or intelligible, or at least endurable, a cot in a dormitory, a meal-ticket – and perhaps, on lucky days, a pair of shoes ...

God Save the King
James Elroy Flecker

God save our gracious King,
Nation and State and King,
   God save the King!

Grant him the Peace divine,
But if his Wars be Thine
Flash on our fighting line
   Victory's Wing!

Thou in his suppliant hands
Hast placed such Mighty Lands:
   Save Thou our King!
As once from golden Skies
Rebels with flaming eyes!
So the King's Enemies
   Doom Thou and fling!

Mountains that break the night
Holds He by eagle right
   Stretching far Wing!
Dawn lands for Youth to reap,
Dim lands where Empires sleep,
His! And the Lion Deep
   Roars for the King.

But most these few dear miles
Of sweetly-meadowed Isles, –
   England all Spring;
Scotland that by the marge
Where the blank North doth charge
Hears Thy Voice loud and large,
   Save, and their King!

Grace on the golden Dales
Of Thine old Christian Wales
   Shower till they sing,
Till Erin's Island lawn
Echoes the dulcet-drawn
Song with a cry of Dawn –
   God save the King!

The Gilded Staff (A Tale of the Old Contemptibles)
From *Front Lines,* Boyd Cable

Broadly speaking, the average regimental officer and man of the
fighting units is firmly convinced beyond all argument that a 'Staff
job' is an absolutely safe and completely *cushy* one, that the Staff-
wallah always has the best of food and drink, a good roof over him,
and a soft bed to lie on, nothing to do except maybe sign his name to
a few papers when he feels so inclined, and perhaps in a casual and
comfortable chat after a good dinner decide on a tactical move, a
strafe of some sort, issue the orders in a sort of brief 'Take Hill 999'
or 'retire by Dead Cow Corner to Two Tree Trench' style, and leave
the regiments concerned to carry on. Briefly, the opinion of the firing
line might be summed up in a short Credo:

'I believe the Staff is No Good.

'I believe the Staff has the cushiest of cushy jobs.

'I believe the Staff never hears a bullet whistle or sees a shell burst
except through a telescope.

'I believe the Staff exists solely to find soft jobs for the wealthy and
useless portion of the aristocracy.

'I believe the Staff does nothing except wear a supercilious manner
and red tabs and trimmings.

'I believe the Staff is No Good.'

As to the average of correctness in this Credo I say nothing, but I
can at least show that these things are not always thus.

The Staff had been having what the General's youthful and
irrepressibly cheerful aide-de-camp called 'a hectic three days'. The
Headquarters signallers had been going hard night and day until one
of them was driven to remark bitterly as he straightened his bent
back from over his instrument and waggled his stiffened fingers that
had been tapping the 'buzzer' for hours on end, 'I'm developin' a
permanent hump on my back like a dog scrapin' a pot, an' if my
fingers isn't to be wore off by inches I'll have to get the farrier to put
a set of shoes on 'em.' But the signallers had some advantages that the
Staff hadn't, and one was that they could arrange spells of duty and

at least have a certain time off for rest and sleep. The Staff Captain would have given a good deal for that privilege by about the third night. The worst of his job was that he had no time when he could be sure of a clear ten minutes' rest. He had messages brought to him as he devoured scratch meals; he was roused from such short sleeps as he could snatch lying fully dressed on a camp bed, by telephone and telegraph messages, or, still worse, by horrible scrawls badly written in faint pencillings that his weary eyes could barely decipher as he sat up on his bed with a pocket electric glaring on the paper; once he even had to abandon an attempt to shave, wipe the lather from his face, and hustle to impart some information to a waiting General. A very hot fight was raging along that portion of front, and almost every report from the firing line contained many map references which necessitated so many huntings of obscure points on the maps that the mere reading and understanding of a message might take a full five or ten minutes; and in the same way the finding of regiments' positions for the General's information or the sending of orders added ten-fold to the map-hunting.

The third day was about the most 'hectic' of all. For the Captain it began before daybreak with a call to the telephone which came just two hours after he had shuffled and shaken together the papers he had been working on without a break through the night, pulled off his boots, blown out his lamp, and dropped with a sigh of relief on his bed in a corner of the room. It was an urgent and personal call, and the first dozen words effectually drove the lingering sleep from the Captain's eyes and brain. 'Yes, yes, "heavily attacked", I got that; go on … No, I don't think I need to refer to the map; I very nearly know the beastly thing by heart now … Yes … Yes … Who? … Killed outright … That's bad … Who's in command now then … Right. The Dee and Don Trenches – wait a minute, which are they? Oh yes, I remember, south from the Pigsty and across to Stink Farm … Right. I'll pass it on at once and let you know in five minutes … Just repeat map references so I can make a note … Yes … Yes … Yes … Right … Bye.'

The urgency of the message, which told of a heavy and partially successful attack on the Divisional Front, wiped out any hope the Captain might have had of a return to his broken sleep. For the next two hours his mind was kept at full stretch reducing to elaborated details the comprehensive commands of the General, locating reserves and supports and Battalion HQs, exchanging long messages with the Artillery, collecting figures of ammunition states, available strengths, casualty returns, collating and sifting them out, reshuffling them and offering them up to the Brigade Major or the General, absorbing or distributing messages from and to concrete personalities or nebulous authorities known widely if vaguely as the DAAG, DAQMG, DADOS, ADMS, CDS, and T, and other strings of jumbled initials.

He washed in the sparing dimensions of a canvas washstand, Field Service, X Pattern, deliberately taking off his coat and rolling up his shirt-sleeves, and firmly turning a deaf and soap-filled ear to the orderly who placed a ruled telephone message form on his table and announced it urgent. Afterwards he attended to the message, and talked into the telephone while his servant cleared one side of his table and served plentiful bacon, and eggs of an unknown period. Immediately after this a concentrated bombardment suddenly developed on a ruined château some three or four hundred yards from the HQ farm. To the youthful aide-de-camp who had arrived from the outer dampness dripping water from every angle of a streaming mackintosh he remarked wrathfully on the prospect of having to move once again in the middle of such beastly waterfall weather. The aide stood at the brown-paper patched window, chuckling and watching the shells rewreck the already wrecked château. 'Looks as if their spies have sold 'em a pup this time,' he said gleefully. I believe they must have been told we were in that old ruin instead of here. Or they were told this place and mistook it on the map for the château. Rather a lark – what!'

'Confound the larks,' said the Captain bitterly, 'especially if they come any nearer this way. This place is quite leaky and draughty enough now without it getting any more shrap or splinter holes punched in it.'

Here the Captain had a short break from his inside job, leaving another officer to look after that and accompanying the General on horseback to a conference with various Brigadiers, Colonels, and Commanding Officers. The ride was too wet to be pleasant, and at no time could a better pace than a jog trot be made because on the road there was too much horse, foot, and wheeled traffic, and off the road in the swimming fields it took the horses all their time to keep their feet.

The conference was held under the remaining quarter-roof of a shell-smashed farm, and the Captain listened and made notes in a damp book, afterwards accompanying the General on a ride round to where something could be seen of the position, and back to HQ. Here, under the General's direction in consultation with the Brigade Major, he elaborated and extended his notes, drafted detailed directions for a number of minor moves next day, and translated them into terms of map-reference language, and a multitude of details of roads to be followed by different units, billeting areas, rationing, and refilling points, and so on.

He made a hasty, tinned lunch, and at the General's request set out to find one of the Battalion Headquarters and there meet some COs and make clear to them certain points of the dispositions arranged. He went in a motor, sped on his way by the cheerful information of the aide that the town through which he must pass had been under 'a deuce of hot fire' all day, had its streets full of Jack Johnson holes, and was in a continual state of blowing up, falling down, or being burnt out. 'I was through there this morning,' said the aide, 'and I tell you it was warmish. Sentry outside on the road wanted to stop me at first; said he'd orders to warn everybody it wasn't safe. Wasn't safe,' repeated the youth, chuckling, 'Lord, after I'd been through there I'd have given that sentry any sort of a certificate of truthfulness. It was *not* safe.'

The Captain went off with his motor skating from ditch to ditch down the greasy road. The guns were rumbling and banging up in front, and as the car bumped and slithered nearer to the town the Captain could hear the long yelling whistle and the deep rolling crashes of heavy shells falling somewhere in it. He too was stopped at the outskirts by a sentry who held up his hand to the driver, and then came and parleyed with the Captain through the window. The Captain impatiently cut his warnings

short. There was no other road that would take him near the point he
desired to reach; he must go through the town; he must ride since he
could not spare time to walk. He climbed out and mounted beside the
driver, with some instinctive and vaguely formed ideas in his mind that if
the driver were hit he might have to take the wheel, that the car might be
upset and pin him underneath, that he might be able to assist in picking a
course through rubbish and shell-holes, to jump out and clear any slight
obstruction from in front of the wheels. The car ran on slowly into the
town. Decidedly the aide had been right, except that 'warmish' was a
mild word for the state of affairs. The Germans were flinging shells into
the town as if they meant to destroy it utterly. The main street through
was littered with bricks and tiles and broken furniture; dead horses were
sprawled in it, some limp and new killed with the blood still running from
their wounds, others with their four legs sticking out post-stiff in the air;
in several places there were broken-down carts, in one place a regular
mass of them piled up and locked in a confused tangle of broken wheels,
splintered shafts, cut harness, and smashed woodwork, their contents
spilled out anyhow and mixed up inextricably with the wreckage.

There was not much traffic in the main street, and such as was
there was evidently, like the Captain himself, only there because no
other road offered. There were half a dozen artillery ammunition
waggons, a few infantry transport carts, several Army Service Corps
vehicles. All of them were moving at a trot, the waggons rumbling
and lumbering heavily and noisily over the cobble-stones, the drivers
stooped forward and peering out anxiously to pick a way between
the obstacles in their path. The shells were coming over continuously,
moaning and howling and yelling, falling with tearing crashes
amongst the houses, blowing them wall from wall, slicing corners
off or cutting a complete top or end away, breaking them down in
rattling cascades of tiles and bricks, bursting them open and flinging
them high and far upwards and outwards in flying fragments. As
the car crawled cautiously through the debris that littered the street,
pieces of brick and mortar, whole or broken slates, chips of wood
and stone, pattered and rapped constantly down about and on the
car; the wheels crunched and ground on splintered glass from the

gaping windows. A shell roared down on the street ahead of them, burst thunderously in a vivid sheet of flame and spurting black cloud of smoke, an appalling crash that rolled and reverberated loud and long up and down the narrow street.

'Go easy,' cautioned the Captain as the black blinding reek came swirling down to meet them, 'or you'll run into the hole that fellow made.'

The driver's face was set and white, and his hands gripped tight on the wheel; the Captain had a sudden compunction that he had brought him, that he had not left the car outside the town and walked through. They edged carefully past the yawning shell-crater with the smoke still clinging and curling up from its edges, and, free of the smoke again, saw a fairly clear stretch ahead of them.

The Captain heard the thin but rising whistle of another heavy shell approaching, and 'Open her out,' he said quickly, 'and let her rip.' The driver, he noticed, for all his white face had his nerves well under control, and steadily caught the change of gear on the proper instant, speeded up sharply but quite smoothly. The car swooped down the clear stretch, the roar of the shell growing louder and closer, and just as they reached and crammed the brakes on to take the corner, they heard the shell crash down behind them. The Captain leaned out and looked back, and had a momentary glimpse of a house on the street spouting black smoke, dissolving and cascading down and out across the road in a torrent of bricks and wreckage. In another two minutes they shot out clear of the town.

A mile farther on a soldier warned them that the crossroads were practically impassable, the roadway being broken and churned up by the heavy shells that all afternoon had been and were still at intervals falling upon it. So the Captain left the car and went on a-foot. He was nearly caught at the crossroads, a shell fragment ripping a huge rent in his mackintosh just over his ribs. Before he reached the communication trenches too he had a highly uncomfortable minute with light high-explosive shells bursting round him while he crouched low in a muddly shell-crater. He reached the meeting-place at last, and spent an hour talking over plans and movements, and by the time he was ready to start back it was rapidly growing dark. It was completely dark before he found his way back to the road again, stumbling over the shell-holed ground, slipping and floundering through the mud, tripping once and falling heavily over some strands of barbed wire. When he found the car again he was so dirty and draggled and dishevelled and ragged – the barbed wire had taken the cap from his head and dropped it in a mud puddle, and left another tear or two in his mackintosh – so smeared and plastered with mud, that his driver at first failed to recognise him. In the town he found parties of the Sappers filling up the worst of the shell-holes and clearing away the debris that blocked the road where he had seen the house blown down, while the shells still screamed up and burst clattering over and amongst the houses, and bullets and splinters whistled and sang overhead, clashed and rattled on the causeway.

He slept snatchily through the rest of the journey, waking many times as the car bumped badly, and once, when it dropped heavily into a shell-hole and bounced out again, flinging him bodily upwards until his head and shoulder banged solidly against the roof, taking half a minute to regain his scattered wits and dissipate a wild dream that the car had been fairly hit by a shell.

And when at last he reached HQ, crawled wearily out of the car, and staggered, half asleep and utterly worn out, into his room, he found there the other officer he had left to handle his work and the youthful aide humped over the table copying out reports.

'Hullo,' said the senior, 'you're late. I say, you do look tucked up.'

The Captain grunted. 'Not more'n I feel,' he said, blinking at the light. 'Thank the Lord my job's over and everything fixed and ready so far's this end goes.'

'You've heard, I suppose?' said the other. 'No? Baddish news. Our left has cracked and the Germ has a slice of their trenches. It upsets all our plans, and we've got 'em all to make over again.'

The Captain stared blankly at him. 'All to make … that means all today's work to begin and go through again. All today's work – well, I'm …'

The aide had been eyeing the mud-bedaubed figure with water dripping from the torn coat, the sopping cap dangling in the dirty hand, the blue unshaven chin and red-rimmed eyes. He giggled suddenly.

'I say, you know what the troops call the Staff?' He spluttered laughter. 'The Gilded Staff,' he said, pointing at the Captain. 'Behold – oh, my aunt – behold the *Gilded Staff*'.

The Secret
G. A. Studdert Kennedy

You were askin' 'ow we sticks it,
Sticks this blarsted rain and mud,
'Ow it is we keeps on smilin'
When the place runs red wi' blood.
Since you're askin' I can tell ye,
And I thinks I tells ye true,
But it ain't official, mind ye,
It's a tip twixt me and you.
For the General thinks it's tactics,
And the bloomin' plans 'e makes.
And the C.O. thinks it's trainin',
And the trouble as he takes.
Sergeant-Major says it's drillin',
And 'is straffin' on parade,
Doctor swears it's sanitation,
And some patent stinks 'e's made.
Padre tells us its religion,
And the Spirit of the Lord;
But I ain't got much religion,
And I sticks it still, by Gawd.
Quarters kids us it's the rations,
And the dinners as we gets.
But I knows what keeps us smilin'
It's the Woodbine Cigarettes.

For the daytime seems more dreary,
And the night-time seems to drag
To eternity of darkness,
When ye 'aven't got a fag.
Then the rain seems some'ow wetter,
And the cold cuts twice as keen,
And ye keeps on seein' Boches,
What the Sargint 'asn't seen.
If ole Fritz 'as been and got ye,
And ye 'ave to stick the pain,
If ye 'aven't got a fag on,
Why it 'urts as bad again.
When there ain't no fags to pull at,
Then there's terror in the ranks.
That's the secret – (yes, I'll 'ave one)
Just a fag – and many Tanks.

The Horse Hospital
From *Over There*, Arnold Bennett

Nor are men the only beings cared for. One of the strangest things
I saw at Boulogne was a horse-hospital, consisting of a meadow of
many acres. Those who imagine that horses are not used in modern
war should see the thousands of horses tethered in that meadow.
Many if not most of them were suffering from shell wounds, and
the sufferers were rather human. I saw a horse operated on under
chloroform. He refused to come to after the operation was over, and
as I left he was being encouraged to do so by movements of the limbs
to induce respiration. Impossible, after that, to think of him as a
mere horse!

The Burial in England
James Elroy Flecker

These then we honour: these in fragrant earth
Of their own country in great peace forget
Death's lion-roar and gust of nostril-flame
Breathing souls across to the Evening Shore.
Soon over these the flowers of our hill-sides
Shall wake and wave and nod beneath the bee
And whisper love to Zephyr year on year,
Till the red war gleam like a dim red rose
Lost in the garden of the Sons of Time.
But ah what thousands no such friendly doom
Awaits – whom silent comrades in full night
Gazing right and left shall bury swiftly
By the cold flicker of an alien moon.

Ye veiled women, ye with folded hands,
    Mourning those you half hoped for Death too dear,
I claim no heed of you. Broader than earth
Love stands eclipsing nations with his wings,
While Pain, his shadow, delves as black and deep
As he e'er flamed or flew. Citizens draw
Back from their dead awhile. Salute the flag!

    If this flag though royally always borne,
Deceived not dastard, ever served base gold;
If the dark children of the old Forest
Once feared it, or ill Sultans mocked it furled,
Yet now as on a thousand death-reaped days
It takes once more the unquestionable road.
O bright with blood of heroes, not a star
Of all the north shines purer on the sea!

Our foes – the hardest men a state can forge,
An army wrenched and hammered like a blade
Toledo-wrought neither to break nor bend,
Dipped in that ice the pedantry of power,
And toughened with wry gospels of dismay;
Such are these who brake down the door of France,
Wolves worrying at the old World's honour,
Hunting Peace not to prison but her tomb.
But ever as some brown song-bird whose torn nest
Gapes robbery, darts on the hawk like fire,
So Peace hath answered, angry and in arms.
And from each grey hamlet and bright town of France
From where the apple or the olive grows,
Or thin tall strings of poplars on the plains,
From the rough castle of the central hills,
From the three coasts – of mist and storm and sun,
And meadows of the four deep-rolling streams,
From every house whose windows hear God's bell
Crowding the twilight with the wings of prayer
And flash their answer in a golden haze,
Stream the young soldiers who are never tired.
For all the foul mists vanished when that land
Called clear, as in the sunny Alpine morn
The jodeler awakes the frosty slopes
To thunderous replies – soon fading far
Among the vales like songs of dead children.
But the French guns' answer, ne'er to echoes weak
Diminished, bursts from the deep trenches yet;
And its least light vibration blew to dust
The weary factions – priest's or guild's or king's,
And side by side troop up the old partisans,
The same laughing, invincible, tough men
Who gave Napoleon Europe like a loaf,
For slice and portion – not so long ago!
Either to Alsace or loved lost Lorraine

They pass, or inexpugnable Verdun
Ceintured with steel, or stung with faith's old cry
Assume God's vengeance for his temple stones.
But you maybe best wish them for the north
Beside you 'neath low skies in loamèd fields,
Or where the great line hard on the duned shore
Ends and night leaps to England's sea-borne flame.
Never one drop of Lethe's stagnant cup
Dare dim the fountains of the Marne and Aisne
Since still the flowers and meadow-grass unmown
Lie broken with the imprint of those who fell,
Briton and Gaul – but fell immortal friends

And fell victorious and like tall trees fell.
    But young men, you who loiter in the town,
Need you be roused with overshouted words,
Country, Empire, Honour, Liége, Louvain?
Pay your own Youth the duty of her dreams
For what sleep shall keep her from the thrill
    Of War's star-smiting music, with its swell
Of shore and forest and horns high in the wind,

Yet pierced with that too sharp piping which if man
Hear and not fear he shall face God unscathed?
What, are you poets whose vain souls contrive
Sorties and sieges spun of the trickling moon
And such a rousing ghost-catastrophe
You need no concrete marvels to be saved?
Or live you here too lustily for change?
Sail you such pirate seas on such high quests,
Hunt you thick gold or striped and spotted beasts,
Or tread the lone ways of the swan-like mountains?
Excused. But if, as I think, breeched in blue,
Stalled at a counter, cramped upon a desk,
You drive a woman's pencraft – or a slave's,

What chain shall hold you when the trumpets play,
Calling from the blue hill behind your town,
Calling over the seas, calling for you!
'But' – do you murmur? – 'we'd not be as those.
Death is a dour recruiting-sergeant: see,
These women weep, we celebrate the dead.'
Boys, drink the cup of warning dry. Face square
That old grim hazard, 'Glory-or-the-Grave.'
Not we shall trick your pleasant years away,
Yet is not Death the great adventure still,
And is it all loss to set ship clean anew
When heart is young and life an eagle poised?
Choose, you're no cowards. After all, think some,
Since we are men and shrine immortal souls
Surely for us as for these nobly dead
The Kings of England lifting up their swords
Shall gather at the gate of Paradise.

A Night in Istanbul
From *The War in Eastern Europe*, John Reed

We dined in the restaurant of the Municipal Garden of the Petit
Champs at Pera, to the blaring ragtime of the band. The striped awning
over the terrace was gay in a flood of yellow light, and electric-lamps
hanging high in the full-leaved trees made a dim, chequered shade on
the people sitting drinking at iron tables, and the cosmopolitan parade
that moved round and round the garden. Vague under the smoky
radiance of an immense yellow moon, the Golden Horn glittered,
speckled with the red and green lights of ships; beyond lay the dim,
obscure mass of Stamboul, like a crouching animal.

The diners were mostly Germans and Austrians – officers on leave,
aide-de-camps on duty at the Seraskierat in full-dress Turkish uniform,
civilian officials, and the highly paid workmen of the Krupp factories;
many of them with wives and children, in comfortable bourgeois dinner-

parties like the restaurants of Berlin. But there were also Frenchmen with smartly dressed wives, English, Italians, and Americans. In the slowly moving throng outside under the trees, were Perote Greeks, Armenians, Levantine Italians, Turks of official rank; German submarine sailors, Germans of the Turkish navy in fezzes, and great rolling ruddy American sailors from the stationnaire *Scorpion*, towering in their white summer uniform head and shoulders above the crowd. It was hard to believe that, just beyond the reach of our ears, the great guns spat and boomed unceasingly day and night across the bitter sands of Gallipoli ...

If I had only space to recount the Homeric battles of those American sailors! The German man-of-war's -men and soldiers were friendly, but the workmen and civilians very quarrelsome. Sometimes an intoxicated or excited Teuton would come over to the American table and begin an argument about munitions of war, or the *Lusitania* case; or a German officer in Turkish uniform would stop them on the street and insist on being saluted. The sailors answered nothing but insults, and then they answered with their fists, Anglo-Saxon fashion. I could write another chapter simply about the night that Seaman Williams broke the German lieutenant's head with a stone beer-mug, and was transferred back to the United States as being 'unfit for diplomatic service.' And then there is the wonderful history of the two sailors who laid out seventeen attacking Germans in a cafe, and were led back to the American Sailors' Club by congratulatory police, while the wounded foe were jailed for three days ... Respect and friendship was mutual between the American sailors and the Turkish police ...

Afterward we got into a cab and drove down the steep, dark streets to the Inner Bridge; the cabman carefully shrouded his lamps, for lights on the bridges were forbidden on account of possible lurking British submarines. Stamboul was black – they were saving coal. Dim lamps in the interiors of little stores and cafés shed a flickering illumination on mysterious figures shrouded in the voluminous garments of the East, who drifted silently by on slippered feet.

Youssof Effendi was in his favourite café in a street behind the Bayazid mosque. We sat there with him, talking and drinking coffee, and puffing lazily at our *narghilehs* – the grey, cool smoke that makes the sweat stand out on your forehead ... Later we walked through the darkness across the city, by ways known to him alone, through arched passages, broken walls, and mosque courtyards. One after the other on mighty minarets, the *muezzins* came out into the heavy night, and cried that quavering singsong which carries so far, and seems the last requiem of an old religion and a worn-out race.

Out of his great courtesy, the Hoja insisted on going with us to Pera; so we invited him to drink a coffee with us at the Petit Champs. On the open-air stage the regular evening vaudeville performance was going on – singing girls, dancing girls, American tramp comedian, Hungarian acrobats, German marionettes – the harsh voices, lascivious gestures, suggestive costumes, ungraceful writhings of the Occident. How vulgar it seemed after the dignified quiet of Stamboul, the exquisite courtesy of Turkish life!

Some Turkish officers from the interior of Asia Minor, who had never before seen women publicly unveiled and showing their legs, sat gaping in the front row, alternately flushing with anger and shame and roaring with laughter at the amazing indecency of the civilised West... The Hoja watched the performance attentively, but his polished politeness gave no sign of embarrassment. Soon it ended, and in spite of many protests on the Hoja's part, we walked down the hill to the bridge with him. He did not speak of the show at all. But I was curious to know his real opinion.

'It was very lovely,' replied Youssof Effendi with the most suave courtesy: 'I shall take my little granddaughter to see it...'

Down at the dark bridge the draw was open, to let pass a contraband ship full of coal and oil which had crept down the coast from Burgas. Now at night it is forbidden for all but high officers to cross the Golden Horn in *caïks,* so there seemed nothing to do but wait for the interminable closing of the draw. Daoud Bey, however, confidently led the way down to the landing-place. Suddenly, out of the shadow popped a soldier-patrol.

'*Dour!* Stop!' cried the officer. 'Where are you going?'

Daoud turned on him rudely. '*Wir sind Deutsche offizieren'* he bellowed. The man saluted hastily, and fell back into the dark. 'The German always does it,' chuckled Daoud ...

Late at night we climbed once more up Pera Hill. In a dark side-street the crowd was already beginning to gather about the front of a bakery, to stand there until it opened in the morning. We were stopped at Tramway Street by a flock of tooting automobiles rushing up, and street-cars one after another with clanging bells. Through the dark windows we glimpsed white faces staring out, bandaged – another Red Crescent ship had arrived from the Front, and they were hurrying the wounded to the hospitals.

'Hell-fire Post'
From *The Kangaroo Marines*, R. W. Campbell

> Bullets here, bullets there,
> Bullets, bullets everywhere.

Such is trench life. Death at every corner, death at every moment of the day. Bullets plunk against the parapet with a monotonous regularity; others crack in the air like a whip, while some whiz past the ear like a great queen bee. At odd intervals a dose of shrapnel heightens the nerves, and now and again a high-explosive comes down with a shuddering boom!

A trench isn't the place for a lady, it isn't the place for a mild-mannered curate. It's the place for blunt, hard and active men. In fact, the nearer man is to the brute creation the better he is at this game. The highly strung, carefully fed, hot-house plant, such as a mamma's darling, hasn't a look in. He finds it a beastly bore, and longs for the drawing-room cushions and afternoon tea. Trench life reveals the best and shows the worst. A man's nature stands out like a statue. For trench life a man needs the stomach of a horse, the strength of a lion, and the nerves of a navvy. Any man can do a bayonet charge; any man can shoot down the charging host; but it takes a braver man to live in a trench month after month. His nostrils are filled with the stench of the fallen, for his parapet is frequently built up with the dead. His tea is made with water polluted with germs, the bully beef stew is generally soaked in dust and sand.

And the flies! They're worse than all, the pestilential breed! Flies kill more men than bullets. Flies were surely invented by some ancient Hun.

Trench life in France is a picnic compared with the Dardanelles. In France, one can get soft bread, fresh coffee and yesterday's *Times*. But, in the Dardanelles it is biscuits and bully, bully and biscuits – without the news of Pollokshields and Mayfair. Yet, despite the severity of things, the Australasians were ever serene. To them it was a sporting game. They had been used to boiling their own billy cans; used to looking for firewood; used to making a shanty wherein to lay their heads. Where the Cockney might die from heat and thirst, the Australasian can thrive like a Zulu or aborigine. City bred troops demand an organisation of things; Australasian troops organise things for themselves. And where our friends of The Kangaroo Marines were certainly demanded all their cunning and courage, it was called 'Hell-Fire Post.' This was on the left of the Australian line, within thirty yards of the Turks. The post had developed from a thin line of holes into a strong redoubt. Many had died, more had been wounded in defending this place, but it was worth it. This was the key of the whole line. That was why The Kangaroo Marines were there. When they took it over, they found the parapets thin and bullets coming in all round.

'Hot shop, by Jove!' said Claud, adjusting his monocle to look through an aperture. Crack! came a bullet, just missing his head.

'Better take that window out of yer face,' said Bill.

'Why?'

'Them ole snipers thinks yer a general.'

'My dear fellow, you're a positive bore – now, lend me a hand.' And Claud, despite the whizzing bullets, filled more sandbags and shoved them up with a shovel. Bill helped him to make a V-shaped aperture. This work was continued all along the line. But all the sandbags and crack shots could not keep the rifle fire down. To move a hand or head above the level of the ground meant a wound.

'This won't do,' said the Colonel, as he made his morning visit on his hands and knees.

'It's like a penny shooting show, Colonel,' said Bill.

'Why?'

'Me an' the boys are doin' running man for them fellers over there. They chip bits on yer head, an' bits on yer chest. It ain't comfortable. It ain't war.'

'It's sudden daith,' chipped in Sandy Brown.

'All right, boys, I'll send up something today. Cheer up, you'll soon be at Manly amongst the girls,' and off went Killem on his rounds. That afternoon a dozen big iron plates came up. These were square with a hole in the centre. This hole was covered by a little iron door, which could be lifted at will. Bill and his pals seized one and commenced to fix it in position. Under a hail of lead they worked sweating, grousing and cursing all the time. At last it was fixed and ready for business.

'This is my shot,' said Bill, taking hold of his rifle. Slowly he opened the door, then peeped through.

'I see one, boys!'

'Where?' they whispered.

'Behind some bags. Gosh, ain't he ugly. He's got a face like a black puddin', and the eyes of a snake. He ain't a bit of Turkish delight, anyhow, I wouldn't like to lick his old face. Wheesht, boys, he's goin' to shoot.'

'At you?'

'No! Some fathead down the line. But I'll get the one-eyed Moslem blighter,' muttered Bill, taking careful aim.

'Mind yis don't hit the ould fellow up in the moon,' said Paddy just as Bill let go.

'Ye spud-faced Paddy. Ye–ye–ye–' blurted out Bill, throwing down his gun in anger.

'Missed, be Jasus – yis couldn't hit the town of Sydney at a hundred yards. Paddy Doolan's the man for that job.' He seized the rifle, but just as he was going to open the little iron door there was a rattle of bullets all over the plate.

'Down, boys, down,' he shouted.

'It's a beastly Maxim,' said Claud, looking up. And a Maxim it was. In ten minutes the so-called armoured plate was riddled. This was the experience with nearly all the other plates – one of the many annoying problems of war. However, the new plates were doubled and bolted. Then they were covered with sandbags and erected so as not to be too obvious on the parapet. This scheme defied the sniper and the Maxim, and, in this way, the Turks' fire was subdued. This was important. In trench warfare the enemy must be terrorised. Not a head must be allowed to bob up, not a rifle and eye seen. Snipers must be hunted to death and given such a hefty and quick dispatch as to intimidate their successors. Water parties and ration parties have to be set on the run; reinforcements spotted and scattered; officers, too, must be kept in their place – below the parapet, if not below the sod. All of this means that the enemy gets demoralised and sickened. And when he has had a month or two of this gentle treatment he is easily dealt with when the time comes for an offensive and bayonet charge.

Of course, the Turks did not let the Australasians have it entirely their own way. When sniping and rifle fire became too dangerous, they resorted to the bomb. The bomb isn't a respectable thing. It sometimes takes your head off, and frequently punctures the system in rather an ugly manner. When a bomb hits, you know it. It is something like a railway engine striking a match-box. These Turkish bomb-throwers had some idea of making a sort of Irish stew out of their opponents' bodies. They bombed *and* bombed *and* bombed. Now, this wasn't at all polite, and it was most uncomfortable, especially when sitting down to a stolen Maconochie – an appetising dish. These bombs burst the parapets, ripped up the sandbags, and knocked men's brains into other men's eyes. Most annoying! One morning a bomb just missed Bill's head.

'What the – who the – why the – These blamed ole Turks think my head's a coconut,' said Bill.

'I hope they'll never hit your head,' remarked Claud.

'Why?'

'It's too full –'

'Of water,' interjected Paddy.

'Yes, there *would* be a flood,' concluded Claud, as he lit his pipe. Just then an order was sent down to pass all empty jam tins to the rear.

'Wot's the jam tins for?'

'Fly traps,' said Paddy.

''Spect we'll have to dig the lead out of the dead men's bodies next,' groused Bill, as he went down the trenches to collect the fly-covered jam tins. These were sent down to the beach in bags, causing many a grouse on the way. Rumour had it that some Jew had made a contract for the empty tins, another yarn was that they were for growing flowers round the General's dugout. But mysterious and resourceful are the ways of the General Staff! These jam tins were redelivered to The Kangaroo Marines next day in the shape of bombs.

'Well I'm jiggered!' said Bill. 'First they puts jam in tins, next they puts bombs in them.'

'And then they'll shove you in them,' interjected Claud.

'What for?'

'Prime Australian beef, fresh tinned, straight from the Dardanelles. That would look well on a label.'

'Yis couldn't do that with Bill,' said Paddy.

'Why?'

'He's a bit high –'

Bang! came a Turkish bomb at that moment, scattering the group into their shelters below the parapets.

'Ye dirty, mouldy-faced sons of dog-eatin', blue-nosed spalpeens – Oi'll bomb yis,' roared Paddy, gripping a jam tin and lighting the fuse.

Bang! it went. Bang! Bang! Bang! went more.

'Some jam,' said Bill, as he watched through the periscope. And then they heard moaning, shrieks, and shouts of 'Allah, Allah.'

'More jam,' ordered Bill. And more jam they received. It wasn't sweet, and certainly unpalatable. And it didn't stick. Tins labeled 'Apricot,' 'Marmalade,' 'Black Currant,' and 'Raspberry,' went hurtling through the air, then burst in a very nasty way above the poor old Turks' trenches. This battle of jam bombs made the Turks much more respectful for a time. Indeed, one of the officers, who must have been a sportsman, flung over a note, on which was written:

DEAR AUSTRALIANS,
We like jam – in fact, we could do with a tin of it, but not that dam-jam-jammy stuff you were putting over last night.

Yours fraternally,
'YUSSEF BEY'

'By Jove! He's a sport – let's chuck him a tin,' said Claud. And over it went. The Turks scattered and waited, but there was no explosion. With a smile the Turkish officer picked up the tin. Unfastening a note tied round it, he read:

DEAR YUSSEF,
This is the real stuff. By the way, you were at Rugby with me. Shall be sorry to kill you.
Yours, etc.,
'CLAUD DUFAIR'

Plunk! came a stone into the Australian lines; round it was fixed a note:

DEAR CLAUD,
Many thanks – it was a god-send. Fancy you being here. I thought you would have been guarding the Marys and Mauds of London from the Zepps. Congrats! Of course, I shall be sorry to kill you.
Yours, etc.,
'YUSSEF BEY'
P.S. There will be no firing today – go to bed.

And there was no firing. This Turkish officer, like every other Turkish soldier, was a gentleman.

It is remarkable how circumstances produce the inventor. At Hell-Fire Post the men found that the ordinary square periscope was almost useless. Every time one went up, bang went a Turk's rifle, and the periscope was blown to smithereens. Indeed, The Kangaroos lost nearly all their periscopes in the first few days. Now this was awkward.

Periscopes are life-savers, for the periscope prevents a man pushing his head above the parapet to see if Johnny Turk is coming over to say 'Good morning.' Something had to be done, so the famous quartette began to cudgel their brains.

'I've got it,' said Claud, picking up a walking-stick.

'Got what,' inquired Bill.

'An idea – you watch.' Taking a penknife out of his pocket, he deftly and quickly cut away the inner portion of the stick. This kept him busy for a couple of hours. When finished, he took a little pocket mirror out of his haversack.

'Too big,' said Bill.

'No, it isn't,' answered Claud, slipping a diamond ring off his finger. He scratched the mirror, then cut two pieces out of it. These he fixed into the walking stick. 'There you are now – a brand new periscope.' And it proved just the thing. The field of vision was quite good. Being small it did not attract attention. The result of this discovery was that every officer's stick was immediately commandeered, and with the aid of Claud's ring and other people's mirrors, a good supply of periscopes were made.

'You think you're smart fellers, I suppose,' said Bill, his envy roused by this success. 'But I'll show you fellers something in a day or two.'

'What is it?'

'"Wait and see," as old Asquith says.' For the next few days Bill was seen in close communion with a fellow Australian. They went about the trenches picking up bits of wood, nails, mirrors, and other odds and ends. These were carried into the little hole of the inventive genius, and there all gradually saw the growth of a wonderful invention. It wasn't Bill's idea exactly. He was simply the managing director, who stimulated curiosity, and fetched the mysterious genius the necessary supplies of material. Anyone who ventured too near the sacred sanctum was told to 'hop it.'

'What's that ould rascal doin'?' Paddy remarked one day.

'A bomb-thrower,' said Sandy.

'Barbed wire burster,' suggested Claud.

'No, it ain't,' interjected Bill, who happened to come along at the time.

'What is it, then?'

'It's a man-killer. You can sit down in yer bed and kill all the ole Turks in front. They can't see who's killin' them.'

'When do you try it?'

'Today.' And he did. That afternoon the inventor allowed Bill to have the trial shot. The instrument, in brief, was a periscope rifle. With the aid of an ordinary rifle, mirrors and wood fixed up in a rough, but ingenious way, there had been produced a killing instrument, which allowed the user to see and to kill without being seen. This was a godsend, for many of the casualties at this post were due to men aiming through the loopholes or over the parapet.

'Here goes,' said Bill, fixing the rifle in position.

'See anything?'

'Yes, a big feller. I'll get him in his ole fat head.' Slowly and steadily he took aim, then bang went his rifle.

'Got him! Got him! Right in his coconut,' shouted Bill with a grim delight.

The invention was hailed as a great success, and the inventor complimented all round. His orders were many, and his instrument soon became general throughout the whole line. Indeed, it was owing to this wonderful invention that the rifle fire of the Turks was again subdued to a remarkable extent.

Other remarkable things were invented by these resourceful fellows. The General Staff also supplied them with new machines of war. One of the finest was the Japanese bomb-thrower, an instrument which threw a great, big bomb like a well-filled melon. This went tumbling over and over, like an acrobat doing a somersault, then burst in the most startling way. The explosion was terrific and destruction amazing. Parapets, trenches, men and Maxims were all destroyed if near the point of contact. 'Some bomb!' as the boys said.

In this sort of warfare it is always the progressive and alert man who wins. It is useless sitting down and grousing. Every means, every trick is justifiable so long as the methods are fair and according to the rules of war. When the history of this war is written special attention ought to be devoted to the many devices which have been employed by the soldier. For example, the Turks opposite to The Kangaroos were always sapping towards the Australasian lines. This was a nuisance. The constant pick! pick! pick! upset everybody. Night after night these Turkish moles had to be bombed away. One evening a sapping party recommenced operations quite near to Claud and his friends.

'At it again,' Bill remarked.

'Yes, they're a beastly nuisance, I'll have to worry them a bit,' said Claud, picking up a little paper bag. He fixed a piece of thin white string round it, then jumped over the parapet. It was quite dark, so he was perfectly safe. Crawling on his hands and knees, he at last reached within ten yards of the sapping Turks. For a few minutes he lay still. His eyes got used to the darkness, enabling him to get a glimpse of the diggers. Pulling out the paper bag, he threw it smartly towards the hole. It burst on the edge of the parapet and the contents scattered all round. Claud waited.

Aitchoo! went one.

Aitchoo! went another.

Aitchoo! went a third.

Aitchoo! Aitchoo! Aitchoo! sneezed all the Turks between their oriental grunts and curses.

Claud burst out laughing and so gave himself away. A head popped out of the hole. Claud was seen. Down it went, and up came a rifle, but before the Turk could fire, Claud, who had a couple of bombs prepared, flung them into the hole. There was a loud bang! bang! followed by a series of shouts, shrieks and moans. The sapping party fled for their lives. This was as Claud desired, so he quietly crawled back to his trench.

'Got 'em that time, Dufair,' said an officer as he tumbled in.

'Yes, sir.'

'By the way, what was all the sneezing about?'

'A little trick, sir,' laughed Claud.

'Was it snuff you chucked at them?'

'No, common or garden pepper, issued with the rations.'

'Good,' said the officer pursuing his rounds.

Now it was on this same evening that Paddy Doolan roused the whole regiment to a state of alarm. He was on sentry go on the extreme left of his regiment's line. Being dark, Paddy began to feel the effects of things supernatural. Every sound, every moving leaf or blade was a Turk. He had fired at a few nothings, and during a spell of silence he was amazed to hear on his left a chattering in a strange tongue.

'Turks, be Jasus, they're in our trenches. Mother of Mary, preserve us,' said Paddy, crossing himself. He listened again. They were chanting a weird dirge. It was something between a Highland lament and a Hindoo snake song. Paddy was amazed. Life seemed to be a shorter affair, and he pictured himself lying dead on the parapet with his throat cut. His teeth were chattering, and his nerves on the run. At last he managed to bellow out, 'Stand to!' The half-sleeping men jumped to their rifles and waited below the parapet.

'What's up, Doolan?' said the officer on reaching them.

'Turks in our trenches, sor. Heaven preserve us.'

'Where?'

'There, sor! There, sor! Listen to them.'

The officer listened. He heard the weird chanting. It wasn't English, it didn't seem Turkish. What on earth was it, he wondered. At last he made up his mind.

'Here, six of you fix bayonets, follow me,' and down the communication trench he crouched and crawled towards the left. They now neared the weird chanting noise. The officer cocked his revolver and whispered back, 'Get ready, boys.' Then, dashing round a bend, he burst on to a dark-skinned group.

'Hands up!' he shouted.

'What's up, boss?' said a smiling dusky gent in khaki, with a New Zealand badge on his shoulder.

'Who the deuce are you?'

'Maoris, boss, Maoris.'

'Hang it all, I thought you were Turks. Good night.'

'Good night, boss,' shouted the laughing Maoris – the finest dark-skinned gentlemen in the world.

Fighting Hard
Henry Lawson

'The Australians are fighting hard in Gallipoli' – Cable.

Rolling out to fight for England, singing songs across the sea;
Rolling North to fight for England, and to fight for you and me;
Fighting hard for France and England, where the storms of Death
are hurled;
Fighting hard for Australasia and the honour of the World!
Fighting hard.

Fighting hard for Sunny Queensland – fighting for Bananaland,
Fighting hard for West Australia, and the mulga and the sand;
Fighting hard for Plain and Wool-track, and the haze of western
heat –
Fighting hard for South Australia and the bronze of Farrar's
Wheat!
Fighting hard.

Fighting hard for fair Victoria, and the mountain and the glen;
(And the Memory of Eureka – there were other tyrants then),
For the glorious Gippsland forests and the World's great Singing
Star –
For the irrigation channels where the cabbage gardens are –
Fighting hard.

Fighting hard for gale and earthquake, and the wind-swept ports
between;
For the wild flax and manuka and the terraced hills of green.
Fighting hard for wooden homesteads, where the mighty kauris
stand –
Fighting hard for fern and tussock! – Fighting hard for Maoriland!
Fighting hard.

Fighting hard for little Tassy, where the apple orchards grow;
(And the Northern Territory just to give the place a show,)
Fighting hard for Home and Empire, while the Commonwealth
prevails –
And, in spite of all her blunders, dying hard for New South Wales.
Dying hard.

Fighting hard for the Pride of Old Folk, and the people that you
know;
And the girl you left behind you – (ah! the time is passing slow).
For the proud tears of a sister! come you back, or never come!
And the weary Elder Brother, looking after things at home –
Fighting hard! *You Lucky Devils!*
Fighting hard.

A Letter to the Cardinals and Bishops of Germany and Austria, from Cardinal Désiré Mercier, Archbishop of Malines, and the Bishops of Namur, Liège and Tournai
From *A Shepherd Among Wolves*, by Arthur Boutwood

24th Nov., 1915. *An important group of German Catholics, under pretext of replying to a French work entitled* The German War and Catholicism, *calumniated the Belgian nation. A professor of Paderborn, Rosenberg, making himself the mouthpiece of his countrymen, frightfully insulted the honour of the Belgian name in a book entitled* The German War and Catholicism: A German reply to French attacks, prepared by German Catholics, *a book all the more perfidious because it is apparently moderate.*

To this book, translated into French and Flemish, and circulated through the Belgian provinces, Mgr. Mercier and the Bishops of Namur, Liège and Tournai replied in the following letter addressed to their colleagues in Germany and Austria-Hungary, inviting them to hold an impartial inquiry into the accusations formulated by Professor Rosenberg:

Eminences, Messeigneurs,

For a whole year, we Catholic Bishops have given to the world
– you bishops of Germany on one side; and we, bishops of Belgium,
France and England, on the other side – a most disconcerting
spectacle.

Hardly had the German armies swarmed over the soil of our
country than the rumour was spread among you that our civilians
were taking part in military operations; that the women of Vise and
Liège tore out the eyes of your soldiers; that the populace had sacked,
in Antwerp and Brussels, the property of expelled Germans.

As early as the first days of August, Dom Ildefons Herwegen, Abbé
of Maria-Laach, addressed to the Cardinal Archbishop of Malines a
telegram in which he implored him, for the love of God, to protect
the German soldiers from the tortures that our countrymen were
supposed to inflict upon them.

Now it was notorious that our Government took precautionary
measures in order that the citizens should all be made acquainted
with the laws of war; in every commune the arms of the inhabitants
had to be deposited at the communal house; by means of placards,
the people were warned that only citizens regularly enrolled under
the flag were authorised to bear arms; and the clergy, anxious to
second the mission of the State, had spread by word of mouth, by
parochial notices and by placards fixed on the church doors, the
instructions issued by the Government.

Accustomed for a century to a *régime* of peace, we could not
imagine it possible that anyone could, in good faith, accuse us of
violent instincts. Strong in our right and in the sincerity of our pacific
intentions, we replied to the calumnies about 'snipers' and 'eyes dug
out' by shrugging our shoulders, persuaded that the truth would not
fail to come to light of itself.

The clergy and episcopate of Belgium were in personal relation with
a great many German and Austrian priests, monks, and bishops; the
Eucharistic Congresses at Cologne in 1909, and at Vienna in 1912,
had furnished opportunities for personal acquaintance and mutual
appreciation. So we felt certain that the Catholics of the nations at

war with us would not judge us lightly; and, without being much disturbed by the contents of Dom Ildefons' telegram, the Cardinal of Malines merely asked him to unite with us in preaching gentleness: for, he added, it has been pointed out to us that the German troops shoot innocent Belgian priests.

As early as the first days of August, crimes had been committed at Battice, at Visé, at Berneau, at Herve and other places; but we tried to hope that they would remain isolated deeds, and, knowing the important position of Dom Ildefons, we had perfect confidence in the following declaration that he was kind enough to send us on 11th August:

'I am informed on the highest authority, that "formal orders" have been given to the German soldiers, by the military authorities, to spare the innocent. As to the very deplorable fact that even priests have lost their lives, I beg to draw the attention of your Eminence to the fact that, latterly, the frocks of priests and monks have become objects of suspicion and disgrace, since French spies have made use of the ecclesiastical habit and even of the costume of nuns to hide their hostile intentions.'

Notwithstanding, hostile acts towards the innocent continued.

On 18th August, 1914, Mgr. the Bishop of Liège, wrote to Commandant Bayer, Governor of the town of Liège:

'One after another, many villages have been destroyed; prominent persons – priests among them – have been shot: others have been arrested, though all of them protested their innocence. I know the priests of my diocese; I cannot believe that a single one of them would be guilty of hostile acts towards the German soldiers. I have visited many ambulances and I have seen the wounded Germans there cared for as zealously as the Belgians. They admit this themselves.'

No reply was made to this letter.

At the beginning of September, the Emperor of Germany lent his authority to the calumnious accusations of which our innocent people were the object. He sent to Mr Wilson, President of the United States, the following telegram, which, to the best of our knowledge, has never been retracted: 'The Belgian Government has publicly encouraged the civil population to take part in this war which it had carefully prepared long before. The cruelties perpetrated in the course of this irregular warfare, by women and even by priests, upon doctors and nurses are such that my generals have finally been compelled to have recourse to the most severe means of chastising the guilty to prevent the blood-thirsty population from continuing these abominably criminal and odious deeds. Many villages, and even the town of Louvain itself, have of necessity been demolished (except the very beautiful Hôtel-de-Ville) in the interest of our defence and for the protection of my troops. My heart bleeds when I realise that such measures have become inevitable, and when I think of the numberless innocents who have lost their homes and their belongings through the criminal deeds in question.'

This telegram was placarded in Belgium by order of the German Government on 11th September. No later than the next day, 12th September, Mgr. the Bishop of Namur asked to be received by the military government of Namur and protested against the reputation that the Emperor sought to give the Belgian clergy; he affirmed the innocence of all the members of the clergy shot or injured, and declared himself ready to publish the guilty deeds that they could succeed in establishing.

The Bishop of Namur's offer was not accepted and nothing came of his protestation. Calumny was consequently free to take its course. The German press fomented it; the *Kölnische Volkzeitung* – organ of the Catholic Centre – vied with the Lutheran press in Chauvinism.

The very day on which thousands of our fellow citizens, ecclesiastics and layman, from Visé, Aerschot, Wesemael, Herent, Louvain, and twenty other localities – as innocent of deeds of war or of cruelties as you and we are – were dragged as prisoners across the railways of Aix-la-Chapelle and Cologne, and were, during deadly hours, made a spectacle for the unwholesome curiosity of the Rhenish metropolis; they had the grief of proving that their Catholic brethren poured forth as many insults upon them as the Lutheran sectaries of Celle, of Soltau or of Magdeburg.

In Germany not one voice was raised in defence of the victims.

The legend which transformed the innocent into the guilty, and crime into an act of justice, thus became accredited, and on 10th May, 1915 the *White Book,* the official organ of the German Empire, dared to take up these odious and cowardly lies on its own account, and to circulate them in neutral countries:

'It is indisputable that wounded Germans have been stripped and killed, yes, horribly mutilated by the Belgian population, and that even women and young girls have taken part in these abominations. Wounded Germans have had their eyes dug out, ears, noses, fingers, sexual organs cut off, or their entrails torn open; in other instances German soldiers have been poisoned, hung from trees, had boiling liquids poured over them, or been burnt, so that they have died in atrocious suffering. These bestial proceedings of the population not only violate the obligations expressly formulated by the Convention of Geneva concerning the respect and care due to the wounded of the enemy army, but are opposed to the fundamental principles of the laws of war and humanity.'

For one moment, dear colleagues in the faith and the priesthood, put yourselves in our place.

We know that these accusations of the imperial Government are calumnies from beginning to end. We know it; we swear it.

Now to justify these accusations, your Government calls upon witnesses who have never been submitted to any checking by examination from the other side.

Is it not your duty, not only out of charity, but in strict justice, to enlighten yourselves, to enlighten your flocks, and to provide us an opportunity for the judicial establishment of our innocence?

You owe us this satisfaction in the name of that Catholic charity which is above national conflicts; you owe it us today in strict justice, because a Committee, sheltered by your – at least tacit – approval, a Committee composed of all that is most distinguished in Germany in politics, science, and religion, has countenanced these official accusations, and has confided to the pen of a Catholic priest, Professor A. J. Rosenberg, of Paderbom, the task of condensing them into a book entitled *Lying Accusations of French Catholics Against Germany*, and has thus saddled Catholic Germany with the responsibility of active and public propagation of calumny against the Belgian people.

When the French book, to which the German Catholics oppose theirs, saw the light, their Eminences Cardinal von Hartmann, Archbishop of Cologne, and Cardinal von Bettinger, Archbishop of Munich, thought it necessary to send a telegram to their Emperor in these words:

> Revolted by the defamations against the German Fatherland and against its glorious army contained in the work *The German War and Catholicism,* our heart feels the need of expressing to your Majesty its sorrowful indignation in the name of the whole German Episcopate. We shall not fail to pour out our complaint to the Supreme Head of the Church.

Well, Most Reverend Eminences, Venerated Colleagues of the German Episcopate, in our turn, we, Bishops of Belgium, revolted by the calumnies against our Belgian country and its glorious army, contained in the *White Book* of the Empire, and reiterated in the reply of the German Catholics to the work of the French Catholics – *we* feel the need of expressing to our King, to our Government, to our army, to our country, our sorrowful indignation and, in order that our protest may not run counter to yours without useful result, we ask you to be so good as to help us to institute a tribunal of impartial inquiry. You will appoint, in your official character, as many members as you wish, and whoever you please to choose: we will appoint as many – three, for example, on each side. And by common agreement, we will ask the Episcopate of a neutral State – Holland, Spain, Switzerland, or the United States – to be so good as to appoint a chairman for us who would preside over the work of the tribunal.

You have carried your complaints to the Supreme Head of the Church. It is not just that he should hear your voice only.

We have, you and us, an identical duty – that is, to place before His Holiness verified documents on which he will be able to found his judgment.

You are not ignorant of the efforts we have made, one after another, to obtain from the Power that is occupying Belgium the constitution of a tribunal of inquiry.

The Cardinal of Malines, on two occasions, in writing – 24th of January, 1915, and the 10th of February, 1915 – and the Bishop of Namur, in a letter addressed to the Military Governor of his province on the 12th of April, 1915, begged for the formation of a tribunal composed of German and Belgian arbitrators in equal numbers, and presided over by a delegate from a neutral State. Our earnest entreaties were met by an obstinate refusal.

Meanwhile, the German authorities were careful to institute inquiries, but they wished them to be one-sided – that is to say, without judicial value.

After having refused the inquiry demanded by the Cardinal of Malines, the German authorities went into various localities where priests had been shot, peaceful citizens massacred or imprisoned, and there, on the deposition of certain witnesses taken by chance or carefully selected – sometimes in the presence of a representative of the local authority who did not know the German language, and thus found himself obliged to accept and to sign on trust the *procès verbaux* – they thought it possible to found conclusions which could afterwards be presented to the public as the result of an impartial examination.

The German inquiry at Louvain in November 1904 was held under these conditions. It is therefore void of authority.

So it is natural that we should turn to you.

The court of arbitration, which the Power in possession has refused us, you will grant us, and you will obtain for us from your Government the public declaration that the witnesses invited by you and by us will be able to say all that they know without having to fear reprisals. Before you, and under protection of your moral authority, they will feel themselves in greater security, and encouraged to testify what they have seen and heard. The world will have confidence in the joint-Episcopate of our two nations; our common superintendence will authenticate the evidence, and will guarantee the accuracy of the *procès verbaux*. The inquiry, conducted thus, will inspire confidence.

Eminences and Venerated Colleagues, we demand this inquiry above all, in order to vindicate the honour of the Belgian people. It has been violated by calumnies started by your people, and by their highest representatives. And you know as well as we do the adage of moral theology, the human, Christian, Catholic adage: Without restitution, no pardon.

Your people, through their political organ and their highest moral authorities, have accused our fellow-citizens of having perpetrated on wounded Germans atrocities and horrors of which the *White Book* and the *Manifesto of the Catholics* drew up the aforesaid details; to all these accusations we oppose a formal denial, and we demand to bring proof that that denial is well founded.

In return, to justify the atrocities committed in Belgium by the German army, the public authorities – by the very heading of the *White Book, Die Völkerrechtswidridge Fährung des Belgischen Volkskriegs*, i.e. *the violation of international law by the proceedings of the Belgian people* – and the hundred Catholic signatories of the work, *The German War and Catholicism: German reply to French attacks,* affirm that the German army is found in Belgium in a position of legitimate defence against a perfidious organisation of *francs-tireurs.*

We declare that nowhere in Belgium has there been an organisation of *francs-tireurs* and, in the name of our calumniated national honour, we demand the right to prove the absolute truth of our affirmation.

You can call before the tribunal of impartial inquiry whoever you like; we shall invite to appear there all the priests of parishes where civilians, priests, monks and laymen were massacred or threatened with death to the cry of *Man hat geschossen,* 'they fired'; if you like, we will ask all these priests to sign their deposition on oath, and then, under pain of professing that the whole Belgian clergy is perjured, you will be obliged to accept it, and the civilized world will not be able to challenge the conclusions of this solemn and decisive inquiry.

But, Eminences and Venerated Colleagues, we may add it is to your interest, as much as to ours, to constitute a tribunal of honour.

For our part, resting upon actual experience, we know and therefore declare that the German army in Belgium, in a hundred different neighbourhoods, gave itself up to pillage, incendiarism, imprisonments, massacre, sacrilege – contrary to all justice and to every feeling of humanity.

We declare this notably of the communes the names of which have figured in our pastoral letters, and in the two Notes written by the Bishops of Namur and of Liège, the 31st of October and the 1st of November, 1915, respectively, to His Holiness Pope Benedict XV, to His Excellency the Nuncio at Brussels, and to the Ministers or representatives of the neutral countries in residence at Brussels.

Fifty innocent priests, thousands of the innocent faithful, were put to death; hundreds of others, whose lives were preserved through circumstances quite independent of the will of their persecutors, were in danger of death; thousands of the innocent, without any preliminary trial, were made prisoners, and, when they were released, it was found that the most searching cross-examination to which they were subjected had not been able to establish any guilt whatever on their part.

These crimes cry to heaven for vengeance.

If, by formulating these denunciations, we calumniate the German army; or if the military authorities have justifiable reasons for ordering or allowing these acts that we call criminal, Germany owes it to her honour and her national interest to *prove* them unfounded. So long as German justice is non-existent, we hold the right and the duty to denounce what, in all conscience, we consider to be a serious attack upon Justice and our honour.

The Chancellor of the German Empire, in the sitting of 4th August, declared that the invasion of Luxembourg and of Belgium was 'contrary to the provisions of international law'; he recognised that, 'in not taking any notice of the justifiable protests of the Governments of Luxembourg and of Belgium, he committed an *injustice* which he promised to make good'; and the Sovereign Pontiff, alluding intentionally to Belgium – as he condescended to write to M. le Ministre Van den Heuvel by His Eminence Cardinal Gaspari, Secretary of State – pronounced in his consistorial allocution of 22nd January, 1915, this irrevocable judgment:

> It is the duty of the Roman Pontiff, whom God has appointed
> sovereign interpreter and avenger of eternal law, to proclaim,
> before all, that *no one must, for any reason whatever, violate
> justice.*

All the same, politicians and casuists have tried, ever since, to
evade or emasculate these decisive words. In their reply to the
French Catholics, the German Catholics employ their usual mean
subtilties, and try to corroborate them by fact. They have, at their
disposition, two witnesses, one anonymous, who says that on 26th
July he saw French officers in conversation with Belgian officers
on the Boulevard Anspach at Brussels; the other, a certain Gustave
Lochard of Rimogne, who deposed that two French regiments of
dragoons – the 28th and the 30th – and one French battery, crossed
the Belgian frontier on the evening of 31st July, 1914, and remained
entirely on Belgian territory during the whole of the following
week.

Now the Belgian Government declares 'that, before the declaration
of war, no French troops, however few, entered Belgium.' And it
adds: 'No honest witness can be found to contradict this declaration.'
Our King's Government, then, accuses the assertion of the German
Catholics of being false.

We have here a question of the first importance, at once political
and moral, on which we ought to enlighten the public conscience.

If, notwithstanding, you decline to examine the general question,
we ask you at least to be so good as to check the witnesses on whom
the German Catholics rely for the decision against us. The deposition
of this Gustave Lochard relates to facts easily checked. The German
Catholics should be anxious to cleanse themselves from the reproach
of falsehood, and should make it a conscientious duty to retract, if
they have allowed themselves to be deceived to our injury.

Of course, we know that it is very repugnant to you to think that
regiments whose discipline, honesty and religious faith you say you
know, have given themselves up to the inhuman acts with which we

reproach them. You wish to persuade yourselves that this is not so, because it cannot be so.

And, we, compelled by evidence, reply to you that it can be so, because it is so.

In face of fact, no presumption holds good.

For you as for us, there is only one issue possible: the verification of fact by a commission whose impartiality is, and is seen by everyone to be, unquestionable.

We have no difficulty in understanding your point of view.

We also respect – please believe this – the spirit of discipline, of work, of faith, of which we have so often met the proofs, and gathered the evidence, among your countrymen. But there is a very large number of Belgians who confess bitterly today how they have been deceived: they have lived through the sinister events of August and September; truth has triumphed over their strongest pre-dispositions. The fact cannot be denied: Belgium has been martyred.

The Battle of the Stories
G. K. Chesterton

In the Caucasus

They came uncounted like the stars that circle or are set,
They circled and they caught us as in a sparkling casting-net
We burst it in the mountain gate where all the guns began,
When the snow stood up at Christmas on the hills of Ardahan.
The guns – and not a bell to tell that God was made a man –
But we did all remember, though all the world forget.

Before Paris

The kings came over the olden Rhine to break an ancient debt,
We took their rush at the river of death in the fields where first we met,
But we marked their millions swaying; then we marked a standard fall;
And far beyond them, like a bird, Maunoury's bugle call:

And there were not kings or debts or doubts or anything at all
But the People that remembers and the peoples that forget.

In Flanders

Empty above your bleating hordes his throne abides the threat,
Who drew the sword of his despair to front your butcher's bet:
You shall scan the empty scabbard; you shall search the empty
seat.
While he along the ruined skies rides royal with retreat,
In the judgment and the silence and the grass upon the street,
And the oath the heavens remember and you would fain forget.

In Poland

A cloud was on the face of God when three kings met,
What hour the worst of men were made the sun hath suffered yet.
We knew them in their nibbling peace or ever they went to war.
In petty school and pilfered field we know them what they are.
And we drank the cup of anguish to the pardon of the Czar,
To the nations that remember and the empires that forget.

In the Dardanelles

To the horned mount of the high Mahound of moon and of
minaret
Labouring go the sieging trains whose tracks are blood and sweat.
The ships break in a sanguine sea; and far to the front a boy
Fallen, and his face flung back to shout with the Son of God for joy.
And the long land under the lifted smoke; and a great light on
Troy,
And all that men remember and madmen can forget.

In the Balkans

They thrice on crags of death were dry and thrice in Danube wet
To prove an old man's empty heart was empty of regret,
For the Turks have taken his city's soul; his spurs of gold are dross,
And the Crescent hangs upon him while we hang upon the Cross.

But we have our tower of pride upon Kossovo of the loss,
For a proof that we remember and the infidels forget.

In the Alps
Master of Arts and mastery of arms, master of all things yet,
For the musket as for the mandolin the master fingers fret;
The news to the noise of the mandolin that all the world comes
home,
And the young are young and the years return and the days of the
kingdom come.
When the wars wearied, and the tribes turned: and the sun rose on
Rome,
And all that Rome remembers when all her realms forget.

In the North Sea
Though the seas were sown with the new dragons that knew not
what they ate,
We broke St George's banner out to the black wind and the wet,
He hath broken all the bridges we could fling, the world and we,
But the bridge of death in heaven that His people might be free,
That we straddled for the saddle of the riders of the sea.
For St George that shall remember if the Dragon shall forget.

All the Voices
Behold, we are men of many lands, in motley seasons set,
From Riga to the rock of Spain, from Orkney to Olivet,
Who stand up in the council in the turning of the year,
And, standing, give the judgment on the evil house of fear;
Knowing the End shall write again what we have written here,
On the day when God remembers and no man can forget.

1916

British Submarines in the Dardanelles
From *Submarine and Anti-Submarine,*
Sir Henry Newbolt

Our submarine campaign in the Sea of Marmora must also have a separate chapter to itself, not only because it is now a closed episode in the history of the War, but because it was conducted under quite unique conditions. The scene of operations was not merely distant from the submarine base, it was divided from it by an approach of unusual danger and difficulty. The channel of the Dardanelles is narrow and winding, with a strong tide perpetually racing down it, and setting strongly into the several bays. It was moreover protected, as will appear in the course of the narrative, by forts with powerful guns and searchlights and torpedo tubes, and by barrages of thick wire and netting. It was also patrolled constantly by armed ships. Yet from the very first all these defences were evaded or broken through with marvellous courage and ingenuity; for nearly a year a succession of brilliant commanders took their boats regularly up and down the passage, and made the transport of Turkish troops and munitions across the Marmora first hazardous, and finally impracticable. Their losses were small; but they passed the weeks of their incredibly long patrols in continual danger, and snatched their successes from the midst of a swarm of vigilant enemies. Two battleships, a destroyer, and five gunboats fell to them, besides over thirty steamers, many of which were armed, nine transports, seven ammunition and store ships, and no less than 188 sailing ships and dhows with supplies. The pages which follow contain notes on the cruise of every British boat which attempted the passage of the Straits; but they are far from giving an account of all their amazing feats and adventures.

Lieutenant Norman Holbrook had the honour of being the first officer to take a British submarine up the Dardanelles. He carefully prepared his boat – B.11 – for the business of jumping over and under obstacles, by devices which have since been perfected but were then experimental. The preliminary trials turned out very satisfactorily, and on Sunday, December 18, 1914, as soon as the mainland searchlights were extinguished at dawn, he trimmed and dived for Seddul Bahr.

His main idea was to put certain Rickmers steamers out of action, and perhaps the actual object of his pursuit was the *Lily Rickmers*. He did not get her, but he got something quite as attractive. It was 9.40 a.m., or rather more than four hours from the start, when at last he put his periscope above water, and saw immediately on his starboard beam a large two-funnelled vessel, painted grey and flying the Turkish ensign. At 600 yards he fired his starboard torpedo, put his helm hard a-starboard, and dipped to avoid remonstrances. The explosion was duly audible a few seconds later, and as B. 11 came quietly up of her own motion her commander took a glimpse through the periscope. The grey ship (she was the battleship *Messudiyeh*) was still on his starboard beam, and firing a number of guns. B. 11 seemed bent on dipping again, but Lieutenant Holbrook was still more bent on seeing what he had done. He got her up once more and sighted his enemy, on the port bow this time. She was settling down by the stem and her guns were no longer firing.

At this moment the man at the helm of B. 11 reported that the lenses of the compass had become fogged, and the instrument was for the time unreadable. Lieutenant Holbrook took a careful survey of his surroundings, calculated that he was in Sari Siglar Bay, and dived for the channel. The boat touched bottom and for ten minutes went hop, skip and jump along it, at full speed, until she shot off into deeper water. Her commander then brought her up again, took a sight of the European shore, steadied her by it, and ran for home. By 2 p.m. he had cleared the entrance. His feat was not only brilliant in itself; it was an act of leadership, an invaluable reconnaissance. In ten hours he had proved all the possibilities of the situation – he had forced a strongly guarded channel, surprised and sunk a battleship in broad daylight, and returned safely, though he had gone up without information and come down without a compass. The V. C. was his manifest destiny.

In the following spring, after the guns of the Allied fleets had failed to reduce the Turkish forts, the submarine campaign was developed. It began with a defeat – one of those defeats which turn to honour, and maintain the invincibility of our Service. On April 17, while attempting a difficult reconnaissance of the Kephez minefield, E. 15 ran ashore in the Dardanelles within a few hundred yards of Fort No. 8. Her crew were captured while trying to get her off, and there was a danger of her falling into the enemy's hands in a serviceable condition. The only remedy was to blow her up. She was no sort of a mark for the battleships at long range; so during the night of the 18th an attack was made by two picket boats, manned by volunteer crews. The boat of HMS *Triumph* was commanded by Lieut. Commander Eric Robinson, who led the expedition, with Lieut. Arthur Brooke Webb, R.N.R., and Midshipman John Woolley, and that of HMS *Majestic* by Lieut. Claud Godwin. The fort gave them over two hundred rounds at short range, mortally wounded one man and sank the *Majestic*'s boat; but Lieut. Commander Robinson succeeded in torpedoing E. 15 and rendering her useless. He brought both crews off, and left even the Germans in Constantinople admiring the pluck of his little enterprise. One officer is reported by Mr Lewis Einstein, of the American Embassy there, to have said, 'I take off my hat to the British Navy.' He was right – this midnight attack by a handful of boys in boats has all the heroic romance of the old cutting-out expeditions, and on Admiral de Robeck's report the leader of it was promoted to commander.

On April 25, A.E. 2 went successfully up and entered the Sea of Marmora; on the 29th, Lieut. Commander Edward Courtney Boyle followed in E. 14. He started at 1.40 a.m., and the searchlight at Suan Dere was still working when he arrived there at 4 o'clock. The fort fired, and he dived, passing clean under the minefield. He then passed Chanak on the surface with all the forts firing at him. Further on there were a lot of small ships patrolling, and a torpedo gunboat at which he promptly took a shot. The torpedo got her on the quarter and threw up a column of water as high as her mast. But Lieut. Commander Boyle could not stop to see more – he became aware that the men in a small steamboat were leaning over and trying to catch hold of the top of his periscope. He dipped and left them; then rounded Nagara Point and dived deep. Again and again he came up and was driven down; destroyers and gunboats were chasing and firing in all directions. It was all he could do to charge his batteries at night. After running continuously for over fifty hours, the motors were so hot that he was obliged to stop. The steadiness of all on board may be judged from the record of the diving necessary to avoid destruction. Out of the first sixty-four hours of the voyage, the boat was kept under for forty-four hours and fifty minutes.

On the afternoon of the 29th, he sighted three destroyers convoying two troopships; fired and dipped – for the destroyers were blazing at his periscope, and he had only that one left – the other had stopped a shot the day before. But even down below a thud was audible, and the depth gauges flicked ten feet; half an hour afterwards he saw through the periscope his own particular transport making for the shore with dense columns of yellow smoke pouring from her. And that was her last appearance. A few hours later he sighted A.E. 2 and spoke her. She had sunk one gunboat, but had had bad luck with her other torpedoes and had only one left. Lieut. Commander Boyle arranged to meet her again next day; but next day the gallant A.E. 2 fell to a Turkish gunboat.

During these days the Sea of Marmora was glassy calm, and the patrol ships were so troublesome that Lieut. Commander Boyle decided to sink one as a deterrent. He picked off a small mine-laying boat, and fired at a larger one twice without success, as the wake of the torpedoes was too easily seen in the clear water.

The first four days of May he spent mainly in being hunted. On the 5th, he got a shot at a destroyer convoying a transport, and made a fine right-angle hit at 600 yards, but the torpedo failed to explode. This only whetted his appetite, and for three days he chased ship after ship. One he followed inshore, but troops on board opened fire on him and hit the boat several times. At last, on the evening of May 10, after being driven down by one destroyer, he sighted another with two transports, and attacked at once. His first torpedo missed the leading transport; his second shot hit the second transport and a terrific explosion followed. Debris and men were seen falling into the water; then night came on rapidly, and he could not mark the exact moment at which she sank.

Inside Constantinople they were already telling each other yarns about E. 14, and for her incredible activity they even promoted her to the plural number. 'One of the English submarines in the Marmora,' Mr Einstein wrote on May 11, 'is said to have called at Rodosto, flying the Turkish flag. The Kaimakam, believing the officers to be German, gave them all the petrol and provisions they required, and it was only after leaving that they hoisted their true colours.' The story will not bear examination from our side; but no doubt it very usefully covered a deficiency in the Kaimakam's store account, whether caused by Germans or by the Faithful themselves.

On May 13, Lieut. Commander Boyle records a rifle duel with a small steamer which he had chased ashore near Panidos. On the 14th he remarks the enemy's growing shyness. 'I think the Turkish torpedo-boats must have been frightened of ramming us, as several times, when I tried to remain on the surface at night, they were so close when sighted that it must have been possible to get us if they had so desired.' The air was so clear that in the daytime he was almost always in sight from the shore, and signal fires and smoke columns passed the alarm continually. He had no torpedoes left and was not mounted with a gun, so that he was now at the end of his tether. On the 17th he was recalled by wireless, and after diving all night ran for Gallipoli at full speed, pursued by a two-funnelled gunboat, a torpedo-boat and a tug, who shepherded him one on each side and one astern, 'evidently expecting,' he thought, 'to get me caught in the nets.' But he adds, 'did not notice any nets,' and after passing another two-funnelled gunboat, a large yacht, a battleship and a number of tramps, the fire of the Chanak forts and the minefield as before, he reached the entrance and rose to the surface abeam of a French battleship of the St. Louis class, who gave her fellow crusader a rousing cheer. Commander Boyle reported that the success of this fine and sustained effort was mainly due to his officers, Lieutenant Edward Stanley and Acting-Lieutenant Lawrence, R.N.R., both of whom received the D.S.C. His own promotion to Commander was underlined by the award of the V. C.

Within twelve hours of E. 14's return, her successor, E. 11, was proceeding towards the Straits. The commanding officer of this boat was Lieut. Commander M. E. Nasmith, who had already been mentioned in despatches for rescuing five airmen while being attacked by a Zeppelin in the Heligoland Bight during the action on Christmas Day, 1914. He had been waiting his turn at the Dardanelles with some impatience, and as E. 11's port engine had been put completely out of action by an accident on the voyage from Malta, he had begged to be allowed to attempt the passage into the Marmora under one engine. This was refused, but his repairs were finished in time for him to take the place of E. 14.

He made the passage of the Straits successfully, reconnoitred the Marmora and made a neat arrangement, probably suggested by the adventures of E. 14, for saving the enemy the trouble of so much hunting. He stopped a small coastal sailing vessel, sent Lieut. D'Oyly Hughes to search her for contraband, and then trimmed well down and made her fast alongside his conning-tower. Being now quite invisible from the eastward, he was able to proceed in that direction all day without interruption. At night he released his stalking-horse and returned westward.

Early on the 23rd, he observed a Turkish torpedo-boat at anchor off Constantinople and sank her with a torpedo; but as she sank she fired a 6-pounder gun, the first shot of which damaged his foremost periscope. He came up for repairs, and all hands took the chance of a bathe. Five hours later he stopped a small steamer, whose crew did a 'panic abandon ship,' capsizing all boats but one. 'An American gentleman then appeared on the upper deck, who informed us that his name was Silas Q. Swing of the *Chicago Sun* and that he was pleased to make our acquaintance... He wasn't sure if there were any stores on board. Lieut. D'Oyly Hughes looked into the matter and discovered a 6-inch gun lashed across the top of the fore hatch, and other gun-mountings in the hold, which was also crammed with 6-inch and other ammunition marked Krupp. A demolition charge sent ship and cargo to the bottom.

Lieut. Commander Nasmith then chased and torpedoed a heavily laden store-ship, and drove another ashore, exchanging rifle fire with a party of horsemen on the cliff above. Altogether the day was a lively one, and the news, brought by Mr Silas Q. Swing and his friends, shook Constantinople up severely. Mr Einstein records that 'the submarine came up at 20 minutes to 2 o'clock, about three hundred yards from where the American guardship *Scorpion* lay moored, and was immediately fired at by the shore batteries. It shot off two torpedoes; the first missed a transport by about fifty yards, the second struck the *Stamboul* fair, passing under a barge moored alongside, which blew up. The *Stamboul* had a gap of twenty feet on her water-line but did not sink. She was promptly towed toward Beshiktash to lie on the bottom in shallow water. The submarine meanwhile, under a perfect hail of fire, which passed uncomfortably close to the *Scorpion*, dived and got away, steering up the Bosphorus. At Galata there was a panic, everyone closing their shops; the troops, who were already on two transports, were promptly disembarked, but later re-embarked, and still later landed once more. The total damage was inconsiderable, but the moral effect was very real.' On the following day he adds, 'S.' (Swing, no doubt – Silas Q. Swing of the *Chicago Sun*) 'came in with an exciting tale. On his way to the Dardanelles the steamer, which carried munitions and a 6-inch gun, had been torpedoed by an English submarine, the E. 11. They allowed the crew to leave, and then sank the ship. The English officer told him there were eleven submarines in the Marmora, and these are holding up all the ships going to the Dardanelles. They had sunk three transports full of troops, out of four which had been sunk, and various other vessels, but do not touch those carrying wounded.'

So, between Lieut. D'Oyly Hughes and Mr Silas Q. Swing, the E. 11 became eleven submarines, and may go down the ages like the eleven thousand virgins of Cologne. Her commander evidently hoped to create a panic, and Mr Einstein leaves us no doubt that the plan succeeded to the full. On May 27 he writes again: 'The Marmora is practically closed by English submarines. Everyone asks where their depot is, and how they are refurnished.' May 28: 'The submarines in the Marmora have frightened the Turks, and all the remaining transports, save one, lie tranquilly in the Golden Horn. Otherwise I have never seen the port so empty. One wonders where the submarines have their base, and when and how it was prepared.' He adds, with some shrewdness: 'Probably, if at all, in some island of the Marmora, though the newer boats can stay out a long time.' E. 11 was far from new, as we have seen, but she was in hands that could make her stand for quality, as well as quantity.

Lieut. Commander Nasmith brought his boat safely back to Mudros on June 7. The last hour of his trip was perhaps the most breathless, for while rushing down by Kilid Bahr he found his trim quite abnormal, and 'observed a large mine preceding the periscope at a distance of about twenty feet; which was apparently hung up by its moorings to the port hydroplane.' He could not come to the surface, as the shore batteries were waiting for him; but when outside Kum Kale, he emptied his after-tanks, got his nose down, and went full speed astern, dropping the mine neatly to the bottom. This was good work, but not better than the skill shown in navigating shoal water, or 'the resource displayed in the delicate operation of recovering two torpedoes' without the usual derrick to hoist them in – an operation which may as well remain for the present undescribed. Admiral de Robeck, in recommending Lieut. Commander Nasmith for the V. C., speaks of his cruise as one 'which will surely find a place in the annals of the British Navy.' It will – there can be no forgetting it. The very log of E. 11 deserves to be a classic. 'Having dived unobserved into Constantinople ...' says her Commander soberly, and so, without a thought of it, adds one to the historic despatches of the Service.

It was now E. 11's turn again. Commander Courtney Boyle took her up on June 10, against a very strong tide. At 9 o'clock next morning he stopped a brigantine, whose crew abandoned ship 'and then all stood up and cursed us. It was too rough to go alongside her, so Acting-Lieut. R. W. Lawrence, R.N.R., swam off to her, climbed aboard, and... set fire to her with the aid of her own matches and paraffin oil.' On the 12th one of the Rickmers steamers was torpedoed. Shortly afterwards there was a big explosion close to the submarine. 'And I think,' says her commander, 'I must have caught the moorings of a mine with my tail as I was turning, and exploded it... The whole boat was very badly shaken.' But *Lily Rickmers* and her sister were now both removed from the Turkish service, for E. 11 had evidently accounted for one of them already. Mr Einstein writes on June 18: 'The German Embassy approached us to cable Washington to protest about the torpedoing without warning of the two Rickmers steamers in the Marmora. One of these was said to be filled with wounded, but their note neglected to say that these had been discharged from hospital and were on their way back to the Dardanelles.' Only a German diplomatist could speak of a ship carrying troops to the Front as 'filled with wounded'; and Mr Einstein adds, 'One cannot but be struck by the German inability to understand our position over the *Lusitania*.' The point is plain, and goes deep. To the modern German mind all such considerations are only a matter of words, useful for argumentative purposes – that there should be any truth of reality or feeling behind them is not imaginable.

The rest of this log is a record of destruction, but destruction on thoroughly un-German methods. 'June 20. – Boarded and sank

8 sailing dhows ... towed the crew inshore and gave them some biscuit, beef, rum, and water, as they were rather wet.' 'June 22. – Let go passenger ship.' 28. – 'Burnt two-master, and started to tow crew in their boat, but had to dive. Stopped two dhows: they were both empty and the crews looked so miserable that I only sunk one and let the other go.' 24. – 'Blew up 2 large dhows: there was another one about a mile off with no boat... and thought I saw two heads in the water. Turned round and found that there were 2 men in the water at least half a mile from their dhow. Picked them up: they were quite exhausted: gave them food and drinks and put them on board their ship. They had evidently seen the other two dhows blown up and were frightened out of their wits.' There is nothing here to boast about – to us, nothing surprising. But it brings to mind inevitably the evidence upon which our enemies stand convicted. We remember the long roll of men and women not only set adrift in stormy seas, but shot and drowned in their open boats without pity and without cause. We admit the courage of the Hun, but we cannot admire it. It is too near to animal ferocity, and stained with a cruelty and callousness which are not even beast-like.

On June 21, Commander Boyle had rendezvoused with E. 12, Lieut. Commander K. M. Bruce. 'I got her alongside, and we remained tied up for 8 hours.' From this time onward the reliefs were arranged to overlap, so that there were nearly always two boats operating at the same time in the Marmora. Lieut. Commander Bruce came up on June 19, and found, like others, that the chief difficulty of forcing the passage was the heating of the main motors on so long and strenuous a run.

The one great day of his nine days' patrol was June 25, when he brought off a hand-to-hand fight on the surface with three enemy ships. At 10.45 in the morning he sighted, in the Gulf of Mudania, a small two-decked passenger steamer. 'She looked,' he says, 'rather like a tram-car, and was towing two sailing-vessels. In the distance was a sister of hers, towing three more.' He chased, and soon stopped the nearer steamer. He could see, as he steamed round her, that she was carrying a lot of stores. She had no boat, and all the crew appeared to be on deck in lifebelts. He could see no sign of guns, so he ran his bow up alongside and sent his first lieutenant, Tristram Fox, to board her. But guns are not the only risk a submarine has to take on such occasions. As the boarding party stepped on board the steamer, a Turk heaved a bomb over the side. It hit E. 12 forward, but did not explode, and no second one followed. The Turks, however, meant fighting, and they opened fire with rifles and a small gun, concealed somewhere aft. The situation was a very anxious one, especially for Lieutenant Fox and his boarding party; for they knew their own ship must open fire in return, and it was difficult to take cover on an enemy ship in action. Lieut. Commander Bruce was in a very tight corner, but he kept his head and played his game without a mistake. He did not hesitate to open fire with his 6-pounder, but he began upon the enemy's stern, where the gun was concealed, and having dealt with that he turned to her other end and put ten shots into her from fore to aft. His men shot steadily, though under gun and rifle fire at a range of only ten yards, and his coxswain, Charles Case, who was with him in the conning-tower, passed up the ammunition. Spare men, with rifles, kept the Turks' heads down, and all seemed to be going well, when the two sailing-ships in tow began a new and very plucky move of their own. They came in to foul the sub-marine's propellers, and at the same time opened fire with rifles, taking E. 12 in flank. But by this time the steamer was beaten, and the British rifles soon silenced those in the sailing-ships. Then, as soon as Lieut. Commander Bruce had cleared the steamer, he sank the three of them. The steamer had probably been carrying ammunition as well as stores, for one of the shots from the 6-pounder touched off something explosive in her forward part. In fifteen minutes she was at the bottom.

Lieut. Commander Bruce was already thinking of the other steamer with the three sailing-ships in tow. She was diligently making for the shore, and he had to open fire at her at 2,000 yards. As he closed, the fire was returned, not only from the ship but from a gun on shore; but by this time he had hit the enemy aft, and set her on fire forward. She beached herself, and as the three sailing-ships had been slipped and were also close under the shore, he had no choice but to leave them. E. 12's injuries were miraculously slight – her commander's account of them is slighter still. 'I was very much hampered,' he says, 'in my movements and took some minutes to get clear of the first steamer. But only one man was hurt, by a splinter from the steamer.' This was quite in accordance with the old English rule of the gun-decks: to hit and be missed there's nothing like closing. The story of this fine little scrimmage ends with the special recommendation by Lieut. Commander Bruce of his first lieutenant, Tristram Fox, 'who behaved exceedingly well under very trying circumstances,' and of his coxswain, Charles Case, and three seamen – they all received the Distinguished Service Medal. Of the commander himself we shall hear again presently.

E. 12 was recalled on June 28, leaving E. 14 still at work; and on the 30th her place was taken by E. 7, Lieut. Commander Cochrane. On the way up, a torpedo from a tube on shore passed over him, and a destroyer made two attempts to ram him, but he got safely through and rendezvoused with E. 14 on the following evening. His misfortunes began next day, when Lieut. Hallifax and an A. B. were badly burned by an explosion in the hold of a captured steamer. Then dysentery attacked the two remaining officers and the telegraphist. Work became very arduous, but work was done notwithstanding. Ship after ship was sunk – five steamers and sixteen sailing-ships in all. One of the steamers was 'a Mahsousie ship, the *Biga*,' of about 8,000 tons. She was lying alongside Mudania Pier, with sailing-vessels moored outside the pier to protect her. But Lieut. Commander Cochrane saw daylight between this barrage and his prey; he dived under the sailing-ships, and up went the *Biga* with a very heavy explosion.

On July 17, he tried a new method of harassing the Turkish army. He came up opposite Kara Burnu and opened fire on the railway cutting west of it, blocking the line – then dived, and went on to Derinjie Burnu. The shipyard there was closed, but he observed a heavy troop train steaming west, towards the block he had so carefully established just before. He followed up at full speed, and after twenty minutes of anxious hope saw the train returning baffled. It eventually stopped in a belt of trees at Yarandji Station; this made spotting difficult, but E. 7's gunnery was good enough. After twenty rounds the three ammunition cars of the train were definitely blown up, and E. 7 could move back to Kara Burnu, where she shelled another train and hit it several times.

All this was very disturbing to the Turks, and they tried every means to stop it at the source. They had already a net in the channel, but it was quite ineffectual. 'Now,' says Mr Einstein on July 15, 'it turns out that they have constructed a barrage of network to keep out the submarines from the Dardanelles, and this explains the removal of the buoys all along the Bosphorus. They need these, and especially their chains, to keep it in place.' A week later, Lieut. Commander Cochrane saw these buoys on his way down. They were in a long line, painted alternately red and black, and stretching from a position a mile north of Maitos village to a steamer moored in Nagara Liman. He dived under them and went on his way; but later on, below Kilid Bahr, the boat fouled a moorings forward and was completely hung up, swinging round, head to tide. By admirable management she was got clear in half an hour, and then the same thing happened again. 'This time,' says her commander coolly, 'I think the boat carried the obstruction with her for some distance. I was expecting to see something foul when we came to the surface, but everything was clear then.' What he and his men saw, during those two half-hours, might also be described as ' something foul.'

The cruise of E. 7 lasted for over three weeks, from June 30 to July 24. On July 21, Commander Courtney Boyle brought up E. 14 once more. He, too, saw the new net near Nagara, 'a line of what looked like lighters half-way across, and one small steamship in the vicinity.' But he passed through the gate in it without touching anything. This was lucky, as he had already scraped against an obstruction off Kilid Bahr and cut his guard wire nearly through. Once up, he got to work at once, and in a busy and adventurous three weeks he sank one steamer, one supply ship, seven dhows and thirteen sailing-vessels. In short, he made himself master of the Marmora.

The complete interruption of the Turkish sea communications was proved by the statements of prisoners. The captain of one ship stated that Constantinople was full of wounded and short of food, and that the troops now all went to Rodosto by rail and then marched to Gallipoli – six hours in the train and three days and nights marching, instead of a short and simple voyage. All the Turkish war-ships were above the second bridge in the Golden Horn, and they never ventured out. There were no steamers going to sea – all supplies to Gallipoli went in sailing craft, towed by destroyers under cover of darkness. It is clear that, to the Turkish imagination, E. 14 was like E. 11 – very much in the plural number. On August 5, E. 11 herself came on duty again, and the two boats met at rendezvous at 2 p.m. next day. Half an hour afterwards, Commanders Boyle and Nasmith started on their first hunt in couples. Their quarry was a gunboat of the Berk-i Satvet class. The chase was a lively one, and it was E. 11, in the end, who made the kill with a torpedo amidships. Then the two boats came alongside again and their commanders concerted a plan for shelling troops next day.

They took up their positions in the early morning hours, and waited for the game to come past. Commander Nasmith had been given the better stand of the two; at 11.30 a.m. he observed troops going towards Gallipoli, rose to the surface and fired. Several of his shots dropped well among them and they scattered. In less than an hour another column approached along the same road. E. 11 had retired, so to speak, into her butt; she now stepped up again, raised her gun, and made good shooting as before. 'The column took cover in open order.'

In the meantime Commander Boyle had been diving up and down all the morning between Fort Victoria and a point four miles up the coast to the east, about a mile from shore. Three times he came to the surface, but each time the troops turned out to be bullocks. At 1.00 p.m. (when he came up for the fourth time) more dust was coming down the road, and this time it was the right kind of dust. As he opened fire he heard E. 11 banging away. She had left the place where he had stationed her, to the N. E. of Dohan Asian Bank, and had come down to join him in his billet. The two boats then conducted a joint action for the best part of an hour. Commander Boyle got off forty rounds, of which about six burst on the road among the troops, and one in a large building. But the distance was almost beyond his 6-pounder's reach. He had to put the full range on the sights, and then aim at the top of the hill, so that his fire was less accurate than that of Commander Nasmith with his 12-pounder. E. 11 had strewed the road with a large number of dead and wounded, when guns on shore came into action and forced her to dive. She came up again an hour and a half later and dispersed the troops afresh, but once more had to dive for her life.

Next day, Commander Boyle ordered E. 11 to change billets with him, and both boats had luck. Commander Boyle destroying a 5,000-ton supply steamer with torpedo and gunfire, and Commander Nasmith bagging a battle-ship. This last was the *Haireddin Barbarossa*. She was passing about five miles N. E. of Gallipoli, escorted by a destroyer. E. 11 was skilfully brought into position on her starboard beam, and the torpedo got home amidships. The *Barbarossa* immediately took a list to starboard, altered course towards the shore, and opened a heavy fire on the submarine's periscope. But she was mortally hit. Within twenty minutes a large flash burst from her fore part, and she rolled over and sank. To lose their last battleship, and so near home, was a severe blow for the Turks, and they made every effort to conceal the depressing details. Mr. Einstein, however, heard them and makes an interesting entry: 'The *Barbarossa* was sunk in the Marmora and not in the Dardanelles, as officially announced. She was convoying barges full of munitions and also two transports, when she found herself surrounded by six submarines.' It is creditable to Commander Nasmith that he did so well with only six of his E. 11 flotilla. Einstein continues: ' The transports were supposed to protect her, but the second torpedo proved effective and she sank in seven minutes. One of the transports and a gunboat were also sunk, the other ran aground. Of crews of 700, only one-third were saved.' And on August 16 he records further successes by Commander Nasmith – a large collier, the *Ispahan*, sunk while unloading in the port of Haidar Pasha, the submarine creeping up under the lee of another boat; and two transports with supplies, the *Chios* and the *Samsoun*, sunk in the Marmora.

Commander Boyle returned to his base on August 12, with no further difficulty than a brush against a mine and a rough-and-tumble encounter with an electric wire obstruction, portions of which be carried away tangled round his periscope and propellers. His boat had now done over 12,000 miles since leaving England and had never been out of running order – a magnificent performance, reported by her commander to be primarily due to the excellence of his chief engine-room artificer, James Hollier Hague, who was accordingly promoted to warrant rank, as from the date of the recommendation.

E. 14 was succeeded on August 13 by E. 2, Commander David Stocks, who met Commander Nasmith at 2 p.m. next day, and handed over a fresh supply of ammunition for E. 11. He also, no doubt, told him the story of his voyage up. Off Nagara his boat had fouled an obstruction, and through the conning-tower scuttles he could see that an 3 ½-inch wire was wound with a half turn round his gun, a smaller wire round the conning-tower itself, and another round the wireless standard aft. It took him ten minutes' plunging and backing to clear this and regain control; and during those ten minutes, small explosions were heard continuously. These were apparently from bombs thrown by guard boats; but a series of loud explosions, a little later, were probably from shells fired by a destroyer which was following up, and was still overhead an hour afterwards.

The two boats parted again, taking separate beats, and spent a week in sinking steamers, boarding hospital ships, and bombarding railway stations. When they met again on the evening of August 21, Commander Nasmith had a new kind of yarn to tell. His lieutenant, D'Oyly Hughes, had volunteered to make an attack on the Ismid Railway, and a whole day had been spent behind Kalolimno Island in constructing a raft capable of carrying one man and a demolition charge of gun-cotton. Then the raft had been tested by a bathing party, and the details of the plan most carefully laid out.

The object was to destroy the viaduct if possible; but, in any case, to blow up part of the line. The risk involved not only the devoted adventurer himself, but the boat as well, for she could not, so long as he had still a chance of returning, quit the neighbourhood or even conceal herself by submerging. The approach was in itself an operation of the greatest delicacy. Commander Nasmith took his boat slowly towards the shore until her nose just grounded, only three yards from the rocks. The cliffs on each side were high enough to prevent the conning-tower being seen while in this position. At 2.10 a.m. Lieut. D'Oyly-Hughes dropped into the water and swam off, pushing the raft with his bale of gun-cotton, and his clothes and accoutrements, towards a spot some sixty yards on the port bow of the boat. His weapons were an automatic service revolver and a sharpened bayonet. He also had an electric torch and a whistle. At the point where he landed he found the cliffs unscalable. So he relaunched his raft and swam along to a better place. He reached the top after a stiff climb, approached the railway line by a careful prowl of half an hour, and went along it for five or six hundred yards, hugging his heavy and cumbersome charge. Voices then brought him up short. He peered about and saw three men sitting by the side of the line. After watching them for some time he decided that they were not likely to move, and that he must make a wide detour in order to inspect the viaduct. He laid down his gun-cotton, and crept inland, making good progress except for falling into a small farmyard, where the fowls, but luckily not the household, awoke and protested. At last he got within three hundred yards of the viaduct. It was easy to see, for there was a fire burning at the near end of it; but there was also a stationary engine working, and a number of workmen moving about. Evidently it would be impossible to bring up and lay his charge there.

He crept back therefore to his gun-cotton and looked about for a convenient spot to blow up the line. The best place seemed to be a low brick-work support over a small hollow. It was only 150 yards from the three men sitting by the line; but there was no other spot where so much damage could be done, and Lieut. D'Oyly Hughes was a volunteer, prepared to take risks. He muffled the pistol for firing the fuse as tightly as possible, with a piece of rag, and pulled

off. On so still a night it made a very loud noise. The three Turks
heard it and he saw them instantly stand up. The next moment they
were running down the line, with Lieutenant D'Oyly Hughes going
his best in front of them. But a chase of this kind was not what he
wanted. His present object was to find a quiet spot on the shore
where he could take to the water undisturbed, and he had no time to
lose. He turned on his pursuers and fired a couple of shots; the Turks
were not hit, but they remembered their own weapons and began
firing too, which was just the relief Lieut. Hughes needed.

He had already decided against trying to climb down by the way
he had come up; but after a considerable run eastward, he struck
the shore more conveniently about three-quarters of a mile from the
small bay in which E. 11 was lying. As he plunged into the water, he
had the joy of hearing the sound of a heavy explosion. His charge had
hung fire for a long time, but when it went it went well; fragments
were hurled between a quarter and half a mile, and fell into the sea
near the boat. There could be no doubt that the line was effectively
cut; and he could now give his whole attention to saving an officer
to the Service.

This was the most desperate part of the affair. After swimming
some four hundred or five hundred yards out to sea, he blew a long
blast on his whistle; but the boat was behind the cliffs in her little bay
and failed to hear him. Day was breaking rapidly; the time of waiting
for him must, he knew, be limited. With a decision and coolness
beyond comment he swam ashore again and rested for a short time
on the rocks – then swam off once more, directly towards the boat.
Before he reached the bay, he had to discard in turn his pistol, his
bayonet, and his electric torch. At last he rounded the point and his
whistle was heard; but, at the same moment, shouts came from the
cliffs overhead, and rifle fire opened on the boat.

She immediately backed, and came slowly astern out of the
bay, intent only upon picking up Lieut. D'Oyly Hughes. But now
came the most extraordinary part of the whole adventure. In the
early morning mist the bow, the gun, and the conning-tower of
the submarine appeared to her distressed officer to be three small

rowing-boats advancing towards him, and rowing-boats could only mean enemies. He turned, swam ashore, and tried to hide himself under the cliffs. But he did not lose his head, and after climbing a few feet he looked back and realised his mistake. He shouted and plunged in again. Forty yards from the rocks he was at last picked up, nearly done, for he had run hard for his life and swum a mile in his clothes. But he had done his work and E. 11 was proud of him, as appears from the concluding sentence in her log: '5.50 a.m. Dived out of rifle fire, and proceeded out of the Gulf of Ismid.'

Commander Nasmith ended his cruise with a brilliant week's work. On August 22 he fought an action with three armed tugs, a dhow, and a destroyer; succeeded most adroitly in evading the destroyer, sinking the dhow and one of the tugs by gunfire, and capturing a number of prisoners, among whom was a German bank manager with a quantity of money for Chanak Bank. The prisoners willingly helped to discharge the cargo of another captured ship – they were apparently much surprised at being granted their lives. On the 25th, two large transports were sunk with torpedoes; on the 28th, E. 11 and E. 2, in company, bombarded the magazine and railway station at Mudania. On September 1, Commander Nasmith had an hour's deliberate shooting at the railway viaduct, scoring a large number of hits; and on the 3rd he returned without misadventure to his base.

Left to herself, E. 2 now found that she also possessed a heroic lieutenant. Under the date September 7 there stands the brief record: 'Lieutenant Lyon swam to and destroyed two dhows.' The story, so well begun, ends next day. At 2.15 a.m. this adventurer, like the other, swam off with a raft and bag of gun-cotton. His object, like the other's, was to destroy a railway bridge. His friends watched him until, at seventy yards' distance, he faded into the dusk. From that moment onwards no sound was ever heard from him. The night was absolutely still, and noises on shore were distinctly audible; but nothing like a signal ever came. It had been agreed that if any trouble arose he should fire his Webley pistol, and the submarine should then show a red light and open fire on the station, which was 800 yards distant. For five hours she remained there waiting. An explosion was heard, but nothing followed, and broad daylight found Commander Stocks still waiting with desperate loyalty. At 7.16 he dived out to sea. An hour later he came to the surface and cruised about the place, hoping that Lyon had managed somehow to get into a boat or dhow. There were several near the village, and he might be lying off in one. But no boat drifted out, then or afterwards. Commander Stocks came again at dawn next day – perhaps, as he said, to bombard the railway station, perhaps for another reason. Six days later he dived for home, breaking right through the Nagara net, by a new and daring method of his own.

It was now Lieut. Commander Bruce's turn again, and he passed all records by patrolling the Marmora successfully in E. 12 for forty days. He had two other boats in company during part of this time – E. 20 and H. 1 – and with the latter's help he carried out a very pretty 'spread attack' on a gunboat off Kalolimno, on October 17. The intended manoeuvre was for E. 12 to rise suddenly and drive the enemy by gunfire over H. 1, who dived at the first gun. The first drive failed, the second was beautifully managed; but, in the bad light of an approaching squall, H. 1's torpedo missed. In a third attempt the bird was reported hit by several shells, but she escaped in the darkness. Lieut. Commander Bruce also did good shooting at a powder factory near Constantinople; sank some shipping, and made some remarkable experiments with a new method of signalling. But his greatest experience was his return journey.

He had passed through the net, he thought, but suddenly observed that he was towing a portion of it with him. The boat began to sink quickly, bows down; the foremost hydroplane jammed. He immediately forced her nose up, by blowing ballast tanks and driving her at full speed. But, even in that position, she continued to sink till she reached 245 feet. At that depth the pressure was tremendous. The conning-tower scuttles burst in, and the conning-tower filled with water. The boat leaked badly, and the fore compartment had to be closed off to prevent the water getting into the battery, where it would have produced the fatal fumes of chlorine gas.

For ten mortal minutes the commander wrestled with his boat. At last, by putting three men on to the hydroplane with hand-gear, he forced the planes to work and the boat rose. He just managed to check her at twelve feet and got her down to fifty, but even at that depth six patrol vessels could be heard firing at her – probably she was still towing something which made a wake on the surface.

Blind, and almost unmanageable, E. 12 continued to plunge up and down, making very little way beyond Nagara. The conning-tower and its compass were out of action, but the commander conned his boat from the main gyro compass, and when both diving gauges failed he used the gauge by the periscope. The climax was reached when at eighty feet, just to the south of Kilid Bahr, another obstruction was met and carried away. But this was a stroke of luck, for when the commander, by real inspiration, put on full speed ahead and worked his helm, the new entanglement slid along the side of the boat and carried away with it the old one from Nagara. The boat rose steeply by the bow and broke surface. Shore batteries and patrols opened fire, and a small shell cracked the conning-tower; others hit the bridge, and two torpedoes narrowly missed her astern. But she came safely through to Helles, and reached her base after a cruise of over 2,000 miles.

H. 1 also put nearly 2,000 miles to her credit, though her cruise lasted only thirty days, as against E. 12's forty. Lieutenant Wilfred Pirie, her commander, took a hand in Lieut. Commander Bruce's signalling experiments and co-operated in several of his military enterprises, as we have already seen. He also worked with E. 20 and was the last to meet her. This was on October 31, the day before he dived for home. After that, nothing more was heard of her till December 5, when Commander Nasmith, who was once more in the Marmora with E. 11, captured a Shirket steamer and obtained much information from the captain, a French-speaking Turk. According to his statement, E. 20 had been ambushed, and her officers and crew taken prisoners. He also gave details of the German submarines based at Constantinople – he thought there were ten of them, including

three large ones. Before accepting this, we shall do well to refer again
to Mr Einstein, who reports four small boats coming from Pola, of
which only three arrived; and one larger one, U. 51, of which he
tells an amusing story. U. 51 had been at Constantinople, but during
August she went out and did not return; it was rumoured that she
had gone home, or been sunk. Then the Turks were electrified by
news of the arrival of a new German super-submarine, over two
hundred feet long. All Constantinople crowded to see her go out on
August 30. 'Departure from Golden Horn of a new giant German
submarine, the U. 54, over 200 feet long and with complete wireless
apparatus.' Next day: ' The U. 54 turns out to be our old friend U. 51,
with another number painted.' On September 2, Mr Einstein adds
sarcastically: 'Report that U. 54 was badly damaged by a Turkish
battery at Silivri ... To mask this, they are spreading the rumour that
an English submarine ran aground, and will doubtless bring in the
German boat under a false number as though she were a captured
prey.' And two days later he was justified – 'U. 64 lies damaged in the
Golden Horn from the fire of a Turkish battery. The reported sinking
of an English boat is a downright lie.'

Commander Nasmith went down the Straits on December 28,
after a record cruise of forty-eight days. In that time he sank no less
than forty-six enemy ships, including a destroyer, the *Var Hissar*,
and ten steamers. A fortnight before he left E. 2, Commander Stocks
came up, and did good work in very bad weather, until she was
recalled on January 2, 1916. The season was over, and she found, in
passing down the Straits, that the Turkish net had apparently been
removed, either by the enemy themselves, or perhaps by the wear
and tear of British submarines repeatedly charging it and carrying it
away piecemeal.

So ended our Eastern submarine campaign – a campaign in which
our boats successfully achieved their military objects – in which, too,
the skill of our officers and men was only surpassed by their courage,
and by their chivalrous regard for the enemies whom they defeated.

Winning the Blue Max
From *An Aviator's Handbook*, Oswald Boelcke

January 15, 1916

Now, events come so fast I cannot keep up with them by writing.

On the 11th we had a little gathering that kept me up later than usual, so I did not feel like getting up in the morning. But, as the weather was good, I strolled out to the field and went up about nine o'clock. I flew over to Lille to lie in wait for any hostile aircraft. At first, I had no luck at all. Finally I saw bombs bursting near Ypres. I flew so far I could see the ocean, but am sorry to say I could not find any enemy 'plane. On my way back, I saw two Englishmen, west of Lille, and attacked the nearer one. He did not appreciate the attention, but turned and ran. Just above the trenches I came within gunshot of him. We greeted each other with our machine guns, and he elected to land. I let him go to get at the second of the pair, and spoil his visit, also. Thanks to my good machine, I gradually caught up with him, as he flew toward the east, north of Lille. When I was still four or five hundred meters away from him, he seemed to have seen all he wanted, for he turned to fly west. Then I went for him. I kept behind him till I was near enough. The Englishman seemed to be an old hand at this game, for he let me come on without firing a shot. He didn't shoot until after I started. I flew squarely behind him, and had all the time in the world to aim, because he did not vary a hair from his straight course. He twice reloaded his gun. Suddenly, after only a short while, he fell. I was sure I had hit the pilot. At 800 metres, his machine righted itself, but then dove on, head-foremost, till it landed in a garden in M_, northeast of S_ The country is very rough there, so I went back to our landing-place and reported by telephone. To my surprise, I heard that at the time Immelmann had shot down an Englishman near P_ I had to laugh.

The greatest surprise came in the evening. We were just at dinner when I was called to the 'phone. At the other end was the Commander-in-Chief's Adjutant, who congratulated me for receiving the order *Pour le mérite*. I thought he was joking. But he told me that Immelmann and I had both received this honour at the telegraphic order of the Kaiser. My surprise and joy were great. I went in and said nothing, but sent Captain K. to the 'phone, and he received the news and broke it to all. First, everyone was surprised, then highly pleased. On the same evening I received several messages of congratulation, and the next day, January 13th, had nothing to do all day but receive other such messages.

Everybody seemed elated. One old chap would not let me go, and I didn't escape till I promised to visit him. From all comers I received messages: by telephone and telegraph. The King of Bavaria, who happened to be in Lille with the Bavarian Crown Prince, invited me to dinner for the 14th of January.

Now comes the best of all. On the 14th, that is, yesterday, it was ideal weather for flying. So I went up at nine o'clock to look around. As it was getting cloudy near Lille, I changed my course to take me south of Arras. I was up hardly an hour, when I saw the smoke of bursting bombs near P_. I flew in that direction, but the Englishman who was dropping the bombs saw me and started for home. I soon overtook him.

When he saw I intended to attack him, he suddenly turned and attacked me. Now, there started the hardest fight I have as yet been in. The Englishman continually tried to attack me from behind, and I tried to do the same to him. We circled 'round and 'round each other. I had taken my experience of December 28th to heart (that was the time I had used up all my ammunition), so I only fired when I could get my sights on him. In this way, we circled around, I often not firing a shot for several minutes. This merry-go-round was immaterial to me, since we were over our lines. But I watched him, for I felt that sooner or later he would make a dash for home. I noticed that while circling around he continually tried to edge over toward his own lines, which were not far away. I waited my chance, and was able to get at him in real style, shooting his engine to pieces. This I noticed when he glided toward his own lines, leaving a tail of smoke behind him. I had to stop him in his attempt to reach safety, so, in spite of his wrecked motor, I had to attack him again. About 200 meters inside our positions I overtook him, and fired both my guns at him at close range (I no longer needed to save my cartridges). At the moment when I caught up to him, we passed over our trenches and I turned back. I could not determine what had become of him, for I had to save myself now. I flew back, and as I had little fuel left, I landed near the village of F_. Here I was received by the Division Staff and was told what had become of the Englishman. To my joy, I learned that, immediately after I had left him, he had come to earth near the English positions. The trenches are only a hundred meters apart at this place. One of the passengers, the pilot, it seems, jumped out and ran to the English trenches. He seems to have escaped, in spite of the fact that our infantry fired at him. Our field artillery quickly opened fire on his machine, and among the first shots one struck it and set it afire. The other aviator, probably the pilot, who was either dead or severely wounded, was burned up with the machine. Nothing but the skeleton of the airplane remains. As my helpers did not come till late, I rode to D_ in the Division automobile, because I had to be with the King of Bavaria at 5.30. From D_ I went directly on to Lille. King and the Crown Prince both conversed with me for quite a while, and they were especially pleased at my most recent success. Once home, I began to see the black side of being a hero. Everyone congratulates you. All ask you questions. I shall soon be forced to carry a printed interrogation sheet with me with answers all filled out. I was particularly pleased by my ninth success, because it followed so close on the *Pour le mérite*.

The Doorway
From *Under Fire*, Henri Barbusse

Soon, passing along this trench whose grassy slopes quiver like the flanks of a fine horse, we come out into our own trench on the Bethune road, and here is our place. Our comrades are there, in clusters. They are eating, and enjoying the goodly temperature.

The meal finished, we clean our aluminium mess-tins or plates with a morsel of bread.

'Tiens, the sun's going!' It is true; a cloud has passed over and hidden it. 'It's going to splash, my little lads,' says Lamuse. 'That's our luck all over! Just as we are going off!'

'A damned country!' says Fouillade. In truth this northern climate is not worth much. It drizzles and mizzles, reeks and rains. And when there is any sun it soon disappears in the middle of this great damp sky.

Our four days in the trenches are finished, and the relief will commence at nightfall. Leisurely we get ready for leaving. We fill and put aside the knapsacks and bags. We give a rub to the rifles and wrap them up.

It is already four o'clock. Darkness is falling quickly, and we grow indistinct to each other. 'Damnation. Here's the rain!' A few drops and then the downpour. *Oh, la, la, la*! We don our capes and tent-cloths. We go back into the dug-out, dabbling, and gathering mud on our knees, hands, and elbows, for the bottom of the trench is getting sticky. Once inside, we have hardly time to light a candle, stuck on a bit of stone, and to shiver all round –

'Come on, *en route*!'

We hoist ourselves into the wet and windy darkness outside. I can dimly see Poterloo's powerful shoulders; in the ranks we are always side by side. When we get going I call to him,

'Are you there, old chap?'

'Yes, in front of you,' he cries to me, turning round. As he turns he gets a buffet in the face from wind and rain, but he laughs.

His happy face of the morning abides with him. No downpour shall rob him of the content that he carries in his strong and steadfast heart; no evil night put out the sunshine that I saw possess his thoughts some hours ago.

We march, and jostle each other, and stumble. The rain is continuous, and water runs in the bottom of the trench. The floor-gratings yield as the soil becomes soaked; some of them slope to right or left and we skid on them. In the dark, too, one cannot see them, so we miss them at the turnings and put our feet into holes full of water.

Even in the greyness of the night I will not lose sight of the slaty shine of Poterloo's helmet, which streams like a roof under the torrent, nor of the broad back that is adorned with a square of glistening oilskin. I lock my step in his, and from time to time I question him and he answers me – always in good humour, always serene and strong.

When there are no more of the wooden floor-gratings, we tramp in the thick mud. It is dark now. There is a sudden halt and I am thrown on Poterloo. Up higher we hear half-angry reproaches –

'What the devil, will you get on? We shall get broken up!'

'I can't get my trotters unstuck!' replies a pitiful voice.

The engulfed one gets clear at last, and we have to run to overtake the rest of the company. We begin to pant and complain, and bluster against those who are leading. Our feet go down haphazardly; we stumble and hold ourselves up by the walls, so that our hands are plastered with mud. The march becomes a stampede, full of the noise of metal things and of oaths.

In redoubled rain there is a second halt; someone has fallen, and the hubbub is general. He picks himself up and we are off again. I exert myself to follow Poterloo's helmet closely that gleams feebly in the night before my eyes, and I shout from time to time,

'All right?'

'Yes, yes, all right,' he replies, puffing and blowing, and his voice always singsong and resonant.

Our knapsacks, tossed in this rolling race under the assault of the elements, drag and hurt our shoulders.

The trench is blocked by a recent landslide, and we plunge into it. We have to tear our feet out of the soft and clinging earth, lifting them high at each step. Then, when this crossing is laboriously accomplished, we topple down again into the slippery stream, in the bottom of which are two narrow ruts, boot-worn, which hold one's foot like a vice, and there are pools into which it goes with a great splash. In one place we must stoop very low to pass under a heavy and glutinous bridge that crosses the trench, and we only get through with difficulty. It obliges us to kneel in the mud, to flatten ourselves on the ground, and to crawl on all fours for a few paces. A little farther there are evolutions to perform as we grasp a post that the sinking of the ground has set at a slope right across our way.

We come to a trench-crossing.

'*Allons*, forward! Look out for yourselves, boys!' says the adjutant, who has flattened himself in a corner to let us pass and to speak to us. 'This is a bad spot.'

'We're done,' shouts a voice so hoarse that I cannot identify the speaker.

'Damn! I've enough of it, I'm stopping here,' groans another, at the end of his wind and his muscle.

'What do you want me to do?' replies the adjutant, 'No fault of mine, eh? *Allons*, get a move on, it's a bad spot – it was shelled at the last relief!'

We go on through the tempest of wind and water. We seem to be going ever down and down, as in a pit. We slip and tumble, butt into the wall of the trench, into which we drive our elbows hard, so as to throw ourselves upright again. Our going is a sort of long slide, on which we keep upright how and where we can. What matters is to stumble only forward, and as straight as possible.

Where are we? I lift my head, in spite of the billows of rain, out of this gulf where we are struggling. Against the hardly discernible background of the buried sky, I can make out the rim of the trench; and there, rising before my eyes all at once and towering over that rim, is something like a sinister doorway, made of two black posts that lean one upon the other, with something hanging from the middle like a torn-off scalp. It is the exit.

'Forward! Forward!'

I lower my head and see no more; but again I hear the feet that sink in the mud and come out again, the rattle of the bayonets, the heavy exclamations, and the rapid breathing.

Once more there is a violent back-eddy. We pull up sharply, and again I am thrown upon Poterloo and lean on his back, his strong and solid back, like the trunk of a tree, like healthfulness and like hope. He cries to me, 'Cheer up, old man, we're there!'

We are standing still. It is necessary to go back a little – *Nom de Dieu!* – No, we are moving on again!

Suddenly a fearful explosion falls on us. I tremble to my skull; a metallic reverberation fills my head; a scorching and suffocating smell of sulphur pierces my nostrils. The earth has opened in front of me. I feel myself lifted and hurled aside – doubled up, choked, and half blinded by this lightning and thunder. But still my recollection is clear; and in that moment when I look wildly and desperately for my comrade-in-arms, I see his body goes up, erect and black, both his arms outstretched to their limit, and a flame in the place of his head!

The Battle of Jutland: The Night Hunt
From *Sea Warfare*, Rudyard Kipling

RAMMING AN ENEMY CRUISER

When the German fleet ran for home, on the night of May 31, it seems to have scattered – 'starred,' I believe, is the word for the evolution – in a general *sauve qui peut*, while the Devil, livelily represented by our destroyers, took the hindmost. Our flotillas were strung out far and wide on this job. One man compared it to hounds hunting half a hundred separate foxes.

I take the adventures of several couples of destroyers who, on the night of May 31, were nosing along somewhere towards the Schleswig-Holstein coast, ready to chop any Hun-stuff coming back to earth by that particular road. The leader of one line was *Gehenna*, and the next two ships astern of her were *Eblis* and *Shaitan*, in the order given. There were others, of course, but with the exception of one *Goblin* they don't come violently into this tale. There had been a good deal of promiscuous firing that evening, and actions were going on all round. Towards midnight our destroyers were overtaken by several three-and four-funnel German ships (cruisers they thought) hurrying home. At this stage of the game anybody might have been anybody – pursuer or pursued. The Germans took no chances, but switched on their searchlights and opened fire on *Gehenna*. Her acting sub-lieutenant reports:

> A salvo hit us forward. I opened fire with the after-guns. A shell then struck us in a steam-pipe, and I could see nothing but steam. But both starboard torpedo-tubes were fired.

Eblis, *Gehenna*'s next astern, at once fired a torpedo at the second ship in the German line, a four-funnelled cruiser, and hit her between the second funnel and the mainmast, when 'she appeared to catch fire fore and aft simultaneously, heeled right over to starboard, and undoubtedly sank.' *Eblis* loosed off a second torpedo and turned aside to reload, firing at the same time to distract the enemy's attention from *Gehenna*, who was now ablaze fore and after. *Gehenna*'s acting sub-lieutenant (the only executive officer who survived) says that by the time the steam from the broken pipe cleared he found *Gehenna* stopped, nearly everybody amidships killed or wounded, the cartridge-boxes round the guns exploding one after the other as the fires took hold, and the enemy not to be seen. Three minutes or less did all that damage, *Eblis* had nearly finished reloading when a shot struck the davit that was swinging her last torpedo into the tube and wounded all hands concerned. Thereupon she dropped torpedo work, fired at an enemy searchlight which winked and went out, and was closing in to help *Gehenna* when she found herself under the noses of a couple of enemy cruisers.

'The nearer one,' he says, 'altered course to ram me apparently.' The Senior Service writes in curiously lawyer-like fashion, but there is no denying that they act quite directly. 'I therefore put my helm hard aport and the two ships met and rammed each other, port bow to port bow.' There could have been no time to think and, for *Eblis*'s commander on the bridge, none to gather information. But he had observant subordinates, and he writes – and I would humbly suggest that the words be made the ship's motto for evermore – he writes, 'those aft noted' that the enemy cruiser had certain marks on her funnel and certain arrangements of derricks on each side which, quite apart from the evidence she left behind her, betrayed her class.

Eblis and she met. Says *Eblis*: 'I consider I must have considerably damaged this cruiser, as 20 feet of her side plating was left in my foc'sle.' Twenty feet of ragged rivet-slinging steel, razoring and reaping about in the dark on a foc'sle that had collapsed like a concertina! It was very fair plating too. There were side-scuttle holes in it – what we passengers would call portholes. But it might have been better, for *Eblis* reports sorrowfully, 'by the thickness of the coats of paint (duly given in 32nds of the inch) she would not appear to have been a very new ship.'

A FUGITIVE ON FIRE
New or old, the enemy had done her best. She had completely demolished *Eblis*'s bridge and searchlight platform, brought down the mast and the fore-funnel, ruined the whaler and the dinghy, split the foc'sle open above water from the stem to the galley which is abaft the bridge, and below water had opened it up from the stem to the second bulkhead. She had further ripped off *Eblis*'s skin-plating for an amazing number of yards on one side of her, and had fired a couple of large-caliber shells into Eblis at point-blank range, narrowly missing her vitals.

Even so, *Eblis* is as impartial as a prize-court. She reports that the second shot, a trifle of eight inches, 'may have been fired at a different time or just after colliding.' But the night was yet young, and 'just after getting clear of this cruiser an enemy battle-cruiser grazed past our stern at high speed' and again the judgmatic mind – 'I think she must have intended to ram us.' She was a large three-funnelled thing, her centre funnel shot away and 'lights were flickering under her foc'sle as if she was on fire forward.' Fancy the vision of her, hurtling out of the dark, red-lighted from within, and fleeing on like a man with his throat cut!

[As an interlude, all enemy cruisers that night were not keen on ramming. They wanted to get home. A man I know who was on another part of the drive saw a covey bolt through our destroyers; and had just settled himself for a shot at one of them when the night threw up a second bird coming down full speed on his other beam.

He had bare time to jink between the two as they whizzed past. One switched on her searchlight and fired a whole salvo at him point blank. The heavy stuff went between his funnels. She must have sighted along her own beam of light, which was about a thousand yards.

'How did you feel?' I asked.

'I was rather sick. It was my best chance all that night, and I had to miss it or be cut in two.'

'What happened to the cruisers?'

'Oh, they went on, and I heard 'em being attended to by some of our fellows. They didn't know what they were doing, or they couldn't have missed me sitting, the way they did.]

THE CONFIDENTIAL BOOKS

After all that *Eblis* picked herself up, and discovered that she was still alive, with a dog's chance of getting to port. But she did not bank on it. That grand slam had wrecked the bridge, pinning the commander under the wreckage. By the time he had extricated himself he 'considered it advisable to throw overboard the steel chest and dispatch-box of confidential and secret books.' These are never allowed to fall into strange hands, and their proper disposal is the last step but one in the ritual of the burial service of His Majesty's ships at sea. *Gehenna*, afire and sinking, out somewhere in the dark, was going through it on her own account. This is her acting Sub-Lieutenant's report: 'The confidential books were got up. The First Lieutenant gave the order: 'Every man aft,' and the confidential books were thrown overboard. The ship soon afterwards heeled over to starboard and the bows went under. The First Lieutenant gave the order: "Everybody for themselves." The ship sank in about a minute, the stern going straight up into the air.'

But it was not written in the Book of Fate that stripped and battered *Eblis* should die that night as *Gehenna* died. After the burial of the books it was found that the several fires on her were manageable, that she 'was not making water aft of the damage,' which meant two thirds of her were, more or less, in commission, and, best of all, that three boilers were usable in spite of the cruiser's shells. So she 'shaped course and speed to make the least water and the most progress towards land.' On the way back the wind shifted eight points without warning – it was this shift, if you remember, that so embarrassed *Cripple* and *Paralytic* on their homeward crawl – and, what with one thing and another, *Eblis* was unable to make port till the scandalously late hour of noon on June 2, 'the mutual ramming having occurred about 11.40 p.m. on May 31.' She says, this time without any legal reservation whatever, 'I cannot speak too highly of the courage, discipline, and devotion of the officers and ship's company.'

Her recommendations are a Compendium of Godly Deeds for the Use of Mariners. They cover pretty much all that man may be expected to do. There was, as there always is, a first lieutenant who, while his commander was being extricated from the bridge wreckage, took charge of affairs and steered the ship first from the engine-room, or what remained of it, and later from aft, and otherwise maneuvered as requisite, among doubtful bulkheads. In his leisure he 'improvised means of signalling,' and if there be not one joyous story behind that smooth sentence I am a Hun!

THE ART OF IMPROVISING

They all improvised like the masters of craft they were. The chief engine-room artificer, after he had helped to put out fires, improvised stops to the gaps which were left by the carrying away of the forward funnel and mast. He got and kept up steam 'to a much higher point than would have appeared at all possible,' and when the sea rose, as it always does if you are in trouble, he 'improvised pumping and drainage arrangements, thus allowing the ship to steam at a good speed on the whole.' There could not have been more than 40 feet of hole.

The surgeon – a probationer – performed an amputation single-handed in the wreckage by the bridge, and by his 'wonderful skill, resource, and unceasing care and devotion undoubtedly saved the lives of the many seriously wounded men.' That no horror might be lacking, there was 'a short circuit among the bridge wreckage for a considerable time.' The searchlight and wireless were tangled up together, and the electricity leaked into everything.

There were also three wise men who saved the ship whose names must not be forgotten. They were Chief Engine-room Artificer Lee, Stoker Petty Officer Gardiner, and Stoker Elvins. When the funnel carried away it was touch and go whether the foremost boiler would not explode. These three 'put on respirators and kept the fans going till all fumes, etc., were cleared away.' To each man, you will observe, his own particular Hell which he entered of his own particular initiative.

Lastly, there were the two remaining Quartermasters – mutinous dogs, both of 'em – one wounded in the right hand and the other in the left, who took the wheel between them all the way home, thus improvising one complete Navy-pattern Quartermaster, and 'refused to be relieved during the whole thirty-six hours before the ship returned to port.' So *Eblis* passes out of the picture with 'never a moan or complaint from a single wounded man, and in spite of the rough weather of June 1st they all remained cheery.' They had one Hun cruiser, torpedoed, to their credit, and strong evidence abroad that they had knocked the end out of another.

But *Gehenna* went down, and those of her crew who remained hung on to the rafts that destroyers carry till they were picked up about the dawn by *Shaitan*, third in the line, who, at that hour, was in no shape to give much help. Here is *Shaitan*'s tale. She saw the unknown cruisers overtake the flotilla, saw their leader switch on searchlights and open fire as she drew abreast of *Gehenna*, and at once fired a torpedo at the third German ship. Shaitan could not see *Eblis*, her next ahead, for, as we know, *Eblis* after firing her torpedoes had hauled off to reload. When the enemy switched his searchlights off *Shaitan* hauled out too. It is not wholesome for destroyers to keep on the same course within a thousand yards of big enemy cruisers.

She picked up a destroyer of another division, *Goblin*, who for the moment had not been caught by the enemy's searchlights and had profited by this decent obscurity to fire a torpedo at the hindmost of the cruisers. Almost as *Shaitan* took station behind *Goblin* the latter was lighted up by a large ship and heavily fired at. The enemy fled, but she left *Goblin* out of control, with a grisly list of casualties, and her helm jammed. *Goblin* swerved, returned, and swerved again; *Shaitan* astern tried to clear her, and the two fell aboard each other, *Goblin*'s bows deep in *Shaitan*'s fore-bridge. While they hung thus, locked, an unknown destroyer rammed *Shaitan* aft, cutting off several feet of her stern and leaving her rudder jammed hard over. As complete a mess as the Personal Devil himself could have devised, and all due to the merest accident of a few panicky salvoes. Presently the two ships worked clear in a smother of steam and oil, and went their several ways. Quite a while after she had parted from *Shaitan*, *Goblin* discovered several of *Shaitan*'s people, some of them wounded, on her own foc'sle, where they had been pitched by the collision. *Goblin*, working her way homeward on such boilers as remained, carried on a one-gun fight at a few cables' distance with some enemy destroyers, who, not knowing what state she was in, sheered off after a few rounds. *Shaitan*, holed forward and opened up aft, came across the survivors from *Gehenna* clinging to their raft, and took them aboard. Then some of our destroyers – they were thick on the sea that night – tried to tow her stern-first, for *Goblin* had cut her up badly forward. But, since *Shaitan* lacked any stern, and her rudder was jammed hard across where the stern should have been, the hawsers parted, and, after leave asked of lawful authority, across all that waste of waters, they sank *Shaitan* by gun-fire, having first taken all the proper steps about the confidential books. Yet *Shaitan* had had her little crumb of comfort ere the end. While she lay crippled she saw quite close to her a German cruiser that was trailing homeward in the dawn gradually heel over and sink.

This completes my version of the various accounts of the four destroyers directly concerned for a few hours, on one minute section of one wing of our battle. Other ships witnessed other aspects of the agony and duly noted them as they went about their business. One of our battleships, for instance, made out by the glare of burning *Gehenna* that the supposed cruiser that *Eblis* torpedoed was a

German battleship of a certain class. So *Gehenna* did not die in vain, and we may take it that the discovery did not unduly depress *Eblis*'s wounded in hospital.

ASKING FOR TROUBLE

The rest of the flotilla that the four destroyers belonged to had their own adventures later. One of them, chasing or being chased, saw *Goblin* out of control just before *Goblin* and *Shaitan* locked, and narrowly escaped adding herself to that triple collision. Another loosed a couple of torpedoes at the enemy ships who were attacking *Gehenna*, which, perhaps, accounts for the anxiety of the enemy to break away from that hornets' nest as soon as possible. Half a dozen or so of them ran into four German battleships, which they set about torpedoing at ranges varying from half a mile to a mile and a half. It was asking for trouble and they got it; but they got in return at least one big ship, and the same observant battleship of ours who identified *Eblis*'s bird reported three satisfactory explosions in half an hour, followed by a glare that lit up all the sky. One of the flotilla, closing on what she thought was the smoke of a sister in difficulties, found herself well in among the four battleships. 'It was too late to get away,' she says, so she attacked, fired her torpedo, was caught up in the glare of a couple of searchlights, and pounded to pieces in five minutes, not even her rafts being left. She went down with her colours flying, having fought to the last available gun.

Another destroyer who had borne a hand in *Gehenna*'s trouble had her try at the four battleships and got in a torpedo at 800 yards. She saw it explode and the ship take a heavy list. 'Then I was chased,' which is not surprising. She picked up a friend who could only do 20 knots. They sighted several Hun destroyers who fled from them; then dropped on to four Hun destroyers all together, who made great parade of commencing action, but soon afterwards 'thought better of it, and turned away.' So you see, in that flotilla alone there was every variety of fight, from the ordered attacks of squadrons under control, to single ship affairs, every turn of which depended on the second's decision of the men concerned; endurance to the hopeless end; bluff and cunning; reckless advance and red-hot flight; clear vision and as much of blank bewilderment as the Senior Service permits its children to indulge in. That is not much. When a destroyer who has been dodging enemy torpedoes and gun-fire in the dark realises about midnight that she is 'following a strange British flotilla, having lost sight of my own,' she 'decides to remain with them,' and shares their fortunes and whatever language is going.

If lost hounds could speak when they cast up next day, after an unchecked night among the wild life of the dark, they would talk much as our destroyers do.

Zion
Rudyard Kipling

The doorkeepers of Zion,
They do not always stand
In helmet and whole armour,
With halberds in their hand;
But, being sure of Zion,
And all her mysteries,
They rest awhile in Zion,
Sit down and smile in Zion;
Ay, even jest in Zion,
In Zion, at their ease.

The gatekeepers of Baal,
They dare not sit or lean,
But fume and fret and posture
And foam and curse between;
For being bound to Baal,
Whose sacrifice is vain,
Their rest is scant with Baal,
They glare and pant for Baal,
They mouth and rant for Baal,

For Baal in their pain.
But we will go to Zion,
By choice and not through dread,
With these our present comrades
And those our present dead;
And, being free of Zion
In both her fellowships,
Sit down and sup in Zion –
Stand up and drink in Zion
Whatever cup in Zion
Is offered to our lips!

Lord Kitchener
Robert Bridges

Unflinching hero, watchful to foresee
And face thy country's peril wheresoe'er,
Directing war and peace with equal care,
Till by long duty ennobled thou wert he
Whom England call'd and bade 'Set my arm free
To obey my will and save my honour fair,'–
What day the foe presumed on her despair
And she herself had trust in none but thee:

Among Herculean deeds the miracle
That mass'd the labour of ten years in one
Shall be thy monument. Thy work was done
Ere we could thank thee; and the high sea swell
Surgeth unheeding where thy proud ship fell
By the lone Orkneys, at the set of sun.

8 June 1916

A Glimpse of the Italian Army
From *A Visit to Three Fronts*, Arthur Conan Doyle

One meets with such extreme kindness and consideration among the Italians that there is a real danger lest one's personal feeling of obligation should warp one's judgment or hamper one's expression. Making every possible allowance for this, I come away from them, after a very wide if superficial view of all that they are doing, with a deep feeling of admiration and a conviction that no army in the world could have made a braver attempt to advance under conditions of extraordinary difficulty.

First a word as to the Italian soldier. He is a type by himself which differs from the earnest solidarity of the new French army, and from the business-like alertness of the Briton, and yet has a very special dash and fire of its own, covered over by a very pleasing and unassuming manner. London has not yet forgotten Durando of Marathon fame. He was just such another easy smiling youth as I now see everywhere around me. Yet there came a day when a hundred thousand Londoners hung upon his every movement – when strong men gasped and women wept at his invincible but unavailing spirit. When he had fallen senseless in that historic race on the very threshold of his goal, so high was the determination within him, that while he floundered on the track like a broken-backed horse, with the senses gone out of him, his legs still continued to drum upon the cinder path. Then when by pure will-power he staggered to his feet and drove his dazed body across the line, it was an exhibition of pluck which put the little sunburned baker straightway among London's heroes. Durando's spirit is alive today, I see thousands of him all around me. A thousand such, led by a few young gentlemen of the type who occasionally give us object lessons in how to ride at Olympia, make no mean battalion. It has been a war of most desperate ventures, but never once has there been a lack of volunteers. The Tyrolese are good men – too good to be fighting in so rotten a cause. But from first to last the Alpini have had the ascendency in the hill fighting, as the line regiments have against the

Kaiserlics upon the plain. Caesar told how the big Germans used to laugh at his little men until they had been at handgrips with them. The Austrians could tell the same tale. The spirit in the ranks is something marvellous. There have been occasions when every officer has fallen and yet the men have pushed on, have taken a position and then waited for official directions.

But if that is so, you will ask, why is it that they have not made more impression upon the enemy's position? The answer lies in the strategical position of Italy, and it can be discussed without any technicalities. A child could understand it. The Alps form such a bar across the north that there are only two points where serious operations are possible. One is the Trentino Salient where Austria can always threaten and invade Italy. She lies in the mountains with the plains beneath her. She can always invade the plain, but the Italians cannot seriously invade the mountains, since the passes would only lead to other mountains beyond. Therefore their only possible policy is to hold the Austrians back. This they have most successfully done, and though the Austrians with the aid of a shattering heavy artillery have recently made some advance, it is perfectly certain that they can never really carry out any serious invasion. The Italians then have done all that could be done in this quarter. There remains the other front, the opening by the sea. Here the Italians had a chance to advance over a front of plain bounded by a river with hills beyond. They cleared the plain, they crossed the river, they fought a battle very like our own battle of the Aisne upon the slopes of the hills, taking 20,000 Austrian prisoners, and now they are faced by barbed wire, machine guns, cemented trenches, and every other device which has held them as it has held everyone else. But remember what they have done for the common cause and be grateful for it. They have in a year occupied some forty Austrian divisions, and relieved our Russian allies to that very appreciable extent. They have killed or wounded a quarter of a million, taken 40,000, and drawn to themselves a large portion of the artillery.

That is their record up to date. As to the future it is very easy to prophesy. They will continue to absorb large enemy armies. Neither side can advance far as matters stand. But if the Russians advance and Austria has to draw her men to the East, there will be a tiger spring for Trieste. If manhood can break the line, then I believe the Durandos will do it.

'*Trieste o morte!*' I saw chalked upon the walls all over North Italy. That is the Italian objective.

And they are excellently led. Cadorna is an old Roman, a man cast in the big simple mould of antiquity, frugal in his tastes, clear in his aims, with no thought outside his duty. Everyone loves and trusts him. Porro, the Chief of the Staff, who was good enough to explain the strategical position to me, struck me as a man of great clearness of vision, middle-sized, straight as a dart, with an eagle face grained and coloured like an old walnut. The whole of the staff work is, as experts assure me, most excellently done.

So much for the general situation. Let me descend for a moment to my own trivial adventures since leaving the British front. Of France I hope to say more in the future, and so I will pass at a bound to Padua, where it appeared that the Austrian front had politely advanced to meet me, for I was wakened betimes in the morning by the dropping of bombs, the rattle of anti-aircraft guns, and the distant rat-tat-tat of a Maxim high up in the air. I heard when I came down later that the intruder had been driven away and that little damage had been done. The work of the Austrian aeroplanes is, however, very aggressive behind the Italian lines, for they have the great advantage that a row of fine cities lies at their mercy, while the Italians can do nothing without injuring their own kith and kin across the border. This dropping of explosives on the chance of hitting one soldier among fifty victims seems to me the most monstrous development of the whole war, and the one which should be most sternly repressed in future international legislation – if such a thing as international law still exists. The Italian headquarter town, which I will call Nemini, was a particular victim of these murderous attacks. I speak with some feeling, as not only was the ceiling of my bedroom shattered some days before my arrival, but a greasy patch with some black shreds upon it was still visible above my window which represented part of the remains of an unfortunate workman, who had been blown to pieces immediately in front of the house. The air defence is very skilfully managed however, and the Italians have the matter well in hand.

My first experience of the Italian line was at the portion which I have called the gap by the sea, otherwise the Isonzo front. From a mound behind the trenches an extraordinary fine view can be got of the Austrian position, the general curve of both lines being marked, as in Flanders, by the sausage balloons which float behind them. The Isonzo, which has been so bravely carried by the Italians, lay in front of me, a clear blue river, as broad as the Thames at Hampton Court. In a hollow to my left were the roofs of Gorizia, the town which the Italians are endeavouring to take. A long desolate ridge, the Carso, extends to the south of the town, and stretches down nearly to the sea. The crest is held by the Austrians and the Italian trenches have been pushed within fifty yards of them. A lively bombardment was going on from either side, but so far as the infantry goes there is none of that constant malignant petty warfare with which we are familiar in Flanders. I was anxious to see the Italian trenches, in order to compare them with our British methods, but save for the support and communication trenches I was courteously but firmly warned off.

The story of trench attack and defence is no doubt very similar in all quarters, but I am convinced that close touch should be kept between the Allies on the matter of new inventions. The quick Latin brain may conceive and test an idea long before we do. At present there seems to be very imperfect sympathy. As an example, when I was on the British lines they were dealing with a method of clearing barbed wire. The experiments were new and were causing great interest. But on the Italian front I found that the same system had been tested for many months. In the use of bullet proof jackets for engineers and other men who have to do exposed work the Italians are also ahead of us. One of their engineers at our headquarters might give some valuable advice. At present the Italians have, as I understand, no military representative with our armies, while they receive a British General with a small staff. This seems very wrong not only from the point of view of courtesy and justice, but also because Italy has no direct means of knowing the truth about our great development. When Germans state that our new armies are made of paper, our Allies should have some official assurance of their own that this is false. I can understand our keeping neutrals from our headquarters, but surely our Allies should be on another footing.

Having got this general view of the position I was anxious in the afternoon to visit Monfalcone, which is the small dockyard captured from the Austrians on the Adriatic. My kind Italian officer guides did not recommend the trip, as it was part of their great hospitality to shield their guest from any part of that danger which they were always ready to incur themselves. The only road to Monfalcone ran close to the Austrian position at the village of Ronchi, and afterwards kept parallel to it for some miles. I was told that it was only on odd days that the Austrian guns were active in this particular section, so determined to trust to luck that this might not be one of them. It proved, however, to be one of the worst on record, and we were not destined to see the dockyard to which we started.

The civilian cuts a ridiculous figure when he enlarges upon small adventures which may come his way – adventures which the soldier endures in silence as part of his everyday life. On this occasion, however, the episode was all our own, and had a sporting flavour in it which made it dramatic. I know now the feeling of tense expectation with which the driven grouse whirrs onwards towards the butt. I have been behind the butt before now, and it is only poetic justice that I should see the matter from the other point of view. As we approached Ronchi we could see shrapnel breaking over the road in front of us, but we had not yet realised that it was precisely for vehicles that the Austrians were waiting, and that they had the range marked out to a yard. We went down the road all out at a steady fifty miles an hour. The village was near, and it seemed that we had got past the place of danger. We had in fact just reached it. At this moment there was a noise as if the whole four tyres had gone simultaneously, a most terrific bang in our very ears, merging into a second sound like a reverberating blow upon an enormous gong. As I glanced up I saw three clouds immediately above my head, two of them white and the other of a rusty red. The air was full of flying metal, and the road, as we were told afterwards by an observer, was all churned up by it. The metal base of one of the shells was found plumb in the middle of the road just where our motor had been. There is no use telling me Austrian gunners can't shoot. I know better.

It was our pace that saved us. The motor was an open one, and the three shells burst, according to one of my Italian companions who was himself an artillery officer, about ten metres above our heads. They threw forward, however, and we travelling at so great a pace shot from under. Before they could get in another we had swung round the curve and under the lee of a house. The good Colonel B. wrung my hand in silence. They were both distressed, these good soldiers, under the impression that they had led me into danger. As a matter of fact it was I who owed them an apology, since they had enough risks in the way of business without taking others in order to gratify the whim of a joyrider. Barbariche and Clericetti, this record will convey to you my remorse.

Our difficulties were by no means over. We found an ambulance lorry and a little group of infantry huddled under the same shelter with the expression of people who had been caught in the rain. The road beyond was under heavy fire as well as that by which we had come. Had the Ostro-Boches dropped a high-explosive upon us they would have had a good mixed bag. But apparently they were only out for fancy shooting and disdained a sitter. Presently there came a lull and the lorry moved on, but we soon heard a burst of firing which showed that they were after it. My companions had decided that it was out of the question for us to finish our excursion. We waited for some time therefore and were able finally to make our retreat on foot, being joined later by the car. So ended my visit to Monfalcone, the place I did not reach. I hear that two 10,000-ton steamers were left on the stocks there by the Austrians, but were disabled before they retired. Their cabin basins and other fittings are now adorning the Italian dugouts.

My second day was devoted to a view of the Italian mountain warfare in the Carnic Alps. Besides the two great fronts, one of defence (Trentino) and one of offence (Isonzo), there are very many smaller valleys which have to be guarded. The total frontier line is over four hundred miles, and it has all to be held against raids if not invasions. It is a most picturesque business. Far up in the Roccolana Valley I found the Alpini outposts, backed by artillery which had been brought into the most wonderful positions. They have taken 8-inch guns where a tourist could hardly take his knapsack. Neither side can ever make serious progress, but there are continual duels, gun against gun, or Alpini against Jaeger. In a little wayside house was the brigade headquarters, and here I was entertained to lunch. It was a scene that I shall remember. They drank to England. I raised my glass to *Italia irredenta* – might it soon be *redenta*. They all sprang to their feet and the circle of dark faces flashed into flame. They keep their souls and emotions, these people. I trust that ours may not become atrophied by self-suppression.

The Italians are a quick high-spirited race, and it is very necessary that we should consider their feelings, and that we should show our sympathy with what they have done, instead of making querulous and unreasonable demands of them. In some ways they are in a difficult position. The war is made by their splendid king – a man of whom every one speaks with extraordinary reverence and love – and by the people. The people, with the deep instinct of a very old civilisation, understand that the liberty of the world and their own national existence are really at stake. But there are several forces which divide the strength of the nation. There is the clerical, which represents the old Guelph or German spirit, looking upon Austria as the eldest daughter of the Church – a daughter who is little credit to her mother. Then there is the old nobility. Finally, there are the commercial people who through the great banks or other similar agencies have got into the influence and employ of the Germans. When you consider all this you will appreciate how necessary it is that Britain should in every possible way, moral and material, sustain the national party. Should by any evil chance the others gain the upper hand there might be a very sudden and sinister change in the international situation. Every man who does, says, or writes a thing which may in any way alienate the Italians is really, whether he knows it or not, working for the King of Prussia. They are a grand people, striving most efficiently for the common cause, with all the dreadful disabilities which an absence of coal and iron entails. It is for us to show that we appreciate it. Justice as well as policy demands it.

The last day spent upon the Italian front was in the Trentino. From Verona a motor drive of about twenty-five miles takes one up the valley of the Adige, and past a place of evil augury for the Austrians, the field of Rivoli. As one passes up the valley one appreciates that on their left wing the Italians have position after position in the spurs of the mountains before they could be driven into the plain. If the Austrians could reach the plain it would be to their own ruin, for the Italians have large reserves. There is no need for any anxiety about the Trentino.

The attitude of the people behind the firing line should give one confidence. I had heard that the Italians were a nervous people. It does not apply to this part of Italy. As I approached the danger spot I saw rows of large, fat gentlemen with long thin black cigars leaning against walls in the sunshine. The general atmosphere would have steadied an epileptic. Italy is perfectly sure of herself in this quarter. Finally, after a long drive of winding gradients, always beside the Adige, we reached Ala, where we interviewed the Commander of the Sector, a man who has done splendid work during the recent fighting. 'By all means you can see my front. But no motorcar, please. It draws fire and others may be hit beside you.' We proceeded on foot therefore along a valley which branched at the end into two passes. In both very active fighting had been going on, and as we came up the guns were baying merrily, waking up most extraordinary echoes in the hills. It was difficult to believe that it was not thunder. There was one terrible voice that broke out from time to time in the mountains – the angry voice of the Holy Roman Empire. When it came all other sounds died down into nothing. It was – so I was told – the master gun, the vast 42-centimetre giant which brought down the pride of

Liège and Namur. The Austrians have brought one or more from Innsbruck. The Italians assure me, however, as we have ourselves discovered, that in trench work beyond a certain point the size of the gun makes little matter.

We passed a burst dugout by the roadside where a tragedy had occurred recently, for eight medical officers were killed in it by a single shell. There was no particular danger in the valley however, and the aimed fire was all going across us to the fighting lines in the two passes above us. That to the right, the Valley of Buello, has seen some of the worst of the fighting. These two passes form the Italian left wing which has held firm all through. So has the right wing. It is only the centre which has been pushed in by the concentrated fire.

When we arrived at the spot where the two valleys forked we were halted, and we were not permitted to advance to the advance trenches which lay upon the crests above us. There was about a thousand yards between the adversaries. I have seen types of some of the Bosnian and Croatian prisoners, men of poor physique and intelligence, but the Italians speak with chivalrous praise of the bravery of the Hungarians and of the Austrian Jaeger. Some of their proceedings disgust them however, and especially the fact that they use Russian prisoners to dig trenches under fire. There is no doubt of this, as some of the men were recaptured and were sent on to join their comrades in France. On the whole, however, it may be said that in the Austro-Italian war there is nothing which corresponds with the extreme bitterness of our western conflict. The presence or absence of the Hun makes all the difference.

Nothing could be more cool or methodical than the Italian arrangements on the Trentino front. There are no troops who would not have been forced back by the Austrian fire. It corresponded with the French experience at Verdun, or ours at the second battle of Ypres. It may well occur again if the Austrians get their guns forward. But at such a rate it would take them a long time to make any real impression. One cannot look at the officers and men without seeing that their spirit and confidence are high. In answer to my inquiry they assure me that there is little difference between the troops of the

northern provinces and those of the south. Even among the snows of
the Alps they tell me that the Sicilians gave an excellent account of
themselves.

That night found me back at Verona, and next morning I was
on my way to Paris, where I hope to be privileged to have some
experiences at the front of our splendid Allies. I leave Italy with
a deep feeling of gratitude for the kindness shown to me, and of
admiration for the way in which they are playing their part in the
world's fight for freedom. They have every possible disadvantage,
economic and political. But in spite of it they have done splendidly.
Three thousand square kilometers of the enemy's country are already
in their possession. They relieve to a very great extent the pressure
upon the Russians, who, in spite of all their bravery, might have been
overwhelmed last summer during the *durchbruch* had it not been for
the diversion of so many Austrian troops. The time has come now
when Russia by her advance on the Pripet is repaying her debt. But
the debt is common to all the Allies. Let them bear it in mind. There
has been mischief done by slighting criticism and by inconsiderate
words. A warm sympathetic hand-grasp of congratulation is what
Italy has deserved, and it is both justice and policy to give it.

Birds on the Western Front
Saki (H. H. Munro)

Considering the enormous economic dislocation which the war
operations have caused in the regions where the campaign is raging,
there seems to be very little corresponding disturbance in the bird
life of the same districts. Rats and mice have mobilised and swarmed
into the fighting line, and there has been a partial mobilisation of
owls, particularly barn owls, following in the wake of the mice, and
making laudable efforts to thin out their numbers. What success
attends their hunting one cannot estimate; there are always sufficient
mice left over to populate one's dug-out and make a parade-ground
and race-course of one's face at night. In the matter of nesting

accommodation the barn owls are well provided for; most of the still intact barns in the war zone are requisitioned for billeting purposes, but there is a wealth of ruined houses, whole streets and clusters of them, such as can hardly have been available at any previous moment of the world's history since Nineveh and Babylon became humanly desolate. Without human occupation and cultivation there can have been no corn, no refuse, and consequently very few mice, and the owls of Nineveh cannot have enjoyed very good hunting; here in Northern France the owls have desolation and mice at their disposal in unlimited quantities, and as these birds breed in winter as well as in summer, there should be a goodly output of war owlets to cope with the swarming generation of war mice.

Apart from the owls one cannot notice that the campaign is making any marked difference in the bird life of the countryside. The vast flocks of crows and ravens that one expected to find in the neighbourhood of the fighting line are non-existent, which is perhaps rather a pity. The obvious explanation is that the roar and crash and fumes of high explosives have driven the crow tribe in panic from the fighting area; like many obvious explanations, it is not a correct one. The crows of the locality are not attracted to the battlefield, but they certainly are not scared away from it. The rook is normally so gun-shy and nervous where noise is concerned that the sharp banging of a barn door or the report of a toy pistol will sometimes set an entire rookery in commotion; out here I have seen him sedately busy among the refuse heaps of a battered village, with shells bursting at no great distance, and the impatient-sounding, snapping rattle of machine-guns going on all round him; for all the notice that he took he might have been in some peaceful English meadow on a sleepy Sunday afternoon. Whatever else German frightfulness may have done it has not frightened the rook of North-eastern France; it has made his nerves steadier than they have ever been before, and future generations of small boys, employed in scaring rooks away from the sown crops in this region, will have to invent something in the way of super-frightfulness to achieve their purpose. Crows and magpies are nesting well within the shell-swept area, and over a small beech-copse I once saw a pair of crows engaged in hot combat with a pair of sparrow-hawks, while considerably higher in the sky, but almost directly above them, two Allied battle-planes were engaging an equal number of enemy aircraft.

Unlike the barn owls, the magpies have had their choice of building sites considerably restricted by the ravages of war: the whole avenues of poplars, where they were accustomed to construct their nests, have been blown to bits, leaving nothing but dreary-looking rows of shattered and splintered trunks to show where once they stood. Affection for a particular tree has in one case induced a pair of magpies to build their bulky, domed nest in the battered remnants of a poplar of which so little remained standing that the nest looked almost bigger than the tree; the effect rather suggested an archiepiscopal enthronement taking place in the ruined remains of Melrose Abbey. The magpie, wary and suspicious in his wild state, must be rather intrigued at the change that has come over the erstwhile fearsome not-to-be-avoided human, stalking everywhere over the earth as its possessor, who now creeps about in screened and sheltered ways, as chary of showing himself in the open as the shyest of wild creatures.

The buzzard, that earnest seeker after mice, does not seem to be taking any war risks, at least I have never seen one out here, but kestrels hover about all day in the hottest parts of the line, not in the least disconcerted, apparently, when a promising mouse-area suddenly rises in the air in a cascade of black or yellow earth. Sparrow-hawks are fairly numerous, and a mile or two back from the firing line I saw a pair of hawks that I took to be red-legged falcons, circling over the top of an oak-copse. According to investigations made by Russian naturalists, the effect of the war on bird life on the Eastern Front has been more marked than it has been over here. 'During the first year of the war rooks disappeared, larks no longer sang in the fields, the wild pigeon disappeared also.' The skylark in this region has stuck tenaciously to the meadows and crop-lands that have been seamed and bisected with trenches and honeycombed with shell-holes. In the chill, misty hour of gloom that precedes a rainy dawn, when nothing seemed alive except a few wary waterlogged sentries and many scuttling rats, the lark would suddenly dash skyward and pour forth a song of ecstatic jubilation that sounded horribly forced and insincere. It seemed scarcely possible that the bird could carry its insouciance to the length of attempting to rear a brood in that desolate wreckage of shattered clods and gaping shell-holes, but once, having occasion to throw myself down with some abruptness on my face, I found myself nearly on the top of a brood of young larks. Two of them had already been hit by something and were in rather a battered condition, but the survivors seemed as tranquil and comfortable as the average nestling.

At the corner of a stricken wood (which has had a name made for it in history, but shall be nameless here), at a moment when lyddite and shrapnel and machine-gun fire swept and raked and bespattered that devoted spot as though the artillery of an entire Division had suddenly concentrated on it, a wee hen-chaffinch flirted wistfully to and fro, amid splintered and falling branches that had never a green bough left on them. The wounded lying there, if any of them noticed the small bird, may well have wondered why anything having wings and no pressing reason for remaining should have chosen to stay in such a place. There was a battered orchard alongside the stricken wood, and the probable explanation of the bird's presence was that it had a nest of young ones whom it was too scared to feed, too loyal to desert. Later on, a small flock of chaffinches blundered into the wood, which they were doubtless in the habit of using as a highway to their feeding-grounds; unlike the solitary hen-bird, they made no secret of their desire to get away as fast as their dazed wits would let them. The only other bird I ever saw there was a magpie, flying low over the wreckage of fallen tree-limbs; 'one for sorrow,' says the old superstition. There was sorrow enough in that wood.

The English gamekeeper, whose knowledge of wild life usually runs on limited and perverted lines, has evolved a sort of religion as to the nervous debility of even the hardiest game birds; according to his beliefs a terrier trotting across a field in which a partridge is nesting, or a mouse-hawking kestrel hovering over the hedge, is sufficient cause to drive the distracted bird off its eggs and send it whirring into the next county.

The partridge of the war zone shows no signs of such sensitive nerves. The rattle and rumble of transport, the constant coming and going of bodies of troops, the incessant rattle of musketry and deafening explosions of artillery, the night-long flare and flicker of star-shells, have not sufficed to scare the local birds away from their chosen feeding grounds, and to all appearances they have not been deterred from raising their broods. Gamekeepers who are serving with the colours might seize the opportunity to indulge in a little useful nature study.

Battles in the Air
From *Flying for France: With the American Escadrille at Verdun*, James R. McConnell

Before we were fairly settled at Bar-le-Duc, Hall brought down a German observation craft and Thaw a Fokker. Fights occurred on almost every sortie. The Germans seldom cross into our territory, unless on a bombarding jaunt, and thus practically all the fighting takes place on their side of the line. Thaw dropped his Fokker in the morning, and on the afternoon of the same day there was a big combat far behind the German trenches. Thaw was wounded in the arm, and an explosive bullet detonating on Rockwell's wind-shield tore several gashes in his face. Despite the blood which was blinding him Rockwell managed to reach an aviation field and land. Thaw, whose wound bled profusely, landed in a dazed condition just within our lines. He was too weak to walk, and French soldiers carried him to a field dressing-station, whence he was sent to Paris for further treatment. Rockwell's wounds were less serious and he insisted on flying again almost immediately.

A week or so later Chapman was wounded. Considering the number of fights he had been in and the courage with which he attacked it was a miracle he had not been hit before. He always fought against odds and far within the enemy's country. He flew more than any of us, never missing an opportunity to go up, and never coming down until his gasolene was giving out. His machine was a sieve of patched-up bullet holes. His nerve was almost superhuman and his devotion to the cause for which he fought sublime. The day he was wounded he attacked four machines. Swooping down from behind, one of them, a Fokker, riddled Chapman's plane. One bullet cut deep into his scalp, but Chapman, a master pilot, escaped from the trap, and fired several shots to show he was still safe. A stability control had been severed by a bullet. Chapman held the broken rod in one hand, managed his machine with the other, and succeeded in landing on a near-by aviation field. His wound was dressed, his machine repaired, and he immediately took the air in pursuit of some more enemies. He would take no rest, and with bandaged head continued to fly and fight.

The escadrille's next serious encounter with the foe took place a few days later. Rockwell, Balsley, Prince, and Captain Thénault were surrounded by a large number of Germans, who, circling about them, commenced firing at long range. Realising their numerical inferiority, the Americans and their commander sought the safest way out by attacking the enemy machines nearest the French lines. Rockwell, Prince, and the captain broke through successfully, but Balsley found himself hemmed in. He attacked the German nearest him, only to receive an explosive bullet in his thigh. In trying to get away by a vertical dive his machine went into a corkscrew and swung over on its back. Extra cartridge rollers dislodged from their case hit his arms. He was tumbling straight toward the trenches, but by a supreme effort he regained control, righted the plane, and landed without disaster in a meadow just behind the firing line.

Soldiers carried him to the shelter of a near-by fort, and later he was taken to a field hospital, where he lingered for days between life and death. Ten fragments of the explosive bullet were removed from his stomach. He bore up bravely, and became the favourite of the wounded officers in whose ward he lay. When we flew over to see him they would say: '*Il est un brave petit gars, l'aviateur américain.*'

[He's a brave little fellow, the American aviator.] On a shelf by his bed, done up in a handkerchief, he kept the pieces of bullet taken out of him, and under them some sheets of paper on which he was trying to write to his mother, back in El Paso.

Balsley was awarded the *Médaille Militaire* and the *Croix de Guerre,* but the honours scared him. He had seen them decorate officers in the ward before they died.

The Nightmare
From *Kangaroo*, D. H. Lawrence

He had known such different deep fears. In Sicily, a sudden fear in the night of some single murderer, some single thing hovering as it were out of the violent past, with the intent of murder. Out of the old Greek past, that had been so vivid, sometimes an unappeased spirit of murderous hate against the usurping moderns. A sudden presence of murder in the air, because of something which the modern psyche had excluded, some old and vital thing which Christianity has cut out. An old spirit, waiting for vengeance. But in England, during the later years of the war, a true and deadly fear of the criminal LIVING spirit which arose in all the stay-at-home bullies who governed the country during those years. From 1916 to 1919 a wave of criminal lust rose and possessed England, there was a reign of terror, under a set of indecent bullies like Bottomley of John Bull and other bottom-dog members of the House of Commons. Then Somers had known what it was to live in a perpetual state of semi-fear: the fear of the criminal public and the criminal government. The torture was steadily applied, during those years after Asquith fell, to break the independent soul in any man who would not hunt with the criminal mob. A man must identify himself with the criminal mob, sink his sense of truth, of justice, and of human honour, and bay like some horrible unclean hound, bay with a loud sound, from slavering, unclean jaws.

This Richard Lovat Somers had steadily refused to do. The deepest part of a man is his sense of essential truth, essential honour, essential justice. This deepest self makes him abide by his own feelings, come what may. It is not sentimentalism. It is just the male human creature, the thought-adventurer, driven to earth. Will he give in or won't he?

Many men, carried on a wave of patriotism and true belief in democracy, entered the war. Many men were driven in out of belief that it was necessary to save their property. Vast numbers of men were just bullied into the army. A few remained. Of these, many became conscientious objectors.

Somers tiresomely belonged to no group. He would not enter the army, because his profoundest instinct was against it. Yet he had no conscientious objection to war. It was the whole spirit of the war, the vast mob-spirit, which he could never acquiesce in. The terrible, terrible war, made so fearful because in every country practically every man lost his head, and lost his own centrality, his own manly isolation in his own integrity, which alone keeps life real. Practically every man being caught away from himself, as in some horrible flood, and swept away with the ghastly masses of other men, utterly unable to speak, or feel for himself, or to stand on his own feet, delivered over and swirling in the current, suffocated for the time being. Some of them to die for ever. Most to come back home victorious in circumstance, but with their inner pride gone: inwardly lost. To come back home, many of them, to wives who had egged them on to this downfall in themselves: black bitterness. Others to return to a bewildered wife who had in vain tried to keep her man true to himself, tried and tried, only to see him at last swept away. And oh, when he was swept away, how she loved him. But when he came back, when he crawled out like a dog out of a dirty stream, a stream that had suddenly gone slack and turbid; when he came back covered with outward glory and inward shame, then there was the price to pay.

And there *is* this bitter and sordid after-war price to pay because men lost their heads, and worse, lost their inward, individual integrity. And when a man loses his inward, isolated, manly integrity, it is a bad day for that man's true wife. A true man should not lose his head. The greater the crisis, the more intense should be his isolated reckoning with his own soul. And *then* let him act, of his own whole self. Not fling himself away: or much worse, let himself be *dragged* away, bit by bit.

Awful years – '16, '17, '18, '19 – the years when the damage was done. The years when the world lost its real manhood. Not for lack of courage to face death. Plenty of superb courage to face death. But no courage in any man to face his own isolated soul, and abide by its decision. Easier to sacrifice oneself. So much easier!

Richard Lovat was one of those utterly unsatisfactory creatures who just would not. He had no conscientious objections. He knew that men *must* fight, sometime in some way or other. He was no Quaker, to believe in perpetual peace. He had been in Germany times enough to know *how* much he detested the German military creatures: mechanical bullies they were. They had once threatened to arrest him as a spy, and had insulted him more than once. Oh, he would never forgive *them*, in his inward soul. But then the industrialism and commercialism of England, with which patriotism and democracy became identified: did not these insult a man and hit him pleasantly across the mouth? How much humiliation had Richard suffered, trying to earn his living! How had they tried, with their beastly industrial self-righteousness, to humiliate him as a separate, single man? They wanted to bring him to heel even more than the German militarist did. And if a man is to be brought to any heel, better a spurred heel than the heel of a Jewish financier. So Richard decided later, when the years let him think things over, and see where he was.

Therefore when the war came, his instinct was against it. When the Asquith government so softly foundered, he began to suffer agonies. But when the Asquith government went right under, and in its place came that John Bull government of '16, '17, '18, then agonies gave way to tortures. He was summoned to join the army: and went. Spent a night in barracks with forty other men, and not one of these other men but felt like a criminal condemned, bitter in dejection and humiliation. Was medically examined in the morning by two doctors, both gentlemen, who knew the sacredness of another naked man: and was rejected.

So, that was over. He went back home. And he made up his mind what he would do. He would never voluntarily make a martyr of himself. His feeling was private to himself, he didn't want to force it on any other man. He would just act alone. For the moment, he was rejected as medically unfit. If he was called up again, he would go again. But he would never serve.

'Once,' he said to Harriet, 'that they have really conscripted me, I will never obey another order, if they kill me.'

Poor Harriet felt scared, and didn't know what else to say.

'If ever,' he said, looking up from his own knees in their old grey flannel trousers, as he sat by the fire, 'if ever I see my legs in khaki, I shall die. But they shall never put my legs into khaki.'

That first time, at the barracks in the country town in the west, they had treated him with that instinctive regard and gentleness which he usually got from men who were not German militarist bullies, or worse, British commercial bullies. For instance, in the morning in that prison barracks room, these unexamined recruits were ordered to make their beds and sweep the room. In obedience, so far, Richard Lovat took one of the heavy brooms. He was pale, silent, isolated: a queer figure, a young man with a beard. The other soldiers – or must-be soldiers – had looked at him as a queer fish, but that he was used to.

'Say, Dad,' said a fattish young fellow older than himself, the only blatherer, a loose fellow who had come from Canada to join up and was already cursing: he was a good deal older than Somers. 'Say, Dad,' said this fellow, as they sat in the train coming up, 'all that'll come off tomorrow – Qck, Qck!' – and he made two noises, and gave two long swipes with his finger round his chin, to intimate that Richard's beard would be cut off tomorrow.

'We'll see,' said Richard, smiling with pale lips.

He said in his heart, the day his beard was shaven he was beaten, lost. He identified it with his isolate manhood. He never forgot that journey up to Bodmin, with the other men who were called up. They were all bitterly, desperately miserable, but still manly: mostly very quiet, yet neither sloppy nor frightened. Only the fat, loose fellow who had given up a damned good job in Canada to come and serve this bloody country, etc., etc., was a ranter and a bragger. Somers saw him afterwards naked: strange, fat, soft, like a woman. But in another carriage the men sang all the time, or howled like dogs in the night:

> I'll be your sweetheart, if you will be mine,
> All my life I'll be you-o-o-ur Valentine.
> Bluebells I'll gather, take them and be true,
> When I'm a man, my plan will be to marry you.

Wailing down the lost corridors of hell, surely, those ghastly melancholy notes – 'All my li-i-i-ife-I'll be you-u-r Valentine.'

Somers could never recall it without writhing. It is not death that matters, but the loss of the integral soul. And these men howled as if they were going to their doom, helplessly, ghastly. It was not the death in front. It was the surrender of all their old beliefs, and all their sacred liberty.

Those bluebells! They were worse than the earlier songs. In 1915, autumn, Hampstead Heath, leaves burning in heaps, in the blue air, London still almost pre-war London: but by the pond on the Spaniards Road, blue soldiers, wounded soldiers in their bright hospital blue and red, always there: and earth-coloured recruits with pale faces drilling near Parliament Hill. The pre-war world still lingering, and some vivid strangeness, glamour thrown in. At night all the great beams of the searchlights, in great straight bars, feeling across the London sky, feeling the clouds, feeling the body of the dark overhead. And then Zeppelin raids: the awful noise and the excitement. Somers was never afraid then. One evening he and Harriet walked from Platts Lane to the Spaniards Road, across the Heath: and there, in the sky, like some god vision, a Zeppelin, and the searchlights catching it, so that it gleamed like a manifestation in the heavens, then losing it, so that only the strange drumming came down out of the sky where the searchlights tangled their feelers. There it was again, high, high, high, tiny, pale, as one might imagine the Holy Ghost, far, far above. And the crashes of guns, and the awful hoarseness of shells bursting in the city. Then gradually, quiet. And from Parliament Hill, a great red glare below, near St. Paul's. Something ablaze in the city. Harriet was horribly afraid. Yet as she looked up at the far-off Zeppelin she said to Somers:

'Think, some of the boys I played with when I was a child are probably in it.'

And he looked up at the far, luminous thing, like a moon. Were there men in it? Just men, with two vulnerable legs and warm mouths. The imagination could not go so far.

Those days, that autumn... people carried about chrysanthemums, yellow and brown chrysanthemums: and the smell of burning leaves: and the wounded, bright blue soldiers with their red cotton neckties, sitting together like macaws on the seats, pale and different from other people. And the star Jupiter very bright at nights over the cup hollow of the Vale, on Hampstead Heath. And the war news coming, the war horror drifting in, drifting in, prices rising, excitement growing, people going mad about the Zeppelin raids. And always the one song:

Keep the home fires burning,
Though your hearts be yearning.

It was in 1915 the old world ended. In the winter 1915–1916 the spirit of the old London collapsed; the city, in some way, perished, perished from being a heart of the world, and became a vortex of broken passions, lusts, hopes, fears, and horrors. The integrity of London collapsed, and the genuine debasement began, the unspeakable baseness of the press and the public voice, the reign of that bloated ignominy, John Bull.

No man who has really consciously lived through this can believe again absolutely in democracy. No man who has heard reiterated in thousands of tones from all the common people during the crucial years of the war: 'I believe in John Bull. Give me John Bull,' can ever believe that in any crisis a people can govern itself, or is ever fit to govern itself. During the crucial years of the war, the people chose, and chose Bottomleyism. Bottom enough.

The well-bred, really cultured classes were on the whole passive resisters. They shirked their duty. It is the business of people who really know better to fight tooth and nail to keep up a standard, to hold control of authority. *Laiser-aller* is as guilty as the actual, stinking mongrelism it gives place to.

It was in mid-winter 1915 that Somers and Harriet went down to Cornwall. The spirit of the war – the spirit of collapse and of human ignominy, had not travelled so far yet. It came in advancing waves.

We hear so much of the bravery and horrors at the Front. Brave the men were, all honour to them. It was at home the world was lost. We hear too little of the collapse of the proud human spirit at home, the triumph of sordid, rampant, raging meanness. 'The bite of a jackal is blood-poisoning and mortification.' And at home stayed all the jackals, middle-aged, male and female jackals. And they bit us all. And blood-poisoning and mortification set in.

We should never have let the jackals loose, and patted them on the head. They were feeding on our death all the while.

Away in the west Richard and Harriet lived alone in their cottage by the savage Atlantic. He hardly wrote at all, and never any propaganda. But he hated the war, and said so to the few Cornish people around. He laughed at the palpable lies of the press, bitterly. And because of his isolation and his absolute separateness, he was marked out as a spy.

'I am not a spy,' he said, 'I leave it to dirtier people. I am myself, and I won't have popular lies.'

So, there began the visits from the policeman. A large, blue, helmeted figure at the door.

'Excuse me, sir, I have just a few enquiries to make.'

The police-sergeant always a decent, kindly fellow, driven by the military.

Somers and Harriet lived now with that suspense about them in the very air they breathed. They were suspects.

'Then let them suspect,' said he. 'I do nothing to them, so what can they do to me.'

He still believed in the constitutional liberty of an Englishman.

'You know,' said Harriet, 'you *do* say things to these Cornish people.'

'I only say, when they tell me newspaper lies, that they *are* lies.'

But now the two began to be hated, hated far more than they knew.

'You want to be careful,' warned one of the Cornish friends. 'I've heard that the coast-watchers have got orders to keep very strict watch on you.'

'Let them, they'll see nothing.'

But it was not till afterwards that he learned that the watchers had lain behind the stone fence, to hear what he and Harriet talked about.

So, he was called up the first time and went. He was summoned to Penzance, and drove over with Harriet, expecting to return for the time at least. But he was ordered to proceed the same afternoon to Bodmin, along with sixteen or seventeen other fellows, farm hands and working men. He said good-bye to Harriet, who was to be driven back alone across the moors, to their lonely cottage on the other side.

'I shall be back tomorrow,' he said.

England was still England, and he was not finally afraid.

The train journey from Penzance to Bodmin with the other men: the fat, bragging other man: the tall man who felt as Somers did: the change at the roadside station, with the porters chaffing the men that the handcuffs were on them. Indeed, it was like being one of a gang of convicts. The great, prison-like barracks – the disgusting evening meal of which he could eat nothing – the little terrier-like sergeant of the regulars, who made them a little encouraging speech: not a bad chap. The lounging about that barracks yard, prisoners, till bed-time: the other men crowding to the canteen, himself mostly alone. The brief talks with men who were for a moment curious as to who and what he was. For a moment only. They were most of them miserable and bitter.

Gaol! It was like gaol. He thought of Oscar Wilde in prison. Night came, and the beds to be made.

'They're good beds, clean beds, you'll sleep quite comfortable in them,' said the elderly little sergeant with a white moustache. Nine o'clock lights out. Somers had brought no night clothes, nothing. He slept in his woollen pants, and was ashamed because they had patches on the knees, for he and Harriet were very poor these years. In the next bed was a youth, a queer fellow, in a sloppy suit of black broadcloth, and down-at-heel boots. He had a degenerate sort of handsomeness too. He had never spoken a word. His face was long and rather fine, but like an Apache, his straight black hair came in a lock over his forehead. And there was an Apache sort of sheepishness, stupidity, in everything he did. He was a long time getting undressed. Then there he stood, and his white cotton day-shirt was long below his knees, like a woman's nightgown. A restless, bitter night, with one man cough, cough, coughing, a hysterical cough, and others talking, making noises in their sleep. Bugle at six, and a scramble to wash themselves at the zinc trough in the wash house. Somers could not crowd in, did not get in till towards the end. Then he had to borrow soap, and afterwards a piece of comb. The men were all quiet and entirely inoffensive, common, but gentle, by nature decent. A sickening breakfast, then wash-up and sweep the floors. Somers took one of the heavy brooms, as ordered, and began. He swept his own floors nearly every day. But this was heavier work. The sergeant stopped him. 'Don't you do that. You go and help to wipe the pots, if you like. Here, you boy, *you* – take that sweeping brush.'

And Somers relinquished his broom to a bigger man.

They were kindly, and, in the essential sense, gentlemen, the little terrier of a sergeant too. Englishmen, his own people.

When it came to Somers' turn to be examined, and he took off his clothes and sat in his shirt in the cold lobby, the fat fellow pointed to his thin, delicate legs with a jeer. But Somers looked at him, and he was quiet again. The queer, soft, pale-bodied fellow, against Somers' thin delicate whiteness. The little sergeant kept saying:

'Don't you catch cold, you chaps.'

In the warm room behind a screen, Richard took off his shirt and was examined. The doctor asked him where he lived – where was his home – asked as a gentleman asks, treated him with that gentle consideration Somers usually met with, save from business people or official people.

'We shall reject you, leave you free,' said the doctor, after consulting with the more elderly, officious little man, 'but we leave it to you to do what you can for your country.'

'Thank you,' said Richard, looking at him.

'Every man must do what he can,' put in the other doctor, who was elderly and officious, but a gentleman. 'The country needs the help of every man, and though we leave you free, we expect you to apply yourself to *some* service.'

'Yes,' said Somers, looking at him, and speaking in an absolutely neutral voice. Things said like that to him were never real to him: more like the noise of a cart passing, just a noise.

The two doctors looked from his face down his thin nakedness again.

'Put your shirt on,' said the younger one.

And Somers could hear the mental comment, 'Rum sort of a fellow,' as he did so.

There was still a wait for the card. It was one of those cards: *A* – Called up for military service. *B* – Called up for service at the front, but not in the lines. *C* – Called up for non-military service. *R* – Rejected. *A*, *B*, and *C* were ruled out in red ink, leaving the Rejected. He still had to go to another office for his pay – two shillings and fourpence, or something like that. He signed for this and was free. Free – with two shillings and fourpence, and pass for a railway ticket – and God's air. The moment he stepped out with his card, he realised that it was Saturday morning, that the sun was shining, filling the big stone yard of the barracks, from which he could look to the station and the hill with its grass, beyond. That hill beyond – he had seemed to look at it through darkened glass, before. Till now, the morning had been a timeless greyness. Indeed, it had rained at seven o'clock, as they stood lounging miserably about in the barracks yard with its high wall, cold and bitter. And the tall man had talked to him bitterly.

But now the sun shone, the dark-green, Cornish hill, hard-looking, was just a near hill. He walked through the great gates. Ah God, he was out, he was free. The road with trees went downhill to the town. He hastened down, a free human being, on Saturday morning, the grey glaze gone from his eyes.

He telegraphed the ignominious word Rejected, and the time of his arrival, to Harriet. Then he went and had dinner. Some of the other men came in. They were reserved now – there was a distance between him and them – he was not of their social class.

'What are you?' they asked him.

'Rejected,' he said.

And they looked at him grudgingly, thinking it was because he was not a working man he had got special favour. He knew what they thought, and he tried not to look so glad. But glad he was, and in some mysterious way, triumphant.

It was a wonderful journey on the Saturday afternoon home – sunny, busy, lovely. He changed at Truro and went into town. On the road he met some of the other fellows, who were called up, but not summoned for service immediately. They had some weeks, or months, of torment and suspense before them. They looked at Somers, and grinned rather jeeringly at him. They envied him – no wonder. And already he was a stranger, in another walk of life.

Rejected as unfit. One of the unfit. What did he care? The Cornish are always horrified of any ailment or physical disablement. 'What's amiss then?' they would ask. They would *say* that you might as well be shot outright as labelled unfit. But most of them tried hard to find constitutional weaknesses in themselves, that would get them rejected also, notwithstanding. And at the same time they felt they must be horribly ashamed of their physical ignominy if they were *labelled* unfit.

Somers did not care. Let them label me unfit, he said to himself. I know my own body is fragile, in its way, but also it is very strong, and it's the only body that would carry my particular self. Let the fools peer at it and put me down, undeveloped chest and what they like, so long as they leave me to my own way.

Then the kindly doctor's exhortation that he should find some way for himself for serving his country. He thought about that many times. But always, as he came near to the fact of committing himself, he knew that he simply could not commit himself to any service whatsoever. In no shape or form could he serve the war, either indirectly or directly. Yet it would have been so easy. He had quite enough influential friends in London to put him into some job, even some quite congenial, literary job, with a sufficient salary. They would be only too glad to do it, for there in his remoteness, writing occasionally an essay that only bothered them, he was a thorn in their flesh. And men and women with sons, brothers, husbands away fighting, it was small pleasure for them to read Mr Somers and his denunciation. 'This trench and machine warfare is a blasphemy against life itself, a blasphemy which we are all committing.' All very well, they said, but we are in for a war, and what are we to do? We hate it as much as he does. But we can't all sit safely in Cornwall.

That was true too, and he knew it, and he felt the most dreary misery, knowing how many brave, generous men were being put through this slaughter-machine of human devilishness. They were doing their best, and there was nothing else to do. But even that was no reason why he should go and do likewise.

If men had kept their souls firm and integral through the years, the war would never have come on. If, in the beginning, there had been enough strong, proud souls in England to concentrate the English feeling into stern, fierce, honourable fighting, the war would never have gone as it went. But England slopped and wobbled, and the tide of horror accumulated.

And now, if circumstances had roped nearly all men into the horror, and it was a case of adding horror to horror, or dying well, on the other hand, the irremediable circumstance of his own separate soul made Richard Lovat's inevitable standing out. If there is outward, circumstantial unreason and fatality, there is inward unreason and inward fate. He would have to dare to follow his inward fate. He must remain alone, outside of everything, everything, conscious of what was going on, conscious of what he was doing and not doing. Conscious he must be, and consciously he must stick to it. To be forced into nothing.

For, above all things, man is a land animal and a thought-adventurer. Once the human consciousness really sinks and is swamped under the tide of events – as the best English consciousness was swamped, pacifist and patriotic alike – then the adventure is doomed. The English soul went under in the war, and, as a conscious, proud, adventurous, self-responsible soul, it was lost. We all lost the war: perhaps Germany least. Lost all the lot. The adventure is always lost when the human conscious soul gives way under the stress, fails to keep control, and is submerged. Then out swarm the rats and the Bottomleys and crew, and the ship of human adventure is a horrible piratic affair, a dirty sort of freebooting.

Richard Lovat had nothing to hang on to but his own soul. So he hung on to it, and tried to keep his wits. If no man was with him, he was hardly aware of it, he had to grip on so desperately, like a man on a plank in a shipwreck. The plank was his own individual self.

Followed that period of suspense which changed his life forever. If the postman was coming plunging downhill through the bushes over the moor, the first thought was: What is he bringing now? The postman was over military age, and had a chuckle of pleasure in handing out those accursed *On His Majesty's Service* envelopes which meant that a man was summoned for torture. The postman was a great Wesleyan and a chapel preacher, and the thought of hell for other men was sweet in him: he had a religious zest added to his natural Cornish zest in other people's disasters.

Again, if there was the glint of a bicycle on the moor road, and if it turned down the bypath towards the cottage, then Somers strained his eyes to see if the rider were fat and blue, or tall and blue. Was it the police sergeant, or the police constable, coming for more identification proofs.

'We want your birth certificate,' said the sergeant. 'They've written from Bodmin asking you to produce your birth certificate.'

'Then tell them to get it. No, I haven't got it. You've had my marriage certificate. You know who I am and where I was born and all the rest. Now let them get the birth certificate themselves.'

Richard Lovat was at the end of all patience. They persisted he was a foreigner – poor Somers, just because he had a beard. One of the most intensely English little men England ever produced, with a passion for his country, even if it were often a passion of hatred. But no, they persisted he was a foreigner. Pah!

He and Harriet did all their own work, their own shopping. One wintry afternoon they were coming home with a knapsack, along the field path above the sea, when two khaki individuals, officers of some sort, strode after them.

'Excuse me,' said one, in a damnatory officious voice. 'What have you got in that sack?'

'A few groceries,' said Lovat.

'I would like to look.'

Somers put the sack down on the path. The tall and lofty officer stooped and groped nobly among a pound of rice and a piece of soap and a dozen candles.

'Ha!' he cried, exultant. 'What's this? A camera!'

Richard peeped in the bag at the groping red military hands. For a moment he almost believed that a camera had spirited itself in among his few goods, the implication of his guilt was so powerful. He saw a block in brown paper.

'A penn'orth of salt,' he said quietly, though pale to the lips with anger and insult.

But the gentlemanly officer – a Captain – tore open the paper. Yes, a common block of salt. He pushed the bag aside.

'We have to be careful,' said the other, lesser man.

'Of course,' said Richard, tying up his bag.

'Good afternoon!' said Harriet.

The fellows half saluted, and turned hastening away. Richard and Harriet had the advantage of sauntering behind them and looking at their noble backs. Oh, they were gentlemen, true English gentlemen: perhaps Cornish.

Harriet gave a pouf of laughter.

'The poor innocent salt!' she exclaimed.

And no doubt that also was chalked up against her.

Boelcke at Gallipoli
From *An Aviator's Handbook*, Oswald Boelcke

JULY 29, 1916

On July 28th I went aboard a gunboat bound for Chanak, with a tow. Gallipoli is a village, with a number of outlying barracks. Several houses on the shore were destroyed by gunfire. Arrived in Chanak toward noon, and went to Merten-Pasha to report. In the afternoon I went to the aviation field and flew over Troy–Kum Kale–Sedil Bar, to the old English position. The flight was beautiful, and the islands of Imbros and Tenedos were as if floating on the clear sea. In the Bay of Imbros we could plainly see the English ships. Outside of the usual maze of trenches we could plainly see the old English camps. Close to Thalaka there was an English U-Boat and a Turkish cruiser, both sunk, and lying partly out of water. At Sedil Bar, a number of steamers and a French battleship were aground. The dead, hilly peninsula was plainly visible. At Kilid Bar, there were large Turkish barracks.

JULY 30, 1916

Went on a small steamer to Sedil Bar. We got off a little before we reached our destination, to go over the whole position with a naval officer, who awaited us. The difference between the Turkish and English positions was striking. The English, of course, had had more and better material to work with. Now it is nothing but a deserted wreck. Then I looked at the English landing places. Here, the Englishmen had simply run a few steamers aground to protect themselves. After a hasty breakfast, I flew... from there, along the north shore of the Sea of Marmora, to St. Stefano.

The Egg
From *Under Fire,* Henri Barbusse

We were badly off, hungry and thirsty; and in these wretched quarters there was nothing!

Something had gone wrong with the revictualing department and our wants were becoming acute. Where the sorry place surrounded them, with its empty doors, its bones of houses, and its bald-headed telegraph posts, a crowd of hungry men were grinding their teeth and confirming the absence of everything:

'The juice has sloped and the wine's up the spout, and the bully's zero. Cheese? Nix. Napoo jam, napoo butter on skewers.'

'We've nothing, and no error, nothing; and play hell as you like, it doesn't help.'

'Talk about rotten quarters! Three houses with nothing inside but draughts and damp.'

'No good having any of the filthy here, you might as well have only the skin of a bob in your purse, as long as there's nothing to buy.'

'You might be a Rothschild, or even a military tailor, but what use'd your brass be?'

'Yesterday there was a bit of a cat mewing round where the 7th are. I feel sure they've eaten it.'

'Yes, there was; you could see its ribs like rocks on the sea-shore.'

'There were some chaps,' says Blaire, 'who bustled about when they got here and managed to find a few bottles of common wine at the bacca-shop at the corner of the street.'

'Ah, the swine! Lucky devils to be sliding that down their necks.'

'It was muck, all the same, it'd make your cup as black as your baccy-pipe.'

'There are some, they say, who've swallowed a fowl.'

'Damn,' says Fouillade.

'I've hardly had a bite. I had a sardine left, and a little tea in the bottom of a bag that I chewed up with some sugar.'

'You can't even have a bit of a drunk – it's off the map.'

'And that isn't enough either, even when you're not a big eater and you're got a communication trench as flat as a pancake.'

'One meal in two days – a yellow mess, shining like gold, no broth and no meat – everything left behind.'

'And worst of all we've nothing to light a pipe with.'

'True, and that's misery. I haven't a single match. I had several bits of ends, but they've gone. I've hunted in vain through all the pockets of my flea-case – nix. As for buying them it's hopeless, as you say.'

'I've got the head of a match that I'm keeping.' It is a real hardship indeed, and the sight is pitiful of the *poilus* who cannot light pipe or cigarette but put them away in their pockets and stroll in resignation. By good fortune, Tirloir has his petrol pipe-lighter and it still contains a little spirit. Those who are aware of it gather round him, bringing their pipes packed and cold. There is not even any paper to light, and the flame itself must be used until the remaining spirit in its tiny insect's belly is burned.

As for me, I've been lucky, and I see Paradis wandering about, his kindly face to the wind, grumbling and chewing a bit of wood.

'Tiens,' I say to him, 'take this.'

'A box of matches!' he exclaims amazed, looking at it as one looks at a jewel. 'Egad! That's capital! Matches!'

A moment later we see him lighting his pipe, his face saucily sideways and splendidly crimsoned by the reflected flame, and everybody shouts,

'Paradis' got some matches!'

Towards evening I meet Paradis near the ruined triangle of a house-front at the corner of the two streets of this most miserable among villages.

He beckons to me:

'Hist!' He has a curious and rather awkward air. 'I say,' he says to me affectionately, but looking at his feet, 'a bit since, you chucked me a box of flamers. Well, you're going to get a bit of your own back for it. Here!' He puts something in my hand. 'Be careful!' he whispers, 'it's fragile!'

Dazzled by the resplendent purity of his present, hardly even daring to believe my eyes, I see an egg!

My First English Victim
From *The Red Baron*, Manfred von Richthofen

We had just arrived at the Front when we recognised a hostile flying squadron that was proceeding in the direction of Cambrai. Boelcke was the first to see it, for he saw a great deal more than ordinary mortals. It was clear to all of us that we should pass our first examination under the eyes of our beloved leader.

Slowly we approached the hostile squadron. It could not escape us. We counted the hostile machines. They were seven in number. We were only five. All the Englishmen flew large bomb-carrying two-seaters. In a few seconds the dance would begin.

Boelcke had come very near the first English machine but he did not yet shoot. I followed. Close to me were my comrades. The Englishman nearest to me was travelling in a large boat painted with dark colours. I did not reflect very long but took my aim and shot. Both of us missed. A struggle began and the great point for me was to get to the rear of the fellow because I could only shoot forward with my gun. He was differently placed for his machine gun was movable. It could fire in all directions.

Apparently he was no beginner, for he knew exactly that his last hour had arrived at the moment when I got at the back of him. At that time I had not yet the conviction 'He must fall!' which I have now on such occasions, but on the contrary, I was curious to see whether he would fall.

My Englishman twisted and turned, going criss-cross. I did not think for a moment that the hostile squadron contained other Englishmen who might come to the aid of their comrade. I was animated by a single thought: 'The man in front of me must come down, whatever happens.' At last a favourable moment arrived. My opponent had apparently lost sight of me. Instead of twisting and turning he flew straight along. In a fraction of a second I was at his back. I give a short series of shots with my machine gun. I had gone so close that I was afraid I might dash into the Englishman. Suddenly, I nearly yelled with joy for the propeller of the enemy machine had stopped turning. I had shot his engine to pieces; the enemy was compelled to land, for it was impossible for him to reach his own lines.

The Englishman landed close to the flying ground of one of our squadrons. I was so excited that I landed also and my eagerness was so great that I nearly smashed up my machine. I rushed to the English machine. My assumption had been correct. I had shot the engine to pieces and both the pilot and observer were severely wounded. The observer died at once and the pilot while being transported to the nearest dressing station. I honoured the fallen enemy by placing a stone on his beautiful grave.

I would mention that since that time no English squadron ventured as far as Cambrai as long as Boelcke's squadron was there.

'The Brave Squares of War'
From *Her Privates We*, Frederic Manning

> *He alone*
> *Dealt on lieutenantry and no practice had*
> *In the brave squares of war.*
>
> SHAKESPEARE

In the morning, the whole camp seethed with hot and angry men, as was always the case when brass hats, and general officers, disturbed the normal routine of their life. Preparations, for the rehearsal of the attack, were complicated by the issue of orders, that blankets were to be handed in, and the camp cleaned up, before the men paraded. They were to parade in full kit with pack complete, and a bread-and-cheese ration was issued to them.

The unnecessary bad temper continued until they fell in on the road; and the colonel came on parade, smiling slightly, as though he were well satisfied, and looked forward to an amusing day. The high, clear voice, which always seemed to carry without much effort, rang out, and the battalion moved off in the direction of Bertrancourt.

After some miles, they turned off the road and continued over reaped fields, finally mounting a ridge and taking up a position with other battalions of their Brigade. There the men were allowed to fall out and eat. They could see at once, more clearly than they had realised from the instructions read out to them, the way they were to be disposed; and started a general discussion on the rival advantages and disadvantages of going over as the first or second wave; a discussion which had no other effect than that of confirming each individual disputant in the opinion with which he had originally started. It proved indirectly, however, that there was a considerable fund of obstinacy, combativeness, and tenacity of purpose among them, and these were clearly assets of military value.

The first excitement was provided by a hare. It was put up by some of the troops in front, who chivvied it about in all directions, until, doubling back, it came straight through their own H.Q. Company, almost running over Bourne's foot. He didn't move, pitying the poor hunted thing. They were in an angle of a field, along the boundaries of which ran a low fence of rabbit wire, and as it was headed into the corner, Martlow flung himself on it, caught it, and broke its neck scientifically with a blow from the edge of his hand.

'Why did you kill it?' exclaimed Bourne, as Martlow buttoned his tunic over the warm quivering body. Bourne thought hares uncanny creatures.

'It'll go into t' pot,' said Martlow, surprised. Mr Sothern came up, and offered him ten francs for it, and after some hesitation Martlow sold it to him.

Presently arrived magnificent people on horseback, glancing superciliously at the less fortunate members of their species whom necessity compelled to walk. Bourne, who loved horses, had seen nothing for months but mules, Rosinante, some sorry hacks ridden by their officers, and a few lusty percherons threshing corn on a kind of treadmill outside a French farm. The sight of these daintily stepping animals, with a sheen on their smooth hides, gave him a thrill of pleasure. He was less favourably impressed by some of the riders.

'That bugger will give his horse a sore back before the day is out,' he said, as one of the great men cantered by importantly.

'You're learnin' a lot o' bad words from us'ns,' said Martlow, grinning.

'Oh, you all swear like so many Eton boys,' replied Bourne, indifferently. 'Have you ever heard an Aussie swear?'

'No, 'n' I don't want,' said Martlow. 'Them buggers 'ave too much spare cash to know what soldierin' means.'

They fell in, and there was another moment of suppressed bad temper. Most of the new signallers went with H.Q. runners, but Weeper Smart, though he was close to them, had to carry the flapper with H.Q. signallers. The flapper was a device by which it was intended to signal to aeroplanes. One could see by now that most of the men were keenly interested; they knew that the plan was intended to supply them with a kind of map, on the actual scale of the trenches they were to attack. Their interest did not fade out completely as they advanced; but they rapidly became aware of the unreality of it all. The files of men moved forward slowly, and, when they reached the tapes, followed the paths assigned to them with an admirable precision. Their formations were not broken up or depleted by any hostile barrage, the ground was not pitted by craters, their advance was not impeded by any uncut wire. Everything went according to plan. It was a triumph of staff work, and these patient, rather unimaginative men tried to fathom the meaning of it all, with an anxiety which only made them more perplexed. They felt there was something incomplete about it. What they really needed was a map of the strange country through which their minds would travel on the day, with fear darkening earth and filling it with slaughter.

Bourne, Shem and Martlow, with the other orderlies, were following close behind the colonel, when the superb individual whose seat on a horse had seemed to Bourne to call for adverse comment, galloped up to them, and reined in his mount.

'What are all these men?' he asked the colonel, pointing almost at the embarrassed Bourne.

'These are my orderlies, sir,' answered the colonel, and Bourne, from the angle at which he stood, saw his cheekbone as he turned to the rider with an amiable smile.

'You seem to have a great many of them,' said god-like Agamemnon, with a supercilious coldness. They kept advancing slowly, and the horse was restive under his strange cargo.

'I don't think more than are usual, sir,' hazarded the colonel with a bland diffidence.

Other important people on horseback, even the most important of them all, on a grey, arrived, and grouped themselves impressively, as though for a portrait. There followed some discussion, first apparently as to the number of the colonel's runners, and then as to why they were not within the imaginary trenches as marked out by the tapes. The colonel remained imperturbable, only saying, in a tone of mild protest, that they would be in the trenches on the day, though there were some advantages in separating them from the other men at the moment. They were all moving forward at a foot's pace, and apparently the Olympian masters of their fate were willing to admit the validity of the colonel's argument, when there was a sudden diversion.

They were passing a small cottage, little more than a hovel, where three cows were tethered to pasture on some rough grass; and the tapes passed diagonally across a square patch of sown clover, dark and green in comparison with the dryer herbage beside it. This was the track taken by a platoon of A Company under Mr Sothern; and as the first few men were crossing the clover, the door of the hovel was flung open, and an infuriated woman appeared.

'*Ces champs sont a moi!*' she screamed, and this was the prelude to a withering fire of invective, which promised to be inexhaustible. It gave a slight tinge of reality to operations which were degenerating into a series of co-ordinated drill movements. The men of destiny looked at her, and then at one another. It was a contingency which had not been foreseen by the staff, whose intention had been to represent, under ideal conditions, an attack on the village of Serre, several miles away, where this particular lady did not live. They felt, therefore, that they had been justified in ignoring her existence. She was evidently of a different opinion. She was a very stubborn piece of reality, as she stood there with her black skirt and red petticoat kilted up to her knees, her grey stockings and her ploughman's boots. She had a perfect genius for vituperation, which she directed against the men, the officers and the *état-major*, with a fine impartiality.

The barrage was effective; and the men, with a thoroughly English respect for the rights of property, hesitated to commit any further trespass.

'Send someone to speak to that woman,' said the divisional general to a brigadier; and the brigadier passed on the order to the colonel, and the colonel to the adjutant; and the adjutant to Mr Sothern, who, remembering that Bourne had once interpreted his wishes to an old woman in Meaulte when he wanted a broom, now thrust him into the forefront of the battle. That is what is called, in the British Army, the chain of responsibility, which means that all responsibility for the errors of their superior officers is borne eventually by private soldiers in the ranks.

For a moment she turned all her hostility on Bourne, prepared to defend her title at the cost of her life, if need should arise. He told her that she would be paid in full for any damage done by the troops; but she replied, very reasonably for all her heat, that her clover was all the feed she had for her cows through the winter, and that mere payment for the clover would be inadequate compensation for the loss of her cows. Bourne knew her difficulties; it was difficult enough, through lack of transport, for these unfortunate peasants to bring up provisions for themselves. He suggested, desperately, to Mr Sothern and the adjutant, that the men should leave the tapes and return to them on the other side of the clover. The adjutant was equal to the situation; and, as the rest of the men doubled round the patch to regain the tapes, and their correct position, on the other side, the general, with all his splendid satellites, moved discreetly away to another part of the field. One of the men shouted out something about '*les Allemands*' to the victorious lady, and she threw discretion to the winds.

'*Les Allemands sont tres bons!*' she shrieked at him.

An aeroplane suddenly appeared in the sky, and, circling over them, signalled with a klaxon horn. The men moved slowly away from her beloved fields, and the tired woman went back into the hovel, and slammed the door on a monstrous world.

When Bourne rejoined the runners he saw the colonel in front of him, with shoulders still shaking, and they all proceeded, slowly and irresistibly, towards the capture of an imaginary Serre. When they had reached their final objective, there was a long pause; and the men, now thoroughly bored and disillusioned, leaned idly on their rifles, waiting. It was a victory for method. Presently there was another movement. Companies fell in on markers, the men seemed to wake out of a dream, and took a spontaneous interest in the proceedings, and the battalion moved off the field. The colonel had a horse waiting for him on the road, and about dusk they came to Bus-les-Artois.

Bourne ran into Sergeant Tozer in Bus, and with Shem and Martlow they made a reconnaissance of the town, visiting the Y.M.C.A., and then an estaminet, where they fell in with Sergeant Morgan, the bombing sergeant. They talked for a little while on the events of the day, and the splendours of the staff.

'Are them buggers coming over the top wi' us?' asked Martlow, innocently; and when the others laughed at him, he continued, indignantly. 'Then what did they come out wi' us today for, swingin' their weight about? That bugger on the black 'orse spoke to the colonel just as tho' 'e took 'im for a lance-jack. Wunner the colonel stood it.'

He and Shem went off to the cinema; so Bourne and the two sergeants found a little place where they could get rum and coffee; after which they went off to bed.

They were signalling with flags in the morning when their work was interrupted, and with others in the field they were fallen in, in two ranks. The adjutant came up from the orderly-room, which was a small hut on the other side of the road. He was followed by two military policemen, between whom was Miller, capless, and no longer with a stripe on his arm. He was white and haggard, but his mouth was half-open in an idiotic grin, and the small furtive eyes wandered restlessly along the line of men drawn up in front of him. Bourne felt a strange emotion rising in him which was not pity, but a revulsion from this degradation of a man, who was now only an abject outcast. In a clear, anxious voice, rather like that of a schoolboy reading a lesson, the adjutant read out a statement that Lance-Corporal Miller had been found guilty of deserting his commanding officer, and had been sentenced to be shot, the sentence being afterwards commuted to one of penal servitude for twenty years. The parade was dismissed again, and the miserable man was marched away to be exhibited to another company. Miller would not, of course, go at once to gaol, the execution of the sentence would be deferred until the war ended. Men could not be allowed to choose gaol as an alternative to military service. That was where the absurdity arose, as Bourne understood the matter; because one could foresee that, when peace was restored, a general amnesty would be granted which would cover all cases of this kind; and the tragedy, but for the act of unspeakable humiliation which they had just witnessed, became a farce.

'We're goin' up to take over trenches tomorrow,' said Corporal Hamley, 'and this is just to encourage any other bugger who thinks o' desertin'.'

'It don't make no differ whether th'art shot be thy own folk or be Germans, if th'art shot,' said Weeper, pessimistically.

The corporal was right. The battalion paraded in fighting order at ten o'clock next morning, and moved up the line to take over trenches. They marched by the divisional artillery H.Q. at Bertrancourt, to Courcelles-aux-Bois, a village the greater part of which was already derelict. From there a road ran up to Colincamps, at the corner of which stood a military policeman as control, beside a red board, the kind of wooden standard used by road-menders as a danger signal, on which was painted in white letters: *Gas Alert On*. The reverse side was painted with the words *Gas Alert Off*; but it seemed a matter of indifference to everyone which way the board was turned.

After that point a wide interval was left between the various platoons. Almost as soon as they left Courcelles, the road, mounting the hill to Colincamps, was under direct observation of the enemy for about three hundred yards, so it had been camouflaged with netting like fishing nets, hung as a curtain between poles on the left side of the road. At the top of the hill was a bend, and, commanding the road, as well as another lesser road, was a more than usually substantial barn, a kind of bastion to the outskirts of Colincamps itself. Bourne thought what an ugly place it would be if it were in the hands of Fritz.

They were moving in dead silence now, not that the Hun could overhear them; and the interval between the various platoons must have been about one hundred yards. It implied a lively sense of favours to come. Passing the barn, there was a sharp bend first to the right then to the left, and they entered the long straight street of Colincamps. Jerry had registered on the church tower, which had a large hole in it, near the top; and the front of a house, on which still hung forlornly a sign, Café de la Jeunesse, had been stove in by another shell. There was not an undamaged house left, and some of the mud-built barns were collapsing, as an effect of repeated explosions in their neighbourhood. The street itself had suffered from heavy shelling, though some of the holes in the roadway had been filled in, when they did not allow of sufficient room for traffic to skirt them; the others had been converted into pools of very liquid mud. The same fine mud coated the whole surface of the roadway, and the mere pressure of one's foot was sufficient to set it oozing from the matrix in which the metalling was, now somewhat loosely, embedded.

The street ended, and the houses with it, on meeting a road linking it with Mailly-Maillet on the right, and on the left continuing to the sugar refinery, where it joined the main road from Mailly-Maillet to Serre. They turned left, downhill, the road curving into the valley, and there was another military control, with a dugout under the road where he could shelter. From that point the road, so long as it was on the slope of the hill, would be visible from the enemy lines. Visibility was poor today, there was a fine ground mist which made the distance vague. Even in the daylight, there was something beautiful and mysterious in that landscape. A line of woods, well away from the road, but gradually converging on it, though of no great depth, and shattered by shelling, curtained their movements once they were down the hill. Leaving the road, and picking their way between gun-pits and dugouts, they came again to Southern Avenue. The shell-crater was now half-full of water, but there was a new one about twenty yards away.

Thence, onward, they followed the route they had taken on working parties, until they came to the big dugout in Legend Trench, which was battalion headquarters. There were two entrances, and about thirty steps to the bottom. Part of it was screened off with blankets for the officers, and the rest was allotted to the men. There was a small recess near the stairs, in which the sergeant-major or quartermaster-sergeant could sit at a table improvised from a box, and where a few stores were kept. Four or five candles stuck on tins lit it, and the air was foul and smoky.

Shem, Bourne and Martlow were sitting close to the door, three minutes after they had taken possession, when the sergeant-major, after the adjutant had spoken to him, turned to them.

''Ere, you three men. You go back to Colincamps, an' in one of the first 'ouses you come to, there's a runner's relay post; you'll find some Gordons there. You'll take over from them, see? Brigade messages will be 'anded to you, an' you'll bring 'em on 'ere; an' our runners will take you messages, which you'll carry on to Brigade at Courcelles. Got it? Well, get a move on.'

They got up, and as they were pulling in their belts, Weeper, who had been sitting next to Shem, looked up at Bourne with a snarling grin, and said something about a cushy job, and some people being always lucky. Bourne did not trouble to reply, thinking, after what he had seen of the road, that headquarters dugout in the support trenches would have satisfied him. Martlow, however, had to say something.

'You 'ave a good sleep, ol' tear gas, an' then you'll feel better.'

They climbed out of the dugout, and set off back to Colincamps.

They had a bread-and-cheese ration in their haversacks. One of them would have to draw their full rations later.

'I wonder why Smart has got a set on me,' said Bourne, reflectively.

''Cause you never take any notice of 'im when 'e starts grousin' at you,' said Martlow.

'I believe you're right,' said Shem; 'but I'm a bit sorry for Weeper. He's always been an awfully good man up the line, at least they all say so in D Company. He hasn't got any friends; and he's so bloody miserable that he never will have any. You see, Bourne, you make friends with everybody, whether he's a cook, or a shoemaker, or a sergeant-major, or only Martlow and myself. Until you came along, well, I mucked in all right with the others, but I didn't have any particular chum, so I know what it feels –'

'*Christ! Look out!*' said Bourne, crouching, but his warning was unheard in the shrieking hiss and explosion which followed almost simultaneously. There was a huge eruption of mud, earth and stones a few yards behind the trench. They waited, tense and white, spattered with mud.

'Let's get out o' this place,' said Martlow, in a shaken whisper, and, as he spoke, another came over. They held their breath as it exploded, further away than the first. Bourne was looking at Martlow, and saw that his underlip had fallen and was trembling a little. A third shell hissed for an appreciably longer time and exploded nearer to the dump. They waited motionless.

'It's bloody lucky that first shell wasn't closer, or we should have been buried,' said Shem, with a rather lopsided grin, after an interval.

'Come on, kid,' said Bourne to Martlow. 'You never hear the one that gets you.'

'I'm not worryin',' said Martlow, quietly.

'It must have been twenty yards off the trench,' said Bourne; 'but I'm not getting out to see. I think it would be better to use Railway Avenue. Fritz seems to have got Southern pretty well taped out; and I shouldn't like to be close to a big dixie like that in Sackville Street.'

'You can't tell,' said Shem, indifferently. 'You've just got to chance it.'

They were moving along at a fair pace, and were soon clear of trenches. The mud along the level by the dump was greasy, and slowed them down a bit; but on reaching the road it was easier going. Bourne asked the control where the relay post was; and they turned into the second yard on the right. There was not a sign of life there, and the houses on that side of the street had suffered more severely than on the other; little of them was left. Most of the buildings abutting on the street were byres and stables, at least at that end of the town. The houses stood farther back, just on the crest of the slope. Not seeing anyone, they shouted, and from a stable came a reply, and a great wooden door opened. They found three Gordons there, very far from gay. They were, however, very decent civil men, and they looked as though they had earned a rest. Their faces had forgotten, at least for the time being, how to smile. They looked at the colours sewn on their successors' haversacks and sleeves, which they knew meant business.

'We've come to take over from you,' said Bourne.

'Thought you weren't comin'. Saw some o' oor chaps gae by...'

'Oh, the relief isn't complete yet,' said Bourne, cheerfully. 'They took us up the trenches and then sent us back. If they can do anything backwards in the army, they will, you know. It's the tradition of the service. What's it like here?'

'Oh, it's cushy enough,' answered the Gordon, in a resigned voice.

'I had a bet with myself you would say that,' said Bourne.

They looked at him curiously, perplexed by his manner, as they completed the business of putting their equipment together, fastening on their water bottles, haversacks, and entrenching tools. Their packs they carried slung, that is, without fastening them to their cross-straps, a practice which is irregular. On active service, however, the authorities allowed the men to use a little intelligence with regard to minor details, except on great occasions. At last, taking up their rifles, they moved to the door.

'Gude day t' ye, an' gude luck, chums,' they said as they went out.

'Good luck,' answered their successors, in more matter-of-fact tones. Bourne looked after them a little wistfully. He didn't grudge them the relief. He wondered when they would all be turning their backs on this desolation.

'I'm goin' to 'ave a peek round the village,' said Martlow. 'You won't want me, there'll be nothin' doin' yet awhile.'

'All right,' said Bourne; 'don't go far away, and don't be long.'

He returned in about twenty minutes with all kinds of luxuries: tea mixed with sugar, four tins of bully-beef, a tin of Maconachie, and tins of pork and beans, the kind in which there was never any pork.

'I scrounged them from some R.E.'s,' he said with a sober pride. 'They're movin' out, an' 'ave a lot o' stuff they don't want to carry. I could 'ave got more if I'd wanted. They're that glad to be goin' they'd give you all they've got. So it don't matter if we don't get no rations till night.'

'Good lad,' said Bourne. 'You are a champion scrounger, Martlow.'

He was thinking that the anxiety of the R.E.'s to get away did not indicate that it was a particularly cushy place. Shem had also been reconnoitring the position, and announced that there was a decent cellar, with most of a house in ruins on top of it, only about twenty yards away. Martlow then decorated the door with a paper on which he had printed with an indelible pencil RELAY POST in block letters.

'Well, we may as well have some tea an' bully,' said Shem.

It was after one o'clock, so they set to and had a good comforting meal and lounged about smoking until a little after two, when a message came from the trenches. One of the regular runners brought it, with Pacey. It was a regulation that two runners should take a message together, in case one might be wounded, but this was often disregarded owing to a shortage of runners: it was tacitly assumed that one of them would go at a time, so that in case of simultaneous messages both ways the post would not be without a man on duty. Shem and Martlow took the message to Brigade H.Q, just the other side of Courcelles, and Pacey and Hankin, the regular runner, sat and yarned with Bourne for a few minutes.

'You look all right 'ere, but Fritz 'as been bashin' the place about, 'asn't 'e?' said Pacey.

Part of the mud wall had come away, leaving only laths. After a cigarette, Pacey and Hankin set off back to the trenches. Bourne sat in a kind of reverie for about half an hour until Shem and Martlow returned, and idle talk continued for a time.

The whole air suddenly became alive, and crash after crash filled the town. They were stunned, and petrified, for a moment. More of the mud wall fell away, and there was a landslide of tiles. They cowered down, as though they wanted to shrink away to nothing. It was heavy stuff coming over. One shell struck the Café de la Jeunesse, and another corner of it went flying in all directions; loose tiles kept falling, and the walls rapidly became threadbare lath, merely from the effects of the concussion.

Bourne felt himself shaking, but they couldn't stay there.

'Get into that cellar!' he shouted to them; and grabbing their rifles and water bottles, which they had taken out, they moved out uncertainly. Bourne felt his breath coming heavily. Shells were bumping practically the whole length of the village. He didn't know what to do about the relay post; and though he felt an awful fool, he decided. 'I'll be after you,' he shouted, and running as a man runs into a rainstorm, he disappeared into the street. He turned the corner and continued downhill to the control's dugout. On the hillside just beyond the control's dugout a man lay dead. His tin hat was blown some yards away, and the top of the head had been taken off, so that at a glance one saw some remnants of the scattered brains. Apparently the whole of Colincamps was going west, clouds of smoke and dust rose from it. Bourne fell down the steps of the dugout. He couldn't say why he was there at first.

'There's a man dead outside, sergeant,' he said, dully.

'What the bloody hell are you doin' out in it? Are you sure 'e's dead?'

'Yes, sergeant; most of the head's gone. I'm at the relay post, runners. I thought I had better tell you that we had left the stable, and gone into the cellar of the house.'

'I'm goin' out to see to that man.'

They doubled out to him, and finding that he was really dead, shifted him off the road; and went into the dugout again.

'I'm going back now, sergeant.'

'You 'ad better wait a bit,' said the sergeant in a kindlier voice. 'You know it's against regulations for you chaps to go alone. There ought to be a pair of you.'

'I had better go back. I didn't know whether we ought to move, as I have not been on the job before. I'll go back to see how my chums are.'

'All right,' said the sergeant, in a curiously irritable way. 'Write up on the door where you are.'

The shelling was still violent, but seemed to be worse at the corner in the direction of Courcelles, and to have extended on this side farther along the Mailly-Maillet road. As Bourne came out, he could see shells exploding by the dump, with some shrapnel bursting, woolly-bears they called them, overhead. He couldn't say whether it was with a prayer or a curse that he made for the corner of Colincamps, doubling up the short rise with difficulty. Collapsing houses had spilt their bricks half across the street. One wall, about sixty yards away from him, suddenly crumpled and fell. He wouldn't look at things. He found himself saying over and over again in soldiers' language: 'I've been out of the bloody shit too long': not uttering the words but thinking them with a curious intensity. His vision seemed narrowed to a point immediately in front of him. When he got to the stable they had left, he went straight to Martlow's notice, and drawing a rough arrow underneath the words 'RELAY POST', wrote in rough blocks the words 'IN CELLAR'. Then he went to it, noticing as he descended that the entrance was turned the wrong way. Shem and Martlow looked at him, but he could scarcely see their faces in the gloom.

'What's it like now?' asked Martlow, with a very slight catch in his voice.

'Oh, it's cushy enough,' said Bourne, with desperate humour.

Suddenly he felt inexpressibly tired. He bowed his head and sat gazing into nothing, emptied of all effort. The shells bumped for some time longer, slackened, and then ceased. Bourne had the sensation that the earth was left steaming.

A drizzle of rain began, and increasing by degrees filled the quiet with little trickling sounds. The cellar was comfortably furnished, as it had apparently been used as a funk-hole before, and by people of more importance than its present occupants. Its sole defect was that the entrance directly faced the Hun lines, and perhaps this inconvenience had prompted them to leave; but during their tenancy they had put in three beds, wooden frames standing about two feet off the floor, over which rabbit-netting had been stretched and nailed, as a substitute for spring mattresses. Some rather thin Wilson canvas curtained the entrance. Bourne remembered that there was some thicker sacking, in the stable which they had left, and he proposed to get it, and nail it over the outside of the doorway.

They went back, together, to their old quarters. Little of the stable was left except its frame, some laths, and a few tiles, still hanging precariously on the slats overhead, through which, now, the rain fell steadily. They wrenched some nails from the timbers, and Shem and Martlow fastened the extra sacking on the doorway of the cellar. Bourne wandered off by himself for a moment. He found that the premises included their own private latrine. He had been silent and preoccupied since coming back from the control, and had said nothing about the man killed on the hillside. He didn't want to talk.

'Bourne's getting windy,' said Shem to Martlow.

''E weren't windy goin' out in that lot,' said Martlow, repelling the suggestion.

'Yes, he was,' said Shem, chuckling; 'that's just why he went.'

'If it comes to that, we're all windy,' grunted Martlow, loyally.

There was some truth in Shem's observation, all the same. Bourne came back in a few minutes, and, having inspected the curtain, he lit a small piece of candle. Martlow was going out, and was told to report if any light were visible from outside.

'There will be a message to take up the line, soon,' said Bourne to Shem. 'I might as well go by myself, I think. I want to try and scrounge a couple of candles from the quarter-bloke.'

'Then I'll take the midnight message to Brigade,' said Shem.

Martlow returned. The light did not show from outside, but it did, of course, when the curtains were twitched aside. They were too close together for them to hope that a man entering would lift first one and then the other. Bourne said they would have to cover or blow out the light on entering or leaving. Then, as the candle was all they had, they blew it out and talked in the dark; Fritz sent three shells over, a regular interval between them.

Our own guns had been completely silent during the strafe. Now, however, after an appreciable pause, a trench-mortar battery sent three back to the Hun; and then, after an interval to give emphasis and point to their reply, added another for luck. Bourne looked at his wristwatch, and saw that it was a couple of minutes after six.

'That sounded like a regular stunt,' he said.

A few minutes later they heard a couple of men shouting above-ground, and Martlow, going halfway up the steps, called to them. Two runners from Brigade came in, and when the sacking curtain had been put in place, Bourne lit the candle.

'Thought you'd all gone west,' said one runner, 'when I saw the bloody barn.'

'I left a notice on the door,' said Bourne, thoughtlessly.

'Well, I can't read it in the bloody dark, can I?' objected the runner. ''Ere's the usual. We'll 'ave a fag, before we go back, chum. You chaps know 'ow to make yourselves comfortable.'

'It's the first duty of a good soldier,' said Bourne.

They talked about the strafe; now that it was over, none of them exaggerated its importance.

'Only a few shells came into Courcelles,' said the runner; 'but we knew Colincamps and the dump were getting it.'

'I'm going now,' said Bourne. 'Don't show any light.'

'You're getting wind-up,' said Shem, laughing.

'Wind-up! 'E's talkin' bloody sense,' said the runner. 'You don't want to take any bloody chances up 'ere, I can tell you. It looks to me as though Jerry 'ad rumbled somethin' already.'

That was Bourne's notion, but he did not pursue the subject.

'D'you go alone?' they asked him.

'Yes, we nearly always go alone,' answered Bourne. 'Goodnight.'

Martlow covered the light with a can, as Bourne moved out into the dark. It was very dark, and the rain was fine, searching and cold. He would keep to the road as far as the dump, it was no use trying a short cut, and the wet surface of the road was at least visible, lots of little pools gleaming in it. The control was not there. Some instinctive scruple moved Bourne to avoid the side of the road where he had found the dead man, and, looking to where they had carried the body, he saw that it had been removed.

The dump was empty. In another couple of hours it would be alive with men and transport. He had a kind of talent for moving about sure-footedly in the dark. He did not mind the rain and he loved the quiet. There were fewer star-shells tonight, and the rain made their expanding and contracting haloes even more mysterious than usual.

He handed in the message, and then spoke to Corporal Hamley, who was with Sergeant-Major Corbet, about the strafe.

'Well, Captain Malet is out of it, now,' said the sergeant-major.

'What happened to Captain Malet, sergeant-major?' he asked, anxiously.

'Dugout blown in; a beam fell on him, an' broke both his legs. They were some time before they got him clear, they had to dig under the beam. They wanted to take a couple of rifles as splints for his legs, until they got him to the dressing-station; but he wouldn't have it. "You may want 'em more than I do," he said. 'You get me a couple of miles away from here and I'm laughing.' When they were getting him out he smoked a cigarette and didn't say a word, though they must have hurt him.'

'Anyone else hurt?' asked Bourne.

'A boy called Bates was killed, and two others wounded or hurt. I haven't heard all the details. B Company had a few casualties. We had a sentry over the dugout wounded. Matheson. D'you know him? You came from A Company, didn't you? Thought so. Someone told me Captain Malet was going to get the colonel to recommend you for a commission, wasn't he? What are you going to do about it, now?'

While the sergeant-major was speaking of Bates having been killed, Bourne tried to remember who Bates was; and, at the effort of memory to recover him, he seemed to hear a high, excited voice suddenly cry out, as though actually audible to the whole dugout: 'What's 'e want to drag me into 't for?'

And it was as though Bates were bodily present there; the sergeant-major's voice seemed less real. In the light of the unsteady candles, each haloed in the fog of smoke, Bourne saw all the quiet men, some half-asleep, some staring in front of them, thinking and waiting. He felt as though he were under some extraordinary hallucination, but he answered the sergeant-major reasonably enough, said he would have a talk to him when they went out of trenches again, suggested speaking to Mr Rhys; and all the time he heard his own voice saying things, which somehow did not seem to concern him, meaningless things which had to be taken very seriously. He knew no more of Bill Bates than that one phrase, passionately innocent: 'What's 'e want to drag me into 't for?'

'Could I get our rations now, sergeant-major?' he said, evenly. 'I have brought a mess-tin, for our rum ration; and I was going to ask if we could have some candles. We left the barn we were in, and moved into a cellar; and we need a bit of light.'

'Who told you to leave the barn an' go into a cellar?'

'Oh, Fritz did. And the barn came unstuck. After the tiles had fallen off, and the walls began to tumble down, I thought we ought to go to ground. I told the sergeant on control duty where we would be, and I left a notice on the door. We're in the same yard, but in the cellar of the house. As all that is left of the house is a couple of thousand bricks, piled up in a heap on top of the cellar, we ought to be fairly safe there; only the entrance faces the line, and we have to be careful to screen the light.'

'I can only let you have a couple of candles,' said the quartermaster-sergeant.

'Oh, make it three, sir,' said Bourne, in a tone of coaxing protest, and a little grudgingly the quarter-bloke dealt him out another, while Bourne talked to keep from thinking.

'Just before I got to the control's dugout, there was a man killed on the road. We lifted him to one side. He was a gunner, I think ... I can take the rum ration in my mess-tin, sir ... It made us all a bit windy, I think. There's not quite so much of Colincamps left as when you last saw it, sergeant-major.'

'It's my belief Fritz has rumbled us,' said the sergeant-major in a whisper.

'What can you expect?' said Bourne, pointing to the bright yellow material sewn on his haversack. 'We are decked out in all the colours of the rainbow, and then marched over the whole countryside in order to advertise the show. Anyone can see we are in war paint. We are put into khaki, so as to be more or less invisible; and then rigged up in colours, so that we can be seen. It's genius.'

'That's so as the artillery can spot us,' said the sergeant-major soberly.

'Whose, sergeant-major?'

'You're a sarky devil, you are.'

'There's your bag o' rations, and don't lose the bag, see?' said the quarter-bloke.

'All right, sir, thank you. I suppose I ought to be moving back. I am sorry about Captain Malet, but I suppose he's lucky. Do you think there's anything to go back, sir? I might save another man a walk.'

'Go and wait inside for a few minutes,' said the sergeant-major; they were all in the recess at the foot of the steps.

'I shall be seeing the adjutant presently. It's all bloody rot having that relay post at Colincamps, in my opinion. The Brigade runners might easily come up here, and our runners go down to Courcelles. Wait a few minutes, and I'll see.'

Bourne went in and sat by Weeper, who neither moved nor spoke to him; and after a few minutes the sergeant-major came in.

'You may go back, Bourne; there probably won't be anything but the report at midnight. Goodnight.'

'Goodnight, sergeant-major,' he said, and, taking up his rifle, climbed up the stairs into the rain and darkness again.

When he got back to the cellar, he found that Martlow had brought in a stray terrier. The dog was obviously suffering from shellshock, he was trembling in a piteous way, and Martlow said that when he had caught him, he had tried to bite. The only domestic animal which Bourne had met among these deserted ruins had been a gaunt and savage cat, which, on seeing him, had cursed the whole human race, and fled precipitately. They had supper, and some hot tea with their rum, persuaded the dog to eat a little bully, and then lay smoking on their beds. They heard trains of limbers passing through the village. Bourne and Martlow curled up to sleep, and Shem waited for the night report to take it back to Courcelles.

In the morning at seven o'clock Fritz sent over his three shells, and the trench mortar battery barked out the same reply as on the previous night. Fritz's shells had fallen very close. Martlow went out first, and then put his head through the doorway to announce that the latrine had been blown up; where it had stood there was nothing but a large hole.

'Well, what do you want,' said Shem; 'a bloody bathroom?'

The dog had another fit of shivering when the shells came over but it recovered later, and Martlow took it outside for a short walk. Exploring the ruins a native instinct got the better of the dog's recently acquired caution, and it disappeared out of history in the pursuit of a cat.

''E were a good dog, that,' said Martlow, regretfully.

Solomon In All His Glory
G. A. Studdert Kennedy

> Still I see them coming, coming,
> In their ragged broken line,
> Walking wounded in the sunlight,
> Clothed in majesty divine.

For the fairest of the lilies,
That God's summer ever sees,
Ne'er was clothed in royal beauty
Such as decks the least of these.
Tattered, torn, and bloody khaki,
Gleams of white flesh in the sun,
Raiment worthy of their beauty,
And the great things they have done.
Purple robes and snowy linen
Have for earthly kings sufficed,
But these bloody sweaty tatters
Were the robes of Jesus Christ.

The Appearance of the Tank
From *The Battle of The Somme: The September Campaign,* John Buchan

On Tuesday, 12th September, a comprehensive bombardment began all along the British front from Thiepval to Ginchy. The whole of Sir Henry Rawlinson's Fourth Army was destined for the action, as well the right corps – the First Canadian – of the Fifth Army, while on the left of the battle to another division was allotted a preliminary attack, which was partly in the nature of a feint and partly a necessary preparatory step. The immediate objective of the different units must be clearly noted. On the left of the main front one Canadian division was directed against Courcelette. On their right a division of the New Army – that Scottish division which had won high honour at Loos – had for its task to clear the remains of the old Switch line and encircle Martinpuich, but not – on the first day at any rate – to attempt the capture of what was believed to be a most formidable stronghold. Going south, two Territorial divisions – Northumbrian and London – had to clear High Wood. On their right the New Zealanders had Flers as their objective, while two divisions of the New Army had to make good the ground east and north of

Delville Wood. Next to them the Guards and a division of the old Regulars were to move north-east from Ginchy against Lesboeufs and Morval, while on the extreme right of the British front another division of London Territorials were to carry Bouleaux Wood and form a defensive flank. It had been agreed between Sir Douglas Haig and General Foch that Combles should not be directly attacked, but pinched by an advance on both sides of it. This advance was no easy problem, for, in Sir Douglas Haig's words, 'the line of the French advance was narrowed almost to a defile by the extensive and strongly fortified wood of St Pierre Vaast on the one side, and on the other by the Combles valley.' The closest co-operation was necessary to enable the two Commands to solve a highly intricate tactical problem.

The British force to be used in the new advance was for the most part fresh. The Guards had not been in action since Loos the previous September, the Canadians were new to the Somme area, while it was the first experience of the New Zealanders on the Western Front. Two of the divisions had been some considerable time already in the front trenches, but the others had been brought up for the purpose only a few days before. All the troops were of the best quality, and had a proud record behind them. More perhaps than any other part of the battle this was an action of the British *corps d'élite*.

In this stage, too, a new weapon was to be used. The 'tanks,' officially known as 'Machine Gun Corps, Heavy Section,' had come out from home some time before, and had been parked in secluded spots at the back of the Front. The world is now familiar with descriptions and pictures of those strange machines, which, shaped like monstrous toads, crawled imperturbably over wire and parapets, butted down houses, shouldered trees aside, and humped themselves over the stoutest walls. They were an experiment which could only be proved in practice, and the design in using them at this stage was principally to find out their weak points, so as to perfect their mechanism for the future. Their main tactical purpose was to clear out redoubts and nests of machine guns which, as we had found to our sorrow at Loos, might hang up the most resolute troops.

For this object they must precede the infantry attack, and the task of assembling them before the parapets were crossed was fraught with difficulty, for they were neither silent nor inconspicuous. The things had been kept a profound secret, and until the very eve of the advance few in the British army had even heard of them. On 14th September, the day before our attack, some of them were seen by German aeroplanes, and the German troops were warned that the British had some strange new engine. Rumours also seem to have reached Germany five or six weeks earlier, for orders had been issued to supply the soldiers with a special kind of armour-piercing bullet. But as to the real nature of the device the Germans had no inkling. They had not grasped the principle, and it is doubtful if they have grasped it yet.

On the night of Thursday, the 14th, the Fifth Army carried out their preliminary task. On a front of a thousand yards south-east of Thiepval a brigade of the New Army stormed the Hohenzollern trench and the strong redoubt which the Germans called the *Wunderwerk*, taking many prisoners and themselves losing little. The fame of this enterprise has been somewhat obscured by the great advance which followed, but it was a most workmanlike and skilful performance, and it had a real effect on the subsequent battle. It deceived the enemy as to the exact terrain of the main assault, and it caused him to launch a counter-attack in an area which was part of the principal battle-ground, with the result that our left wing, after checking his attack, was able to catch him on the rebound.

The morning of Friday, 15th September, was perfect autumn weather, with a light mist filling the hollows and shrouding the slopes. At 6 a.m. the British bombardment, which had now lasted for three days, rose to the fury of hurricane fire. The enemy had a thousand guns of all calibres massed against us, and his defences consisted of a triple line of entrenchments and a series of advanced posts manned by machine guns. Our earlier bombardment had cut his wire and destroyed many of his trenches, besides hampering greatly his bringing up of men, rations, and shells. The final twenty minutes of intense fire, slowly creeping forward with our infantry close under its shadow, pinned him to his positions and interfered with his counter-barrage. To an observer it seemed that the deafening crescendo all round the horizon was wholly British.

At twenty minutes past six our men crossed the parapets and moved forward methodically towards the enemy. The Germans, manning their trenches as our guns lengthened, saw through the thin mist inhuman shapes crawling towards them, things like gigantic slugs, spitting fire from their mottled sides. They had been warned of a new weapon, but what mortal weapon was this terror that walked by day? And ere they could collect their dazed wits the British bayonets were upon them.

On the left and centre the attack was instantly successful. The Canadians, after beating off the German counter-attack, carried Courcelette in the afternoon. In this advance French-Canadian troops played a distinguished part in winning back some miles of French soil for their ancient motherland. On their right the Scottish division, which had already been six weeks in line, performed something more than the task allotted it. The capture of Martinpuich was not part of the programme of the day's operations, but the Scots pushed east and west of the village, and at a quarter past five in the evening had the place in their hands. Farther south there was fierce fighting in the old cockpit of High Wood. It was two months since we had first effected an entrance into its ill-omened shades, but we had been forced back, and for long had to be content with its southern corner. The strong German third line – which ran across its northern half on the very crest of the ridge – and the endless craters and machine-gun redoubts made it a desperate nut to crack. We had pushed out horns to east and west of it, but the northern stronghold in the wood itself had defied all our efforts. It was held on that day by troops of the 2nd Bavarian Corps, and the German ranks have shown no better fighting stuff. Our first attack failed, but on a second attempt the London Territorials, a little after noon, swept the place clear, though not without heavy losses.

Beyond them the New Zealand Division, with a New Army Division on its right, carried the Switch line and took Flers with little trouble. They were preceded by a tank, which waddled complacently up the main street of the village, with the enemy's bullets rattling harmlessly off its sides, followed by cheering and laughing British troops. Farther south we advanced our front for nearly a mile and a half. A light division of the New Army, debouching from Delville Wood, cleared Mystery Corner on its eastern side before the general attack began, and then with splendid élan pushed forward north of Ginchy in the direction of Lesboeufs.

Only on the right wing was the tale of success incomplete. Ginchy, it will be remembered, had been carried by Irish troops on 9th September, but its environs were not yet fully cleared, and the enemy held the formidable point known as the Quadrilateral. This was situated about 700 yards east of Ginchy at a bend of the Morval road, where it passed through a deep wooded ravine. One of the old Regular divisions was directed against it, with the Guards on their left and the London Territorials on their right. The business of the last-named was to carry Bouleaux Wood and form a defensive flank north of Combles, while the Guards were to advance from Ginchy on Lesboeufs. But the strength of the Quadrilateral foiled the plan. The Londoners did indeed enter Bouleaux Wood, but the division on their left was fatally hung up in front of the Quadrilateral, and this in turn exposed the right flank of the Guards. The Guards Brigades advanced, as they have always advanced, with perfect discipline and courage. But both their flanks were enfiladed; the front of attack was too narrow; the sunken road before them was strongly held by machine guns; they somewhat lost direction; and, in consequence, no part of our right attack gained its full objective. There, and in High Wood, we incurred most of the casualties of the day. The check was the more regrettable since complete success in this area was tactically more important than elsewhere.

But after all deductions were made the day's results were in a high degree satisfactory. We had broken in one day through three of the enemy's main defensive systems, and on a front of over six miles had advanced to an average depth of a mile. It was the most effective blow yet dealt at the enemy by British troops. It gave us not only the high ground between Thiepval and the Combles valley, but placed us well down the forward slopes. 'The damage to the enemy's *morale*,' said the official summary, 'is probably of greater consequence than the seizure of dominating positions and the capture of between four and five thousand prisoners.' Three famous Bavarian divisions had been engaged and completely shattered, and the whole enemy front thrown into a state of disorder. The tanks had, for a new experiment, done wonders. Some of them broke down on the way up, and, of the twenty-four which crossed the German lines, seven came to grief early in the day. The remaining seventeen did brilliant service, some squatting on enemy trenches and clearing them by machine-gun fire, some flattening out uncut wire, others destroying machine-gun nests and redoubts or strong points like the sugar factory at Courcelette. But their moral effect was greater than the material damage they wrought. The sight of those deliberate, impersonal engines ruthlessly grinding down the most cherished defences put something like panic into troops who had always prided themselves upon the superior merit of their own fighting 'machine.' Beyond doubt, too, the presence of the tanks added greatly to the zeal and confidence of our assaulting infantry. An element of sheer comedy was introduced into the grim business of war, and comedy is dear to the heart of the British soldier. The crews of the tanks – which they called His Majesty's Landships – seemed to have acquired some of the light-heartedness of the British sailor. Penned up in a narrow stuffy space, condemned to a form of motion compared with which that of the queasiest vessel was steady, and at the mercy of unknown perils, these adventurers faced their task with the zest of a boy on holiday. With infinite humour they described how the enemy had surrounded them when they were stuck, and had tried in vain to crack their shell, while they themselves sat laughing inside.

In the achievements of the day our aircraft nobly co-operated. They destroyed thirteen hostile machines and drove nine more in a broken condition to ground. They bombarded enemy headquarters and vital points on all his railway lines. They destroyed German kite balloons and so put out the eyes of the defence. They guided our artillery fire and they brought back frequent and accurate reports of every stage in the infantry advance. Moreover, they attacked both enemy artillery and infantry with their machine-gun fire from a low elevation. Such performances were a proof of that resolute and exalted spirit of the offensive which inspired all arms of the service. In the week of the action on the whole Somme battleground only fourteen enemy machines managed to cross our lines, while our airplanes made between two thousand and three thousand flights far behind the German front.

When I Come Home
Leslie Coulson

When I come home, dear folk o' mine,
We'll drink a cup of olden wine;
And yet, however rich it be,
No wine will taste so good to me
As English air. How I shall thrill
To drink it in on Hampstead Hill
When I come home!

When I come home, and leave behind
Dark things I would not call to mind,
I'll taste good ale and home-made bread,
And see white sheets and pillows spread.
And there is one who'll softly creep
To kiss me, ere I fall asleep,
And tuck me 'neath the counterpane,
And I shall be a boy again,
 When I come home!

When I come home from dark to light,
And tread the roadways long and white,
And tramp the lanes I tramped of yore,

And see the village greens once more,
The tranquil farms, the meadows free,
The friendly trees that nod to me,
And hear the lark beneath the sun,
'Twill be good pay for what I've done,
When I come home!

1917

Returning, We Hear the Larks
Isaac Rosenberg

Sombre the night is.
And though we have our lives, we know
What sinister threat lies there.

Dragging these anguished limbs, we only know
This poison-blasted track opens on our camp –
On a little safe sleep.

But hark! joy – joy – strange joy.
Lo! heights of night ringing with unseen larks.
Music showering our upturned list'ning faces.

Death could drop from the dark
As easily as song –
But song only dropped,
Like a blind man's dreams on the sand
By dangerous tides,
Like a girl's dark hair for she dreams no ruin lies there,
Or her kisses where a serpent hides.

Claude Enlists
From *One of Ours*, Willa Cather

During the bleak month of March, Mr Wheeler went to town in his buckboard almost every day. For the first time in his life he had a secret anxiety. The one member of his family who had never given him the slightest trouble, his son Bayliss, was just now under a cloud.

Bayliss was a Pacifist, and kept telling people that if only the United States would stay out of this war, and gather up what Europe was wasting, she would soon be in actual possession of the capital of the world. There was a kind of logic in Bayliss' utterances that shook Nat Wheeler's imperturbable assumption that one point of view was as good as another. When Bayliss fought the dram and the cigarette, Wheeler only laughed. That a son of his should turn out a Prohibitionist, was a joke he could appreciate.

But Bayliss' attitude in the present crisis disturbed him. Day after day he sat about his son's place of business, interrupting his arguments with funny stories. Bayliss did not go home at all that month. He said to his father, 'No, Mother's too violent. I'd better not.'

Claude and his mother read the papers in the evening, but they talked so little about what they read that Mahailey inquired anxiously whether they weren't still fighting over yonder. When she could get Claude alone for a moment, she pulled out Sunday supplement pictures of the devastated countries and asked him to tell her what was to become of this family, photographed among the ruins of their home; of this old woman, who sat by the roadside with her bundles.

'Where's she goin' to, anyways? See, Mr Claude, she's got her iron cook pot, pore old thing, carryin' it all the way!'

Pictures of soldiers in gas-masks puzzled her; gas was something she hadn't learned about in the Civil War, so she worked it out for herself that these masks were worn by the army cooks, to protect their eyes when they were cutting up onions!

'All them onions they have to cut up, it would put their eyes out if they didn't wear somethin',' she argued.

On the morning of the eighth of April Claude came downstairs early and began to clean his boots, which were caked with dry mud. Mahailey was squatting down beside her stove, blowing and puffing into it. The fire was always slow to start in heavy weather. Claude got an old knife and a brush, and putting his foot on a chair over by the west window, began to scrape his shoe. He had said good morning to Mahailey, nothing more. He hadn't slept well, and was pale.

'Mr Claude,' Mahailey grumbled, 'this stove ain't never drawed good like my old one Mr Ralph took away from me. I can't do nothin' with it. Maybe you'll clean it out for me next Sunday.'

'I'll clean it today, if you say so. I won't be here next Sunday. I'm going away.'

Something in his tone made Mahailey get up, her eyes still blinking with the smoke, and look at him sharply. 'You ain't goin' off there where Miss Enid is?' she asked anxiously.

'No, Mahailey.' He had dropped the shoebrush and stood with one foot on the chair, his elbow on his knee, looking out of the window as if he had forgotten himself. 'No, I'm not going to China. I'm going over to help fight the Germans.'

He was still staring out at the wet fields. Before he could stop her, before he knew what she was doing, she had caught and kissed his unworthy hand.

'I knowed you would,' she sobbed. 'I always knowed you would, you nice boy, you! Old Mahail' knowed!'

Her upturned face was working all over; her mouth, her eyebrows, even the wrinkles on her low forehead were working and twitching. Claude felt a tightening in his throat as he tenderly regarded that face; behind the pale eyes, under the low brow where there was not room for many thoughts, an idea was struggling and tormenting her. The same idea that had been tormenting him.

'You're all right, Mahailey,' he muttered, patting her back and turning away. 'Now hurry breakfast.'

'You ain't told your mudder yit?' she whispered.

'No, not yet. But she'll be all right, too.' He caught up his cap and went down to the barn to look after the horses.

When Claude returned, the family were already at the breakfast table. He slipped into his seat and watched his mother while she drank her first cup of coffee. Then he addressed his father.

'Father, I don't see any use of waiting for the draft. If you can spare me, I'd like to get into a training camp somewhere. I believe I'd stand a chance of getting a commission.'

'I shouldn't wonder.' Mr Wheeler poured maple syrup on his pancakes with a liberal hand. 'How do you feel about it, Evangeline?'

Mrs Wheeler had quietly put down her knife and fork. She looked at her husband in vague alarm, while her fingers moved restlessly about over the tablecloth.

'I thought,' Claude went on hastily, 'that maybe I would go up to Omaha tomorrow and find out where the training camps are to be located, and have a talk with the men in charge of the enlistment station. Of course,' he added lightly, 'they may not want me. I haven't an idea what the requirements are.'

'No, I don't understand much about it either.' Mr Wheeler rolled his top pancake and conveyed it to his mouth. After a moment of mastication he said, 'You figure on going tomorrow?'

'I'd like to. I won't bother with baggage – some shirts and underclothes in my suitcase. If the Government wants me, it will clothe me.'

Mr Wheeler pushed back his plate. 'Well, now I guess you'd better come out with me and look at the wheat. I don't know but I'd best plough up that south quarter and put it in corn. I don't believe it will make anything much.'

When Claude and his father went out of the door, Dan sprang up with more alacrity than usual and plunged after them. He did not want to be left alone with Mrs Wheeler. She remained sitting at the foot of the deserted breakfast table. She was not crying. Her eyes were utterly sightless. Her back was so stooped that she seemed to be bending under a burden. Mahailey cleared the dishes away quietly.

Out in the muddy fields Claude finished his talk with his father. He explained that he wanted to slip away without saying good-bye to anyone. 'I have a way, you know,' he said, flushing, 'of beginning things and not getting very far with them. I don't want anything said about this until I'm sure. I may be rejected for one reason or another.'

Mr Wheeler smiled. 'I guess not. However, I'll tell Dan to keep his mouth shut. Will you just go over to Leonard Dawson's and get that wrench he borrowed? It's about noon, and he'll likely be at home.' Claude found big Leonard watering his team at the windmill. When Leonard asked him what he thought of the President's message, he blurted out at once that he was going to Omaha to enlist. Leonard reached up and pulled the lever that controlled the almost motionless wheel.

'Better wait a few weeks and I'll go with you. I'm going to try for the Marines. They take my eye.'

Claude, standing on the edge of the tank, almost fell backward.

'Why, what – what for?'

Leonard looked him over. 'Good Lord, Claude, you ain't the only fellow around here that wears pants! What for? Well, I'll tell you what for,' he held up three large red fingers threateningly; 'Belgium, the *Lusitania*, Edith Cavell. That dirt's got under my skin. I'll get my corn planted, and then Father'll look after Susie till I come back.'

Claude took a long breath. 'Well, Leonard, you fooled me. I believed all this chaff you've been giving me about not caring who chewed up who.'

'And no more do I care,' Leonard protested, 'not a damn! But there's a limit. I've been ready to go since the *Lusitania*. I don't get any satisfaction out of my place any more. Susie feels the same way.'

Claude looked at his big neighbour. 'Well, I'm off tomorrow, Leonard. Don't mention it to my folks, but if I can't get into the army, I'm going to enlist in the navy. They'll always take an able-bodied man. I'm not coming back here.' He held out his hand and Leonard took it with a smack.

'Good luck, Claude. Maybe we'll meet in foreign parts. Wouldn't that be a joke! Give my love to Enid when you write. I always did think she was a fine girl, though I disagreed with her on Prohibition.'

Claude crossed the fields mechanically, without looking where he went. His power of vision was turned inward upon scenes and events wholly imaginary as yet.

The Jazz Bird
Vachel Lindsay

The Jazz Bird sings a barnyard song,
A cock-a-doodle bray,
A jingle-bells, a boiler works,
A he-man's roundelay.

The eagle said: 'Son Jazz Bird,
I send you out to fight.
And the Jazz Bird spread out his sunflower wings,
And roared with all his might,

And they woke to it in Oregon,
In Florida and Maine
And the land was dark with airships
In the darting Jazz Bird's train.

Crossing the roaring ocean
His bell-mouth shook the sky,
And the Yankees in the trenches
Gave back the hue and cry.

And Europe had not heard the like,
And Germany went down.
The Jazz Bird with the headlight eyes
Tore off the Kaiser's crown.

At midnight on a haunted road
A star bends low and sees

The Kaiser and his row of sons
Marching at their ease.

Their necks are broken by the hemp,
They goose-step in a line,
Their stripped bones strutting in the wind
Swinging as a sign

That Jazz Birds come on sunflower wings
When loathsome tyrants rise...
The Jazz Bird guards the gallows,
He lights it with his eyes.

A Children's Hospital in Wartime
J. M. Barrie

What should I write about, O Princess Elizabeth, in this, your Gift Book? About hospitals, I think, as, behold, you have now a hospital of your own. Or perhaps I should write about children, and in compliment to you, about poor children, as yours is a hospital for these, and the compliment lies in this, that since your earliest years poor children have been the people about whom you have most wondered. Yes, and so practical was your curiosity that, in the far past when you were only four, you drew for me a picture of what you thought a hospital for such children should be like. It was a triumphant rural edifice, though at the time I could not discover that it had any back to it. Now I see that you meant this to be its chiefest glory. You were signifying that your hospital was to extend indefinitely in that direction among trees and buttercups until all the ailing ones were roped in.

There is a competition these days in children's hospitals between you and a still younger Princess, for you have now a hospital apiece, hers being in Edinburgh, and it comes to my mind that I might tell now in print, as once before in talk, of a third, an odd little hospital that was mine. This hospital was in France during the war. It was on the river Marne, not very far from Verdun, and had some peculiarities that made it different from other war hospitals. It began because I have a lamentable weakness for children and old ladies, and it was largely staffed (as you would now say) in a pretty château by kind voluntary nurses. (I shall tell you what a voluntary is some other day, but you are one.) I regret to say that it had often to be run in ways that would be promptly shown the door in your hospital. Nevertheless I beg to decline to disparage my hospital.

It started with eight beds, which you may consider made it no more than a nursery, but in a few months there were nearly a hundred, although I dare say the inmates of your hospital would not have called them all beds. The procedure, you see, was to begin constructing another bed, woodwork and all, when another stretcher was seen coming down the avenue. Bedrooms for extra nurses were knocked up with the same rapidity by the male staff, for outside help could not be obtained. If you had an hour off you immediately became a carpenter or a glazier or a plumber. It was a hospital for French children wounded by bombs or guns, and many of them had lost a leg or an arm. The oldest patient, I suppose, was not ten years of age, and others were little more than babes. On the evening of the day the hospital opened the first eight were all asleep in one room, which afterwards became Ward No. 1. At this time the château was damp, and that night part of the ceiling fell down. There was a hastening of grown-ups to the room, who wondered at hearing no screaming, for it had sounded like the falling of a bomb. The children indeed had thought it a bomb, but they were used to bombs, and when their elders opened the door they found these eight little Roman Catholics by their bedsides praying so neatly.

When the hospital was at its fullest a Zeppelin fell into the grounds, brought down by the guns at Bar-le-Duc. I think it was one of the first airships brought down in the war. It had been coming and going occasionally dropping bombs, and I feel sure the airmen had no idea that there were these small people below. The children were put to bed at an unusually early hour, while it was still light, the blinds pulled down, and they were told it was night-time and to go to sleep. Next morning when they woke they knew, though an attempt was made to conceal it from them, that the Zeppelin was lying in the grounds of the hospital with some fragments of men who had once been as brave as ours. They were very frightened children at first, but the staff had the happy thought of giving the equivalent of threepence in French coins to each, whereupon they skipped and sang, and with the awful sarcasm of early years they called their threepences 'The tears of William'.

Being now people of means they gave financial gifts to forty old ladies who had mostly been living in holes in the ground with some planks over them for a roof, ladies whom we were afterwards to supply with forty beds in another château. I was not there, but must it not have been great fun to see the children tipping the old ladies?

These little patients were not sad all the time. They invented games in which to have a limb missing was a help rather than a hindrance: indeed if I was there they expected me to invent the games and to play in them also. I taught them cricket with rules never conceived by the M.C.C., in which the bat was a crutch and the ball was made out of lint purloined from the medical stores. I hope you won't draw back from me with a shudder when I say that I fear I was the purloiner. They developed regrettable artifice to bring me down to join them in these pastimes in the early morning. Thus they learned a few Scots words from a nurse who I am sure never picked them up at Glamis, words like 'dagont' and 'Tam Shanter,' which they thought was the friendly Scottish for 'potatoes.' Me they called 'Monsieur Auld Reekie,' and armed with such words they gathered beneath my window at dawn and suddenly shouted them in chorus as a tempting way of luring me from sleep. Sometimes their parents journeyed to the château to take them in their arms and weep over the parts of them that were not there, but the convalescents wriggled away from all such fondling in order to get back to their games. And upstairs at windows were other patients looking out wistfully and cunningly 'holding their breath' so that the nurse with thermometer should be deceived into thinking their temperatures were normal and so let them down to play. How gay that little hospital is to look back upon now, but it was not always gay. In that way and in some others I dare say it was rather like yours. If we cannot always be gay we can always make pretend.

'Mesopotamian Alphabet'
From *The B. E. F. Times,* Anon.

The following has been sent us from the Indian Army by one of our old Divisional friends. He suggests that someone should have a shot at the 'B.E.F. Alphabet Up-to-date.' Will some please try and submit efforts early? Ed.

A was an Apple that grew so they say,
In the Garden of Eden down Kurna way,
Till Eve came along and ate it one day,
And got thrown out of Mesopotamia.

B is the Biscuit that's made in Delhi,
It breaks your teeth and bruises your belly,
And grinds your intestines into a jelly,
In the land of Mesopotamia.

C is the poor old Indian Corps,
Which went to France and fought in the war,
Now it gathers the crops and fights no more
In the land of Mesopotamia.

D is the Digging we've all of us done
Since first we started to fight the Hun,
By now we've shifted ten thousand ton
Of matter in Mesopotamia.

E was the Energy shown by the Staff
Before the much-advertised Hanna strafe.

Yet the net result was the Turks had a laugh
At our Staff in Mesopotamia.

F stands for 'Fritz' who flies in the sky.
To bring down the brute we've had many a try,
But the shells we shoot with, all pass him by
And fall in Mesopotamia.

G is the Grazing we do all the day.
We fervently hope that someday we may
Get issued again with a ration of hay,
'Though we're still in Mesopotamia.

H are the Harems, which it appears
Have flourished in Baghdad for hundreds of years,
We propose to annex all the destitute dears –
When their husbands leave Mesopotamia.

I is the Indian Government, but
About this I'm told I must keep my mouth shut.
For it's all due to them that we failed to reach
Kut-El-Atnara in Mesopotamia.

J is the Jam, with the label that lies,
And states that in Paris it won the First Prize,
But out here we use it for catching the flies
That swarm in Mesopotamia.

K are the Kisses from lips sweet and fair,
Waiting for us around Leicester Square,
When we wend our way home, after wasting a year
 Or two in Mesopotamia.

L is the Loot we hope we shall seize –
Wives and wine and bags of rupees,

When the Mayor of Baghdad hands over the keys
To the British in Mesopotamia.

M is the local Mosquito, whose bite
Keeps us awake all the hours of the night,
And makes all our faces a horrible sight
In the land of Mesopotamia.

N is the Navy that's tied to the shore,
They've lashings of beer, and provisions galore,
How I wish I had joined as a sailor before
I came out to Mesopotamia.

O are the Orders we get from the Corps,
Thank goodness by now we are perfectly sure
If issued at three they'll be cancelled by four–
In this land of Mesopotamia.

P are the Postal officials who fail
To deliver each week more than half of our mail.
If they had their deserts they'd all be in jail
Instead of in Mesopotamia.

Q's the Quinine which we take everyday
To keep the Malarial fever away,
Which we're bound to get sooner or later, they say,
If we stop here in Mesopotamia.

R is for the Rations they give us to eat,
For brekker there's biscuits, for dinner there's meat;
And if we've been good we get jam as a treat
For our tea in Mesopotamia.

S & T are supposed to supply
The Army with food, we all hope when they die

They will go to a spot as hot and as dry
As this rotten old Mesopotamia.

U is the Lake known as Um-el-Brahm,
Which guards our left flank from all possible harm,
And waters old G____s barley farm
In the middle of Mesopotamia.

V is the Victory won at Dijailah,
I heard it first from a pal who's a sailor,
Who read it in Reuter on board his Mahola
On the Tigris in Mesopotamia.

W stands for Wonder and pain,
With which we regard the infirm and insane
Old *____ this campaign
We're waging in Mesopotamia.
(*censored – Ed)

X are the 'Xtras the Corps say we get,
But so far there isn't a unit I've met
That has drawn a single one of them yet
Since they landed in Mesopotamia.

Y is the Yearning we feel every day
For a passage to Basrah, and so to Bombay,
If we get there we'll see that we stop right away
From this wilderness Mesopotamia.

Z I've tried very hard, and at last I had hit
On a verse which this damnable letter would fit,
But the Censor deleted it – every bit
Save the last word 'Mesopotamia.'

Chahels is really a horrible spot,
Where there isn't a drop of drink to be got,
Yet here we're going to be left till we rot
In the Middle of Mesopotamia.

Vimy Ridge
From *Over the Top with the 25th*, R. Lewis

Zero hour (5.30 a.m., Easter Monday, 1917) had come! The VIMY RIDGE attack was on! Whistles blew and over the top went the Canadians. The artillery started their work. Hundreds and hundreds of guns commenced drum fire simultaneously. Looking towards the Hun trenches it appeared as if the whole line was afire. It was a grand and impressive sight. The gallant pipers leading the 25th could be seen but it was impossible with the din to hear what they were playing. Gradually we advanced our ground – nothing but holes filled with mud and water to make the going very difficult. At last we reached the German line which had been taken by the 24th and 26th Battalion. We jumped into what was left of the trench and waited until the set time to move forward. Looking at the Hun trench one could easily see what good work the gunners were doing. Everything was smashed in; dugouts were gone and many of the enemy with them. Our next objective was the TU ROP GRABEN trench. By this time the Boche realised that he had no small attack to deal with and his artillery, helped with many machine guns, started causing us many casualties. Just about this stage of the advance Major Delancy was killed and also R. S. M. Hinchcliffe. We could see our boys for miles advancing with confidence and determination. The Hun shells and bullets were coming swift but that did not stay the Canadians. Parties of the enemy were trying to put up a fight but they were soon settled. Major A. O. Blois, though wounded, took command of the Battalion and for this and other good work he was awarded the D.S.O.

Finally we reached our last objective and commenced to consolidate. This trench, like the others, was in an awful condition.

We found a large dugout named CRAEMER HOUSE which was a Battalion headquarters. By this time we had lost not only Major Delancy, but Lieuts. Hallesy, Sheriff, Feindel, Barber, as well as other officers wounded, and a good number of men both killed and wounded.

Then came the long hours of waiting. It had rained during the morning and everybody was more or less wet and as the evening drew on it became very cold, and by the time the morning came again the Battalion, having no overcoats or shelter, were in a sorry plight, with but little food or water except what the Hun had left behind.

On the evening of the attack Col. S. Bauld came with Lieuts. Lewis and Fisher and Capt. and Q. M. Ingraham, who having heard of the casualties amongst the officers volunteered to come and help out. The following night water was sent up, and although it tasted more like petrol we were glad to get it.

That night we moved back to the rear trench and everyone felt a lot happier when a rumour went around that the Battalion was going to be relieved. After holding the position for less than two days we were sent for two days' rest, prior to being relieved, into a larger German tunnel known as FOLKER TUNNEL.

Lieut. Dryden was detailed to take charge of the burial party and sad work it was, collecting friend and foe from all over the battlefield.

After a night in the tunnel the order came that instead of going out to be relieved we were again to go forward. The people at home will never realise what this order meant to our men. After four days without sleep, wet clothing and mud right next to the skin, with very little food or water, our men were not anxious to move forward, but did they grumble? Not they. When the word came to move forward they were ready once more for another go at the Hun.

We came out of the trenches for a short rest. We had to travel about two miles over shell-torn ground and we were about all in, having been in the line for quite a few days doing our duty regardless of shells, snow and rain. After what seemed to us to be a long time we arrived out at our resting place not so very far from the front line. We bivouacked here in tents and had one beautiful rest. Rain and mud the entire four days that we were out here. Col. Bauld was in charge of the Battalion and Major Blois was acting as second in command. But we were quite happy despite the rain and mud. One night the German aeroplanes came overhead. The order came to put out the lights and just to show you how little the boys thought of Fritz's bombs, a crowd of men in a few of the tents who had just came back from a working party and were turning in when the signal went to put out lights ignored it saying: 'Just wait a few minutes as we have to turn in.' I wonder if Fritz's planes would wait? I guess not. Anyway he did not get us that night. Now and again Fritz would drop an occasional shell over quite close to us but he never did us any damage.

We had come through one of the heaviest engagements that had taken place up until this time and though very muddy, we were as happy as anyone could be.

The Duck Board
Sivori Levey

It's a long way to Tipperary,
  Or so it always seems;
There's a long, long trail awinding
  Into the land of dreams.
And there's a long and narrow path
Our Warriors know well,
For one way leads to Blighty,
  And the other way to – well!

It's the Duck Board Glide,
It's the Duck Board Slide,
  On a cold and frosty night;
For it's over a mile
In single file
  Out in the pale moon-light.

It's nippy; slippy;
Bumpy; jumpy;
* Shell-holes either side;*
And when machine guns cough
You can all drop off
That Duck Board Glide.

It's very dark and lonely,
  And you see, when on the top,
A Very Light; so in the trench
  You very lightly drop.
But when you want to reach the line,
That's done as best you may,
There's only one path that you have to take,
  It is the only way.

  It's the Duck Board Glide, etc.

When you were young, and went to Church,
  Or Chapel, it may be,
The *Padre* used to take some text
  To *strafe* you all with glee.
'The path is long and narrow
Along which you ought to go!'
We did not know then what it was,
  But now, of course, we know.

  It's the Duck Board Glide, etc.

Drill
From *Action Front*, Boyd Cable

'*Yesterday one of the enemy's heavy guns was put out of action by our artillery.*' Extract from despatch.

'Stand fast!' the instructor bellowed, and while the detachment stiffened to immobility he went on, without stopping to draw breath, bellowing other and less printable remarks. After he had finished these he ordered 'Detachment rear!' and taking more time and adding even more point to his remarks, he repeated some of them and added others, addressing abruptly and virulently the 'Number' whose bungling had aroused his wrath.

'You've learnt your gun drill,' he said, 'learned it like a sulphur-crested cockatoo learns to gabble "Pretty Polly scratch a poll"; why in the name of Moses you can't make your hands do what your tongue says 'as me beat. You, Donovan, that's Number Three, let me hear you repeat the drill for Action Front.'

Donovan, standing strictly to attention, and with his eyes fixed straight to his front, drew a deep breath and rattled off:

'At the order or signal from the battery leader or section commander, "Halt action front!" One orders "Halt action front!" At the order from One, the detachment dismounts, Three unkeys, and with Two lifts the trail; when the trail is clear of the hook, Three orders "Limber drive on."'

The instructor interrupted explosively.

'You see,' he growled, 'you know it. Three orders "Limber drive on." You're Three! But did you order limber drive on, or limber drive off, or drive anywhere at all? Did you expect drivers that would be sitting up there on their horses, with their backs turned to you, to have eyes in the backs of their heads to see when you had the trail lifted, or did you be expectin' them to thought-read that you wanted them to drive on!'

Three, goaded at last to a sufficiency of daring, ventured to mutter something about 'was going to order it.'

The instructor caught up the phrase and flayed him again with it.

' "Was going to," he repeated, "was going to order it." Perhaps someday, when a bullet comes along and drills a hole in your thick head, you will want to tell it you "was going to" get out of the way. You maybe expect the detachment to halt and stand easy, and light a cigarette, and have a chat while you wait to make up your mind what you're going to say, and when you're going to say it! And if ever you get past recruit drill in the barracks square, my lad, and smell powder burnt in action, you'll learn that there's no such thing as "going to" in your gun drill. If you're slow at it, if you fumble your fingers, and tie knots in your tongue, and stop to think about your "going to," you'll find maybe that "going to" has gone before you make up your mind, and the only thing "going to" will be you and your detachment; and its Kingdom Come you'll be "going to" at that. And now we'll try it again, and if I find any more "going to" about it this time it's an hour's extra drill a day you'll be "going to" for the next week.'

He kept the detachment grilling and grinding for another hour before he let them go, and at the end of it he spent another five minutes pointing out the manifold faults and failings of each individual in the detachment, reminding them that they belonged to the Royal Regiment of Artillery that is 'The right of the line, the terror of the world, and the pride of the British Army,' and that any man who wasn't a shining credit to the Royal Regiment was no less than a black disgrace to it.

When the detachment dismissed, and for the most part gravitated to the canteen, they passed some remarks upon their instructor almost pungent enough to have been worthy of his utterance.

'Him an' his everlastin'. "Cut the Time!"'

'I'm just about fed up with him,' said Gunner Donovan bitterly, 'and I'd like to know where's all the sense doing this drill against a stop-watch. You'd think from the way he talks that a man's life was hanging on the whiskers of a half-second. Blanky rot, I call it.'

'I wouldn't mind so much,' said another gunner, 'if ever he thought to say we done it good, but not 'im. The better we does it and the faster, the better and the faster he wants it done. It's my belief that if he had a gun detachment picked from the angels above he'd tell 'em their buttons and their gold crowns was a disgrace to Heaven, that they was too slow to catch worms or catch a cold, and that they'd 'ave to cut the time it took 'em to fly into column o' route from the right down the Golden Stairs, or to bring their 'arps to the 'alt action front.'

These were the mildest of the remarks that passed between the smarting Numbers of the gun detachment, but they would have been astonished beyond words if they could have heard what their instructor Sergeant 'Cut-the-Time' was saying at that moment to a fellow-sergeant in the sergeants' mess.

'They're good lads,' he said, 'and it's me, that in my time has seen the making and the breaking and the handling and the hammering of gun detachments enough to man every gun in the Army, that's saying it. I had them on the "Halt action front" this morning, and I tell you they've come on amazing since I took 'em in hand. We cut three solid seconds this morning off the time we have been taking to get the gun into action, and a second a round off the firing of ten rounds. They'll make gunners yet if they keep at it.'

'Three seconds is good enough,' said the other mildly.

'It isn't good enough,' returned the instructor, 'if they can make it four, and four's not good enough if they can make it five. It's when they can't cut the time down by another split fraction of a second that I'll be calling them good enough. They won't be blessing me for it now, but come the day maybe they will.'

The battery was moving slowly down a muddy road that ran along the edge of a thick wood. It had been marching most of the night, and, since the night had been wet and dark, the battery was splashed and muddy to the gun-muzzles and the tops of the drivers' caps. It was early morning, and very cold. Gunners and drivers were muffled in coats and woollen scarves, and sat half-asleep on their horses and wagons. A thick and chilly mist had delayed the coming of light, but now the mist had lifted suddenly, blown clear by a quickly risen chill wind. When the mist had been swept away sufficiently for something to be seen of the surrounding country, the Major, riding at the head of the battery, passed the word to halt and dismount, and proceeded to 'find himself on the map.' Glancing about him, he picked out a church steeple in the distance, a wayside shrine, and a cross-road near at hand, a curve of the wood beside the road, and by locating these on the squared map, which he took from its mud-splashed leather case, he was enabled to place his finger on the exact spot on the map where his battery stood at that moment. Satisfied on this, he was just about to give the order to mount when he heard the sound of breaking brushwood and saw an infantry officer emerge from the trees close at hand.

The officer was a young man, and was evidently on an errand of haste. He slithered down the steep bank at the edge of the wood, leaped the roadside ditch, asked a question of the nearest man, and, getting an answer from him, came at the double past the guns and teams towards the Major. He saluted hastily, said 'Mornin', sir,' and went on breathlessly:

'My colonel sent me across to catch you. We are in a ditch along the edge of the far side of this wood, and could just see enough of you between the trees to make out your battery. From where we are we can see a German gun, one of their big brutes, with a team of about twenty horses pulling it, plain and fair out in the open. The Colonel thinks you could knock 'em to glory before they could reach cover.'

'Where can I see them from?' said the Major quickly.

'I'll show you,' said the subaltern, 'if you'll leave your horse and come with me through this wood. It's only a narrow belt of trees here.'

The Major turned to one of his subalterns who was with him at the head of the battery.

'Send back word to the captain to come up here and wait for me!' he said rapidly. 'Tell him what you have just heard this officer say, and tell him to give the word, "Prepare for action." And now,' he said, turning to the infantryman, 'go ahead.'

The two of them jumped the ditch, scrambled up the bank, and disappeared amongst the trees.

A message back to the captain who was at the rear of the battery brought him up at a canter. The subaltern explained briefly what he had heard, and the captain, after interrupting him to shout an order to 'Prepare for action,' heard the finish of the story, pulled out his map, and pointing out on it a road shown as running through the trees, sent the subaltern off to reconnoiter it.

The men were stripping off their coats, rolling them and strapping them to the saddles and wagon seats; the Numbers One, the sergeants in charge of each gun, bustling their gunners, were seeing everything about the guns made ready: the gunners were examining the mechanism and gears of the gun, opening and closing the hinged flaps of the wagons, and tearing the thin metal cover off the fuses.

It was all done smartly and handily, and one after another the sergeants reported their subsections as ready. Immediately the captain gave the order to mount, drivers swung themselves to their saddles, and the gunners to their seats on the wagons, and all sat quietly waiting for whatever order might come next.

The lifting of the mist had shown a target to the gunners on both sides apparently, and the roar and boom of near and distant guns beat and throbbed quicker and at closer intervals.

In three minutes the Major came running back through the wood, and the captain moved to meet him.

'We've got a fair chance!' said the Major exultingly. 'One of their big guns clear in the open, and moving at a crawl. I want you to take the battery along the road here, sharp to the right at the cross-road, and through the wood. The Inf. tell me there is just a passable road through. Take guns and firing battery wagons only; leave the others here. When you get through the wood, turn to the right again, and along its edge until you come to where I'll be waiting for you. I'll take the range-taker with me. The order will be "open sights"; it's the only way – not time to hunt a covered position! Now, is all that clear?'

'Quite clear,' said the captain tersely.

'Off you go, then,' said the Major; 'remember, it's quick work. Trumpeter, come with me, and the range-taker. Sergeant-major, leave the battery staff under cover with the first line.'

He swung into the saddle, set his horse at the ditch, and with a leap and scramble was over and up the bank and crashing into the undergrowth, followed by his trumpeter and a man with the six-foot tube of a range-finder strapped to the saddle.

Before he was well off the road the captain shouted the order to walk march, and as the battery did so the subaltern who had been sent out to reconnoiter the road came back at a canter.

'We can just do it,' he reported; 'it's greasy going, and the road is narrow and rather twisty, but we can do it all right.'

The captain sent back word to section commanders, and the other two subalterns spurred forward and joined him.

'We go through the wood,' he explained, 'and come into action on the other side. The order is "open sights," so I expect we'll be in an exposed position. You know what that means. There's a gun to knock out, and if we can do it and get back quick before they get our range we may get off light. If we can't –' and he broke off significantly. 'Get back and tell your Numbers One, and be ready for quick moving.'

Immediately they had fallen back the order was given to trot, and the battery commenced to bump and rumble rapidly over the rough road. As they neared the cross-roads they were halted a moment, and then the guns and their attendant ammunition wagons only went on, turned into the wood, and recommenced to trot.

They jolted and swayed and slid over the rough, wet road, the gunners clinging fiercely to the handrails, the drivers picking a way as best they could over boulders and between ruts. They emerged on the far side of the wood, found themselves in an open field, turned sharply to the right, and kept on at a fast trot. A line of infantry were entrenched amongst the trees on the edge of the wood, but their shouted remarks were drowned in the clatter and rattle and jingle of wheels and harness. Out on their left the ground rose very gently, and far beyond a low crest could be seen clumps of trees, patches of fields, and a few scattered farmhouses. At several points on this distant slope the white smoke-clouds of bursting shells were puffing and breaking, but so far there was no sign to be seen of any man or of any gun. When they came to where the Major was waiting he rode out from the trees, blew sharply on a whistle, and made a rapid signal with hand and arm. The guns and wagons had been moving along the edge of the wood in single file, but now at the shouted order each team swung abruptly to its left and commenced to move in a long line out from the wood towards the low crest, the whole movement being performed neatly and cleanly and still at a trot. The Major rode to his place in the centre of the line, and the battery, keeping its place close on his heels, steadily increased its pace almost to a canter. The Major's whistle screamed again, and at another signal and the shouted orders the battery dropped to a walk. Every man could see now over the crest and into the shallow valley that fell away from it and rose again in gentle folds and slopes. At first they could see nothing of the gun against which they had expected to be brought into action, but presently someone discovered a string of tiny black dots that told of the long team and heavy gun it drew. Another sharp whistle and the Major's signal brought the battery up with a jerk.

'Halt! Action front!' The shouted order rang hoarsely along the line.

For a moment there was wild commotion; a seething chaos, a swirl of bobbing heads and plunging horses. But in the apparent chaos there was nothing but the most smooth and ordered movement, the quick but most exact following of a routine drill so well ground in that its motions were almost mechanical. The gunners were off their seats before the wheels had stopped turning, the key snatched clear, and the trail of the gun lifted, the wheels seized, and the gun whirled round in a half-circle and dropped pointing to the enemy. The ammunition wagon pulled up into place beside the gun, the traces flung clear, and the teams hauled round and trotted off. As Gunner Donovan's trail was lifted clear his yell of 'Limber, drive on,' started the team forward with a jerk, and a moment later, as he and the Number Two slipped into their seats on the gun the Number Two grinned at him. 'Sharp's the word,' he said: 'D'you mind the time –' He was interrupted roughly by the sergeant, who had just had the target pointed out to him, jerking up the trail to throw the gun roughly into line.

'Shut yer head, and get on to it, Donovan. You see that target there, don't you?'

'See it a fair treat!' said Donovan joyfully; 'I'll bet I plunk a bull in the first three shots.'

Back in the wood the infantry colonel, from a vantage-point half-way up a tall tree, watched the ensuing duel with the keenest excitement.

The battery's first two ranging shots dropped in a neat bracket, one over and one short; in the next two the bracket closed, the shorter shot being almost on top of the target. This evidently gave the range closely enough, and the whole battery burst into a roar of fire, the blazing flashes running up and down the line of guns like the reports of a gigantic Chinese cracker. Over the German gun a thick cloud of white smoke hung heavily, burst following upon burst and hail after hail of shrapnel sweeping the men and horses below. Then through the crashing reports of the guns and the whimpering rush of their shells' passage, there came a long whistling scream that rose and rose and broke off abruptly in a deep rolling cr-r-r-rump. A spout of brown earth and thick black smoke showed where the enemy shell had burst far out in front of the battery.

The infantry colonel watched anxiously. He knew that out there somewhere another heavy German gun had come into action; he knew that it was a good deal slower in its rate of fire, but that once it had secured its line and range it could practically obliterate the light field guns of the battery. The battery was fighting against time and the German gunners to complete their task before they could be silenced. The first team was crippled and destroyed, and another team, rushed out from the cover of the trees, was fallen upon by the shrapnel tornado, and likewise swept out of existence.

Then another shell from the German gun roared over, to burst this time well in the rear of the battery.

The colonel knew what this meant. The German gun had got its bracket.

The battery had ceased to fire shrapnel, and was pouring high-explosive about the derelict gun. The white bursts of shrapnel had given place to a series of spouting volcanoes that leaped from the ground about the gun itself. Another German shell fell in front of the battery and a good 200 yards nearer to it. A movement below attracted the colonel's attention, and he saw the huddled teams straighten out and canter hard towards the guns. He turned his glasses on the German gun again, and could not restrain a cry of delight as he saw it collapsed and lying on its side, while high-explosive shells still pelted about it.

The teams came up at a gallop, swept round the guns, and halted. Instantly they were hooked in, the buried spades of the guns wrenched free, the wheels manned, the trails dropped clashing on the limber hooks. And as they dropped, another heavy shell soared over, burst behind the battery, so close this time that the pieces shrieked and spun about the guns, wounding three horses and a couple of men. The Major, mounted and waiting, cast quick glances from gun to gun. The instant he saw they were ready he signaled an order, the drivers' spurs clapped home, and the whips rose and fell whistling and snapping. The battery jerked forward at a walk that broke immediately into a trot, and from that to a hard canter.

Even above the clatter and roll of the wheels and the hammering hoof-beats, the whistle and rush of another heavy shell could be heard. Gunner Donovan, twisted sideways and clinging close to the jolting seat, heard the sound growing louder and louder, until it sounded so close that it seemed the shell was going to drop on top of them. But it fell behind them, and exactly on the position where the battery had stood. Donovan's eye caught the blinding flash of the burst, the springing of a thick cloud of black smoke. A second later something shrieked hurtling down and past his gun team, and struck with a vicious thump into the ground.

'That was near enough,' shouted Mick, on the seat beside him. Donovan craned over as they passed, and saw, half-buried in the soft ground, the battered brass of one of their own shell cartridges. The heavy shell had landed fairly on top of the spot where their gun had stood, where the empty cartridge cases had been flung in a heap from the breech. If they had been ten or twenty seconds later in getting clear, if they had taken a few seconds longer over the coming

into action or limbering up, a few seconds more to the firing of their
rounds, the whole gun and detachment...

Gunner Donovan leaned across to Mick and shouted loudly. But his
remark was so apparently irrelevant that Mick failed to understand.
A sudden skidding swerve as the team wheeled nearly jerked him
off his seat, the crackling bursts of half a dozen light shells over the
plain behind him distracted his attention for a moment further. Then
he leaned in towards Donovan, 'What was that?' he yelled. 'What
didjer say?'

Donovan repeated his remark. 'Gawd–bless–old "Cut-the-Time".'

The battery plunged in amongst the trees, and into safety.

Dumb Heroes
T. A. Girling

There's a D.S.O. for the Colonel,
A Military Cross for the Sub,
A medal or two, when we all get through,
And a bottle of wine with our grub.

There's a stripe of gold for the wounded,
A rest by the bright sea-shore,
And a service is read as we bury our dead,
Then our country has one hero more.

And what of our poor dumb heroes
That are sent without choice to the fight,
That strain at the load on the shell-swept road
As they take up the rations at night.

They are shelling on Hell Fire Corner,
There's shrapnel just burst in the Square,
And their bullets drum as the transports come
With the food for the soldiers there.

The halt till the shelling is over,
The rush through the line of fire,
The glowing light in the dead of night,
And the terrible sights in the mire.

It's the daily work of the horses
And they answer the spur and rein,
With quickened breath, 'mid the toll of death,
Through the mud, and the holes, and the rain.

There's a fresh treated wound in the chestnut,
The black mare's neck has a mark,
The brown mule's new mate won't keep the same gait
As the one killed last night in the dark.

But they walk with the spirit of heroes,
They care not for medals or cross,
But for duty alone, into perils unknown,
They go, never counting the loss.

There's a swift painless death for the hopeless,
With a grave in a shell-hole or field,
There's a hospital base for the casualty case,
And a Vet. for those easily healed.

But there's never a shadow of glory,
A cheer, or a speech, in their praise,
While patient and true they carry us through
With the limbers in shot-riven ways.

So here's to 'Dumb Heroes' of Britain,
Who serve her as nobly and true,
As the best of her boys, 'mid the roar of the guns
And the best of her boys on the blue.

They are shell-shocked, they're bruised, and they're broken,
They are wounded and torn as they fall,
But they're true and they're brave to the very grave,
And they're heroes, one and all.

Fighting Beyond Baghdad
From *With a Highland Regiment in Mesopotamia,*
Anon.

The battle was now divided into two parts. On our left the Turks
had been forced to retire from their advanced positions, but on the
right they still held some trenches among the broken ground near
the railway, two hundred yards in advance of the main position on
the ridge; but on the right our losses had not been so severe, nor was
our line so extended.

On the left the Turk occupied no advanced positions, but he
outflanked our line, and the enfilade fire from his commanding
positions was causing such losses that it seemed impossible for
our men to continue the advance without strong artillery support.
Unfortunately this was not forthcoming at the time, because our
covering batteries had found they were at extreme range, and were
now in the act of moving to a more forward position. If an attacking
line wavers and halts within close range of an enemy entrenched,
that attack is done until supports come up and give it again an
impetus forward. But there were now few supports available, and
the moment most critical.

Yet all along our front small sections of Highlanders still continued
to rise up, make a rush forward, and fling themselves down, weaker
perhaps by two or three of their number, but another thirty yards
nearer the enemy. Now the last supports pressed into the firing line,
and as one leader fell, another took his place. One platoon changed
commanders six times in as many minutes, but a lance-corporal
led the remaining men with the same dash and judgment as his
seniors.

It was at this time our Lewis gun teams lost so heavily. The weight of the gun and the extra ammunition carried renders their movements slower than that of their comrades, and consequently the teams offer a better target as well as one specially sought for by the enemy. The officer in charge, Lieut. Gillespie, had brought up two of our guns in the endeavour to subdue the fire from Sugar Loaf Hill, but at the very moment of giving the range his left arm was shattered. He had been light-weight champion of India, and as he now continued fighting, I could not but compare him to his famous predecessor in the Ring, who carried on the fight with one arm broken. I know those brave, brown eyes of his never flinched in pain, nor wavered in doubt, as he made his way back, not to the Aide Post, but in order to bring forward two more guns for the same purpose. But, alas! while directing their fire he was seen by some Turkish riflemen and fell, never again to rise, his breast pierced by two bullets.

A number of staff and artillery officers witnessed this attack by a Highland regiment. Some were chiefly impressed by so much individual gallantry, others at the example of what can be achieved by collective determination. Was it the result of hard and constant training, perfect discipline, or *esprit de corps* that at this moment of trial made these thin extended lines work as if by clockwork to their own saving and the victory of our arms?

It was during this advance of five hundred yards that the regiment met with its heaviest losses. With four officers and half his men killed or wounded, and an enemy machine-gun pouring a continuous stream of bullets on to the remainder, the situation is not a happy one for a company sergeant-major, and this was the situation which the young Sergeant-Major Ben Houston of our left company had now to face. He turned round, as so often in battle one does turn round, hoping to see supports pushing forward, and a bullet seared an ugly line across both shoulders. Without waiting, he led his men on, and another bullet struck his bayonet; fragments cut his face and made his eye swell, so that he could not see out of it. Yet when I met him at midnight after the last charge, he told me much of the battle and nothing of his wounds. High praise is due to those who, although weakened by wounds, continue fighting and undertaking fresh responsibilities.

The company next on the left fared little better, but these two companies forced the enemy back, and occupied the low sandhills some two hundred yards in advance of his main position, and there waited, by order, before making the final assault. The left company lost two signallers killed, and the next company had four signallers all wounded in the act of calling for more ammunition. Ammunition was brought up, but, though many brave men fell and many brave deeds were done, nothing was carried out with greater bravery, nothing contributed more to our success, than the maintenance of communication throughout the battle.

The left half battalion, reduced to less than half of its original numbers, was in need of help. This help it now gained from the action of the companies on the right. Undismayed by the enemy shell and rifle fire, these two companies, gallantly assisted by the Indian battalion on the east side of the railway, pressed forward, and at five o'clock charged the enemy, and drove him out of his advanced trenches at the point of the bayonet. The very quickness of the manoeuvre had ensured its success, though it was only achieved with considerable loss to ourselves as well as to the Turk. But the gain was great. Small parties of Highlanders now crept forward among the sand-dunes, two Lewis guns were taken to the east side of the railway embankment, and a hot enfilade fire was brought to bear on the enemy main position. So effective was this that the Turks were forced to evacuate the ridge for some 400 yards nearest the railway, and even from Sugar Loaf Hill his fire weakened, and the relief to our left half battalion and to the Gurkhas was correspondingly great. Streams of wounded Turks were also seen passing from the ridge to the rear: it was not only the British who suffered losses on the 14th of March.

The situation was now greatly in our favour, and it only wanted a final charge to complete the success. But this assault could not be made without either artillery support or the arrival of fresh troops to fill up our depleted and extended ranks. Our Colonel, therefore, ordered all companies to wait in the positions they had gained, but

to be ready to charge immediately after the batteries had bombarded
the enemy trenches. Consequently, during the next hour both sides
remained on the defensive.

During this hour rifle fire grew less and less, artillery firing ceased.
High above the battlefield some crested larks were singing, even as
they sing on a quiet evening over the trenches in France, as they sing
over the fields at home. A few green and bronze bee-eaters hovered
almost like hawks over the sand-dunes, and a cloud of sandgrouse
were swinging and swerving across the open ground that divided
Highlander from Turk. The wind had died quite away, and a scent
of alyssum filled the air. There was no movement among the troops,
there was none even among the slender wild grasses of the plain.
The sun, that had been blazing all through the day, now hung low in
the western sky. The sound of battle was dying, even as the day was
dying. 'The world was like a nun, breathless in adoration.' And we
soldiers, absorbed in this remote corner of the world war, intent on
the hour immediately before us, lay there breathless in expectancy.

Suddenly our 18-pounders opened gun fire. With rare precision
shrapnel burst all along the enemy trenches, and at 6.30, as the
shelling slackened in intensity, the Highlanders rose as one man, their
bayonets gleaming in the setting sun, and, with the Gurkhas on their
left, rushed across the open. There was little work for the bayonet.

The Turk fled as our men closed, and the position so long and
hardly fought for was won.

The Highlanders had gained their objective, but had lost heavily
in officers and men. The remainder were exhausted by the labours
of the past twenty-four hours and by lack of water; but when orders
came to push forward and capture Mushaidie railway station there
was no feeling of doubt or hesitation. Some time was spent in
reorganisation, in bringing up and distributing reserve ammunition;
the two left companies were amalgamated, and an officer detailed to
act with the right wing of the Gurkhas, since that battalion, though
it had not suffered such heavy losses in men, had only two officers
left unwounded. The two companies of the supporting Highland

battalion now arrived and were detailed as a reserve to our attacking line. The third regiment of our brigade had been operating far out on the left flank, and were now occupying Sugar Loaf Hill, from which they had driven the last remaining Turks, and the Indian regiment on the right of the railway, which had fought so well with us throughout the battle, received orders to halt for the night.

And thus we advanced alone; but though hungry, thirsty, weary, worn, there was full confidence among all ranks, and one resolve united all; the determination to press forward and complete the rout of the enemy.

A mile ahead we passed a position, strongly entrenched but luckily deserted by the Turks, and it was not for another two miles, when our patrols came close to the station, that the enemy was reported in any numbers. There the patrols described a scene of considerable confusion. A train was shunting, and many Turks rushing about and shouting orders. Our patrols were working half a mile ahead of the regiment, so in spite of every effort it was half an hour later before we filed silently past the station, formed up once again for the attack, and charged with the bayonet. The enemy fired a few shots, one of our men and a few Turks were killed and a few more made prisoners; but the rest fled and disappeared into the night, leaving piles of saddlery, ammunition, and food behind them. But the last train had left Mushaidie, and with it vanished our hopes of captured guns and prisoners. However, we had achieved the task allotted to us, and the moment the necessary pickets had been posted the rest of us forgot exhaustion, forgot victory, in the most profound sleep.

Two Tuppenny Ones, Please
From *Something Childish*, Katherine Mansfield

Lady: Yes, there is, dear; there's plenty of room. If the lady next to me would move her seat and sit opposite... Would you mind? So that my friend may sit next to me... Thank you so much! Yes, dear, both the cars on war work; I'm getting quite used to 'buses. Of course, if we go to the theatre, I 'phone Cynthia. She's still got one car. Her chauffeur's been called up... Ages ago... Killed by now, I think. I can't quite remember. I don't like her new man at all. I don't mind taking any reasonable risk, but he's so obstinate – he charges everything he sees. Heaven alone knows what would happen if he rushed into something that wouldn't swerve aside. But the poor creature's got a withered arm, and something the matter with one of his feet, I believe she told me. I suppose that's what makes him so careless. I mean – well! ... Don't you know! ...

Friend...?

Lady: Yes, she's sold it. My dear, it was far too small. There were only ten bedrooms, you know. There were only ten bedrooms in that house. Extraordinary! One wouldn't believe it from the outside – would one? And with the governesses and the nurses – and so on. All the menservants had to sleep out... You know what that means.

Friend...!!

Conductor: Fares, please. Pass your fares along.

Lady: How much is it? Tuppence, isn't it? Two tuppenny ones, please. Don't bother – I've got some coppers, somewhere or other.

Friend...!

Lady: No, it's all right. I've got some – if only I can find them.

Conductor: Parse your fares, please.

Friend...!

Lady: Really? So I did. I remember now. Yes, I paid coming. Very well, I'll let you, just this once. War time, my dear.

Conductor: 'Ow far do you want ter go?

Lady: To the Boltons.

Conductor: Another 'a'penny each.

Lady: No – oh, no! I only paid tuppence coming. Are you quite sure?

Conductor (savagely): Read it on the board for yourself.

Lady: Oh, very well. Here's another penny. (To friend): 'Isn't it extraordinary how disobliging these men are? After all, he's paid to do his job. But they are nearly all alike. I've heard these motor buses affect the spine after a time. I suppose that's it... You've heard about Teddie – haven't you?'

Friend...

Lady: He's got his... He's got his... Now what is it? Whatever can it be? How ridiculous of me!

Friend...?

Lady: Oh, no! He's been a Major for ages.

Friend...?

Lady: Colonel? Oh, no, my dear, it's something much higher than that. Not his company – he's had his company a long time. Not his battalion...

Friend...?

Lady: Regiment! Yes, I believe it is his regiment. But what I was going to say is he's been made a... Oh, how silly I am! What's higher than a Brigadier-General? Yes, I believe that's it. Chief of Staff: Of course, Mrs T.'s frightfully gratified.

Friend...

Lady: Oh, my dear, everybody goes over the top nowadays. Whatever his position may be. And Teddy is such a sport, I really don't see how... Too dreadful – isn't it!

Friend...?

Lady: Didn't you know? She's at the War Office, and doing very well. I believe she got a rise the other day. She's something to do with notifying the deaths, or finding the missing. I don't know exactly what it is. At any rate, she says it is too depressing for words, and she has to read the most heartrending letters from parents, and so on. Happily, they're a very cheery little group in her room – all officers' wives, and they make their own tea, and get cakes in turn from Stewart's. She has one afternoon a week off, when she shops or has her hair waved. Last time she and I went to see Yvette's Spring Show.

Friend...?

Lady: No, not really. I'm getting frightfully sick of these coat-frocks, aren't you? I mean, as I was saying to her, what is the use of paying an enormous price for having one made by Yvette, when you can't really tell the difference, in the long run, between it and one of those cheap ready-made ones. Of course, one has the satisfaction for oneself of knowing that the material is good, and so on – but it looks nothing. No; I advised her to get a good coat and skirt. For, after all, a good coat and skirt always tells. Doesn't it?

Friend...!

Lady: Yes, I didn't tell her that – but that's what I had in mind. She's much too fat for those coat-frocks. She goes out far too much at the hips. I half ordered a rather lovely indefinite blue one for myself, trimmed with the new lobster red... I've lost my good Kate, you know.

Friend...!

Lady: Yes, isn't it annoying! Just when I got her more or less trained. But she went off her head, like they all do nowadays, and decided that she wanted to go into munitions. I told her when she gave notice that she would go on the strict understanding that if she got a job (which I think is highly improbable), she was not to come back and disturb the other servants.

Conductor (savagely): Another penny each, if you're going on.

Lady: Oh, we're there. How extraordinary! I never should have noticed...

Friend...?

Lady: Tuesday? Bridge on Tuesday? No, dear, I'm afraid I can't manage Tuesday. I trot out the wounded every Tuesday you know. I let cook take them to the Zoo, or some place like that – don't you know. Wednesday – I'm perfectly free on Wednesday.

Conductor: It'll be Wednesday before you get off the 'bus if you don't 'urry up.

Lady: That's quite enough, my man.

Friend...!!

Blowing Up a Train
From *Seven Pillars of Wisdom: Book VI – The Failure of the Bridges*, T. E. Lawrence

Food was going to be our next preoccupation, and we held a council in the cold driving rain to consider what we might do. For lightness' sake we had carried from Azrak three days' rations, which made us complete until tonight; but we could not go back empty-handed. The Beni Sakhr wanted honour, and the Serahin were too lately disgraced not to clamour for more adventure. We had still a reserve bag of thirty pounds of gelatine, and Ali ibn el Hussein who had heard of the performances below Maan, and was as Arab as any Arab, said, 'Let's blow up a train'. The word was hailed with universal joy, and they looked at me: but I was not able to share their hopes, all at once.

Blowing up trains was an exact science when done deliberately, by a sufficient party, with machine-guns in position. If scrambled at it might become dangerous. The difficulty this time was that the available gunners were Indians; who, though good men fed, were only half-men in cold and hunger. I did not propose to drag them off without rations on an adventure which might take a week. There was no cruelty in starving Arabs; they would not die of a few days' fasting, and would fight as well as ever on empty stomachs; while, if things got too difficult, there were the riding-camels to kill and eat: but the Indians, though Moslems, refused camel-flesh on principle.

I explained these delicacies of diet. Ali at once said that it would be enough for me to blow up the train, leaving him and the Arabs with him to do their best to carry its wreck without machine-gun support. As, in this unsuspecting district, we might well happen on a supply train, with civilians or only a small guard of reservists aboard, I agreed to risk it. The decision having been applauded, we sat down in a cloaked circle, to finish our remaining food in a very late and cold supper (the rain had sodden the fuel and made fire not possible) our hearts somewhat comforted by chance of another effort.

At dawn, with the unfit of the Arabs, the Indians moved away for Azrak, miserably. They had started up country with me in hope of a really military enterprise, and first had seen the muddled bridge, and now were losing this prospective train. It was hard on them; and to soften the blow with honour I asked Wood to accompany them. He agreed, after argument, for their sakes; but it proved a wise move for himself, as a sickness which had been troubling him began to show the early signs of pneumonia.

The balance of us, some sixty men, turned back towards the railway. None of them knew the country, so I led them to Minifir, where, with Zaal, we had made havoc in the spring. The re-curved hill-top was an excellent observation post, camp, grazing ground and way of retreat, and we sat there in our old place till sunset, shivering and staring out over the immense plain which stretched map-like to the clouded peaks of Jebel Druse, with Um el Jemal and her sister-villages like ink-smudges on it through the rain.

In the first dusk we walked down to lay the mine. The rebuilt culvert of kilometre 172 seemed still the fittest place. While we stood by it there came a rumbling, and through the gathering darkness and mist a train suddenly appeared round the northern curve, only two hundred yards away. We scurried under the long arch and heard it roll overhead. This was annoying; but when the course was clear again, we fell to burying the charge. The evening was bitterly cold, with drifts of rain blowing down the valley.

The arch was solid masonry, of four metres span, and stood over a shingle water-bed which took its rise on our hill-top. The winter rains had cut this into a channel four feet deep, narrow and winding, which served us as an admirable approach till within three hundred yards of the line. There the gully widened out and ran straight towards the culvert, open to the sight of anyone upon the rails.

We hid the explosive carefully on the crown of the arch, deeper than usual, beneath a tie, so that the patrols would not feel its jelly softness under their feet. The wires were taken down the bank into the shingle bed of the watercourse, where concealment was quick; and up it as far as they would reach. Unfortunately, this was only sixty yards, for there had been difficulty in Egypt over insulated cable and no more had been available when our expedition started.

Sixty yards was plenty for the bridge, but little for a train: however, the ends happened to coincide with a little bush about ten inches high, on the edge of the watercourse, and we buried them beside this very convenient mark. It was impossible to leave them joined up to the exploder in the proper way, since the spot was evident to the permanent-way patrols as they made their rounds.

Owing to the mud the job took longer than usual, and it was very nearly dawn before we finished. I waited under the draughty arch till day broke, wet and dismal, and then I went over the whole area of disturbance, spending another half-hour in effacing its every mark, scattering leaves and dead grass over it, and watering down the broken mud from a shallow rain-pool near. Then they waved to me that the first patrol was coming, and I went up to join the others.

Before I had reached them they came tearing down into their prearranged places, lining the watercourse and spurs each side. A train was coming from the north. Hamud, Feisal's long slave, had the exploder; but before he reached me a short train of closed box-wagons rushed by at speed. The rainstorms on the plain and the thick morning had hidden it from the eyes of our watchman until too late. This second failure saddened us further and Ali began to say that nothing would come right this trip. Such a statement held risk as prelude of the discovery of an evil eye present; so, to divert attention, I suggested new watching posts be sent far out, one to the ruins on the north, one to the great cairn of the southern crest.

The rest, having no breakfast, were to pretend not to be hungry. They all enjoyed doing this, and for a while we sat cheerfully in the rain, huddling against one another for warmth behind a breastwork of our streaming camels. The moisture made the animals' hair curl up like a fleece, so that they looked queerly dishevelled. When the rain paused, which it did frequently, a cold moaning wind searched out the unprotected parts of us very thoroughly. After a time we found our wetted shirts clammy and comfortless things. We had nothing to eat, nothing to do and nowhere to sit except on wet rock, wet grass or mud. However, this persistent weather kept reminding me that it would delay Allenby's advance on Jerusalem, and rob him of his great possibility. So large a misfortune to our lion was a half-encouragement for the mice. We would be partners into next year.

In the best circumstances, waiting for action was hard. Today it was beastly. Even enemy patrols stumbled along without care, perfunctorily, against the rain. At last, near noon, in a snatch of fine weather, the watchmen on the south peak flagged their cloaks wildly in signal of a train. We reached our positions in an instant, for we had squatted the late hours on our heels in a streaming ditch near the line, so as not to miss another chance. The Arabs took cover properly. I looked back at their ambush from my firing point, and saw nothing but the grey hillsides.

I could not hear the train coming, but trusted, and knelt ready for perhaps half an hour, when the suspense became intolerable, and I signalled to know what was up. They sent down to say it was coming very slowly, and was an enormously long train. Our appetites stiffened. The longer it was the more would be the loot. Then came word that it had stopped. It moved again.

Finally, near one o'clock, I heard it panting. The locomotive was evidently defective (all these wood-fired trains were bad), and the heavy load on the up-gradient was proving too much for its capacity. I crouched behind my bush, while it crawled slowly into view past the south cutting, and along the bank above my head towards the culvert. The first ten trucks were open trucks, crowded with troops. However, once again it was too late to choose, so when the engine was squarely over the mine I pushed down the handle of the exploder. Nothing happened. I sawed it up and down four times.

Still nothing happened; and I realised that it had gone out of order, and that I was kneeling on a naked bank, with a Turkish troop train crawling past fifty yards away. The bush, which had seemed a foot high, shrank smaller than a fig-leaf; and I felt myself the most distinct object in the countryside. Behind me was an open valley for two hundred yards to the cover where my Arabs were waiting and wondering what I was at. It was impossible to make a bolt for it, or the Turks would step off the train and finish us. If I sat still, there might be just a hope of my being ignored as a casual Bedouin.

So there I sat, counting for sheer life, while eighteen open trucks, three box-wagons, and three officers' coaches dragged by. The engine panted slower and slower, and I thought every moment that it would break down. The troops took no great notice of me, but the officers were interested, and came out to the little platforms at the ends of their carriages, pointing and staring. I waved back at them, grinning nervously, and feeling an improbable shepherd in my Meccan dress, with its twisted golden circlet about my head. Perhaps the mud-stains, the wet and their ignorance made me accepted. The end of the brake van slowly disappeared into the cutting on the north.

As it went, I jumped up, buried my wires, snatched hold of the wretched exploder, and went like a rabbit uphill into safety. There I took breath and looked back to see that the train had finally stuck. It waited, about five hundred yards beyond the mine, for nearly an hour to get up a head of steam, while an officers' patrol came back and searched, very carefully, the ground where I had been seen sitting. However the wires were properly hidden: they found nothing; the engine plucked up heart again, and away they went.

Mifleh was past tears, thinking I had intentionally let the train through; and when the Serahin had been told the real cause they said 'Bad luck is with us'. Historically they were right; but they meant it for a prophecy, so I made sarcastic reference to their courage at the bridge the week before, hinting that it might be a tribal preference to sit on camel-guard. At once there was uproar, the Serahin attacking me furiously, the Beni Sakhr defending. Ali heard the trouble, and came running.

When we had made it up the original despondency was half forgotten. Ali backed me nobly, though the wretched boy was blue with cold and shivering in an attack of fever. He gasped that their ancestor the Prophet had given to Sherifs the faculty of 'sight', and by it he knew that our luck was turning. This was comfort for them: my first instalment of good fortune came when in the wet, without other tool than my dagger, I got the box of the exploder open and persuaded its electrical gear to work properly once more.

We returned to our vigil by the wires, but nothing happened, and evening drew down with more squalls and beastliness, everybody full of grumbles. There was no train; it was too wet to light a cooking fire; our only potential food was camel. Raw meat did not tempt anyone that night; and so our beasts survived to the morrow.

Ali lay down on his belly, which position lessened the hunger-ache, trying to sleep off his fever. Khazen, Ali's servant, lent him his cloak for extra covering. For a spell I took Khazen under mine, but soon found it becoming crowded. So I left it to him and went downhill to connect up the exploder. Afterwards I spent the night there alone by the singing telegraph wires, hardly wishing to sleep, so painful was the cold. Nothing came all the long hours, and dawn, which broke wet, looked even uglier than usual. We were sick to death of Minifir, of railways, of train watching and wrecking, by now. I climbed up to the main body while the early patrol searched the railway. Then the day cleared a little. Ali awoke, much refreshed, and his new spirit cheered us. Hamud, the slave, produced some sticks which he had kept under his clothes by his skin all night. They were nearly dry. We shaved down some blasting gelatine, and with its hot flame got a fire going, while the Sukhur hurriedly killed a mangy camel, the best spared of our riding-beasts, and began with entrenching tools to hack it into handy joints.

Just at that moment the watchman on the north cried a train. We left the fire and made a breathless race of the six hundred yards downhill to our old position. Round the bend, whistling its loudest, came the train, a splendid two-engined thing of twelve passenger coaches, travelling at top speed on the favouring grade. I touched off under the first driving wheel of the first locomotive, and the explosion was terrific. The ground spouted blackly into my face, and I was sent spinning, to sit up with the shirt torn to my shoulder and the blood dripping from long, ragged scratches on my left arm. Between my knees lay the exploder, crushed under a twisted sheet of sooty iron. In front of me was the scalded and smoking upper half of a man. When I peered through the dust and steam of the explosion the whole boiler of the first engine seemed to be missing.

I dully felt that it was time to get away to support; but when I moved, learnt that there was a great pain in my right foot, because of which I could only limp along, with my head swinging from the shock. Movement began to clear away this confusion, as I hobbled towards the upper valley, whence the Arabs were now shooting fast into the crowded coaches. Dizzily I cheered myself by repeating aloud in English 'Oh, I wish this hadn't happened'.

When the enemy began to return our fire, I found myself much between the two. Ali saw me fall, and thinking that I was hard hit, ran out, with Turki and about twenty men of his servants and the Beni Sakhr, to help me. The Turks found their range and got seven of them in a few seconds. The others, in a rush, were about me – fit models, after their activity, for a sculptor. Their full white cotton drawers drawn in, bell-like, round their slender waists and ankles; their hairless brown bodies; and the love-locks plaited tightly over each temple in long horns, made them look like Russian dancers.

We scrambled back into cover together, and there, secretly, I felt myself over, to find I had not once been really hurt; though besides the bruises and cuts of the boiler-plate and a broken toe, I had five different bullet-grazes on me (some of them uncomfortably deep) and my clothes ripped to pieces.

From the watercourse we could look about. The explosion had destroyed the arched head of the culvert, and the frame of the first engine was lying beyond it, at the near foot of the embankment, down which it had rolled. The second locomotive had toppled into the gap, and was lying across the ruined tender of the first. Its bed was twisted. I judged them both beyond repair. The second tender had disappeared over the further side; and the first three wagons had telescoped and were smashed in pieces.

The rest of the train was badly derailed, with the listing coaches butted end to end at all angles, zigzagged along the track. One of them was a saloon, decorated with flags. In it had been Mehmed Jemal Pasha, commanding the Eighth Army Corps, hurrying down to defend Jerusalem against Allenby. His chargers had been in the first wagon; his motor-car was on the end of the train, and we shot it up. Of his staff we noticed a fat ecclesiastic, whom we thought to be Assad Shukair, Imam to Ahmed Jemal Pasha, and a notorious pro-Turk pimp. So we blazed at him till he dropped.

It was all long bowls. We could see that our chances of carrying
the wreck were slight. There had been some four hundred men on
board, and the survivors, now recovered from the shock, were under
shelter and shooting hard at us. At the first moment our party on the
north spur had closed, and nearly won the game. Mifleh on his mare
chased the officers from the saloon into the lower ditch. He was too
excited to stop and shoot, and so they got away scatheless. The Arabs
following him had turned to pick up some of the rifles and medals
littering the ground, and then to drag bags and boxes from the train.
If we had had a machine-gun posted to cover the far side, according
to my mining practice, not a Turk would have escaped.

Mifleh and Adhub rejoined us on the hill, and asked after Fahad.
One of the Serahin told how he had led the first rush, while I lay
knocked out beside the exploder, and had been killed near it. They
showed his belt and rifle as proof that he was dead and that they
had tried to save him. Adhub said not a word, but leaped out of the
gully, and raced downhill. We caught our breaths till our lungs hurt
us, watching him; but the Turks seemed not to see. A minute later he
was dragging a body behind the left-hand bank.

Mifleh went back to his mare, mounted, and took her down behind
a spur. Together they lifted the inert figure on to the pommel, and
returned. A bullet had passed through Fahad's face, knocking out
four teeth, and gashing the tongue. He had fallen unconscious, but
had revived just before Adhub reached him, and was trying on hands
and knees, blinded with blood, to crawl away. He now recovered
poise enough to cling to a saddle. So they changed him to the first
camel they found, and led him off at once.

The Turks, seeing us so quiet, began to advance up the slope. We
let them come half-way, and then poured in volleys which killed
some twenty and drove the others back. The ground about the train
was strewn with dead, and the broken coaches had been crowded:
but they were fighting under eye of their Corps Commander, and
undaunted began to work round the spurs to outflank us.

We were now only about forty left, and obviously could do no
good against them. So we ran in batches up the little stream-bed,

turning at each sheltered angle to delay them by pot-shots. Little Turki much distinguished himself by quick coolness, though his straight-stocked Turkish cavalry carbine made him so expose his head that he got four bullets through his head-cloth. Ali was angry with me for retiring slowly. In reality my raw hurts crippled me, but to hide from him this real reason I pretended to be easy, interested in and studying the Turks. Such successive rests while I gained courage for a new run kept him and Turki far behind the rest.

At last we reached the hill-top. Each man there jumped on the nearest camel, and made away at full speed eastward into the desert, for an hour. Then in safety we sorted our animals. The excellent Rahail, despite the ruling excitement, had brought off with him, tied to his saddle-girth, a huge haunch of the camel slaughtered just as the train arrived. He gave us the motive for a proper halt, five miles farther on, as a little party of four camels appeared marching in the same direction. It was our companion, Matar, coming back from his home village to Azrak with loads of raisins and peasant delicacies.

So we stopped at once, under a large rock in Wadi Dhuleil, where was a barren fig-tree, and cooked our first meal for three days. There, also, we bandaged up Fahad, who was sleepy with the lassitude of his severe hurt. Adhub, seeing this, took one of Matar's new carpets, and, doubling it across the camel-saddle, stitched the ends into great pockets. In one they laid Fahad, while Adhub crawled into the other as make-weight: and the camel was led off southward towards their tribal tents.

The other wounded men were seen to at the same time. Mifleh brought up the youngest lads of the party, and had them spray the wounds with their piss, as a rude antiseptic. Meanwhile we whole ones refreshed ourselves. I bought another mangy camel for extra meat, paid rewards, compensated the relatives of the killed, and gave prize-money, for the sixty or seventy rifles we had taken. It was small booty, but not to be despised. Some Serahin, who had gone into the action without rifles, able only to throw unavailing stones, had now two guns apiece. Next day we moved into Azrak, having a great welcome, and boasting – God forgive us – that we were victors.

Munition Wages
Madeline Ida Bedford

Earning high wages? Yus,
Five quid a week.
A woman, too, mind you,
I calls it dim sweet.

Ye'are asking some questions –
But bless yer, here goes:
I spends the whole racket
On good times and clothes.

Me saving? Elijah!
Yer do think I'm mad.
I'm acting the lady,
But – I ain't living bad.

I'm having life's good times.
See 'ere, it's like this:
The 'oof come o' danger,
A touch-and-go bizz.

We're all here today, mate,
Tomorrow – perhaps dead,
If Fate tumbles on us
And blows up our shed.

Afraid! Are yer kidding?
With money to spend!
Years back I wore tatters,
Now – silk stockings, mi friend!

I've bracelets and jewellery,
Rings envied by friends;

A sergeant to swank with,
And something to lend.

I drive out in taxis,
Do theatres in style,
And this is mi verdict –
It is jolly worthwhile.

Worthwhile, for tomorrow
If I'm blown to the sky,
I'll have repaid mi wages
In death – and pass by.

Christmas Up the Line
From *Notes of a Camp Follower on the Western Front*,
E. W. Hornung

Soon the shy wintry sun was wearing a veil of frosted silver. The eye
of the moon was on us early in the afternoon, ever a little wider open
and a degree colder in its stare. All one day our mud rang like an
anvil to the tramp of rubicund customers in greatcoats and gloves;
and the next day they came and went like figures on the film next-
door, silent and outstanding upon a field of dazzling snow.

But behind the counter we had no such seasonable sights to cheer
us; behind the counter, mugs washed overnight needed wrenching
off their shelf, and three waistcoats were none too many. In our
room, for all the stove that reddened like a schoolgirl, and all the
stoking that we did last thing at night, no amount of sweaters,
blankets, and miscellaneous wraps was excessive provision against
the early morning. By dawn, which leant like lead against our canvas
windows, and poked sticks of icy light through a dozen holes and
crannies, the only unfrozen water in the hut was in the kitchen boiler
and in my own hot-water bottle. I made no bones about this trusty
friend; it hung all day on a conspicuous nail; and it did not prevent

me from being the first up in the morning, any more than modesty shall deter me from trumpeting the fact. One of us had to get up to lay the stove and light the fire, and it was my chance of drawing approximately even with my brisk commander. No competing with his invidious energy once he had taken the deck; but here was a march I could count on stealing while he slept the sleep of the young. Often I was about before the orderlies, and have seen the two rogues lying on their backs in the dim light of their kitchen, side by side like huge dirty children. As for me, blackened and bent double by my exertions, swaddled in fleece lining and other scratch accoutrements, no doubt I looked the lion grotesque of the party; but, by the time the wood crackled and the chimney drew, I too had my inner glow.

So we reached the shortest day; then came a break, and for me the Christmas outing of a lifetime.

The Y.M.C.A. in that sector had just started an outpost of free cheer in the support line. It was a new departure for the winter only, a kind of cocoa-kitchen in the trenches, and we were all very eager to take our turn as cooks. The post was being manned by relays of the workers in our area, one at a time and for a week apiece; but at Christmas there were to be substantial additions to the nightly offering. It was the obvious thing to suggest that extra help would be required, and to volunteer for the special duty. But one may jump at such a chance and yet feel a sneaking thrill of morbid apprehension, and yet again enjoy the whole thing the more for that very feeling. Such was my case as I lit the fire on the morning of the 21st of December, foolishly wondering whether I should ever light it again. By all accounts our pitch up the Line was none too sheltered in any sense, and the severity of the weather was not the least intimidating prospect. But for forty mortal months I would have given my right eye to see trench life with my left; and I was still prepared to strike that bargain and think it cheap.

The man already on the spot was coming down to take me back with him: we met at our headquarters over the mid-day meal, by which time my romantic experience had begun. I had walked the ruined streets in a shrapnel helmet, endeavouring to look as though it belonged to me, and had worn a gas-mask long enough to hope I might never have to do so for dear life. The other man had been wearing his in a gas-alarm up the Line; he had also been missed by a sniper, coming down the trench that morning; and had much to say about a man who had not been missed, but had lain, awaiting burial, all the day before on the spot where we were to spend our Christmas... It was three o'clock and incipient twilight when we made a start.

Our little headquarters Ford 'bus took us the first three miles, over the snow of a very famous battlefield, not a whole year old in history, to the mouth of a valley planted with our guns. Alighting here we made as short work of that valley as appearances permitted, each with a shifty eye for the next shell-hole in case of need; there were plenty of them, including some extremely late models, but it was not our lot to see the collection enlarged. Neither had our own batteries anything to say over our heads; and presently the trenches received us in fair order, if somewhat over-heated. I speak for myself and that infernal fleece lining, which I had buttoned back into its proper place. It alone precluded an indecent haste.

But in the trenches we could certainly afford to go slower, and I for one was not sorry. It was too wonderful to be in them in the flesh. They were almost just what I had always pictured them; a little narrower, perhaps; and the unbroken chain of duck-boards was a feature not definitely foreseen; and the printed sign-boards had not the expected air of a joke, might rather have been put up by order of the London County Council. But the extreme narrowness was a surprise, and indeed would have taken my breath away had I met my match in some places. An ordinary gaunt warrior caused me to lean hard against my side of the trench, and to apologise rather freely as he squeezed past; a file of them in leather jerkins, with snow on their toe-caps and a twinkle under their steel hat-brims, almost tempted me to take a short cut over the top. I wondered would I have got very far, or dropped straight back into the endless open grave of the communication trench.

Seen from afar, as I knew of old, that was exactly what the trenches looked like; but from the inside they appeared more solid and rather deeper than any grave dug for the dead. The whole thing put me more in mind of primitive ship-building – the great ribs leaning outwards, flat timbers in between – and over all sand-bags and sometimes wire-work with the precise effect of bulwarks and hammock-netting. Even the mouths of dug-outs were not unlike port-holes flush with the deck; and many a piquant glimpse we caught in passing, bits of faces lit by cigarette-ends and half-sentences or snatches of sardonic song; then the trench would twist round a corner into solitude, as a country road shakes off a hamlet, and on we trudged through the thickening dusk. Once, where the sand-bags were lower than I had noticed, I thought some very small bird had chirped behind my head, until the other man turned his and smiled.

'Hear that?' he said. 'That was a bullet! It's just about where they sniped at me this morning.'

I shortened my stick, and crept the rest of the way like the oldest inhabitant of those trenches, as perhaps I was.

It was nearly dark when our journey ended at one of those sunken roads which make a name for themselves on all battlefields, and duly complicate the Western Front. Sometimes they cut the trench as a level crossing does a street, and then it is not a bad rule to cross as though a train were coming. Sometimes it is the trench that intersects the sunken road; this happened here. We squeezed through a gap in the sand-bags, a gap exactly like a stile in a stone fence, and from our feet the bleak road rose with a wild effect into the wintry sunset.

It was a road of some breadth, but all crinkled and misshapen in its soiled bandage of frozen snow. Palpable shell-holes met a touchy eye for them on every side; one, as clean-cut as our present footprints, literally adjoined a little low sand-bagged shelter, of much the same dimensions as a blackfellow's gunyah in the bush. This inviting habitation served as annex to a small enough hut at least three times its size; the two cowered end to end against the sunken roadside, each roof a bit of bank-top in more than camouflage, with real grass doing its best to grow in real sods.

'No,' said the other man, 'only the second half of the hut's our hut. This first half's a gum-boot store. The sand-bagged hutch at the end of all things is where we sleep.'

CHRISTMAS DAY

The tiny hut is an abode of darkness made visible by a single candle, mounted in its own grease in the worst available position for giving light, lest the opening of the door cast the faintest beam into the sunken road outside. On the shelf flush with the door glimmer parental urns with a large family of condensed-milk tins, opened and unopened, full and empty; packing-cases in similar stages litter the duck-board flooring, or pile it wall-high in the background; trench-coats, gas-masks, haversacks and helmets hang from nails or repose on a ledge of the inner wall, which is the sunken roadside, naked and unashamed. Two weary figures cower over the boiler fire; they are the other man and yet another who has come up for the night. A third person, who may look more like me than I feel like him, hovers behind them, smoking and peering at his watch. It is the last few minutes of Christmas Eve, and for a long hour there has been little or nothing doing. Earlier in the evening, from seven or so onwards, there seemed no end to the queue of armed men, calling for their mug of cocoa and their packet of biscuits, either singly, each for himself, or with dixies and sand-bags to be filled for comrades on duty in the trenches.

The quiet has been broken only by the sibilant song of the boiler, by desultory conversation and bursts of gunfire as spasmodic and inconsequent. Often a machine-gun has beaten a brief but furious tattoo on the doors of darkness; but now come clogged and ponderous footfalls – mud to mud on the duck-boards leading from the communication trench – and a chit is handed in from the outer moonlight.

24–12–17.

To Y.M.C.A. Canteen,
_____ Avenue.

DEAR SIRS,

I will be much obliged if you will supply the bearer with hot cocoa (sufficient for 90 men) which I understand you are good enough to issue to units in this line. The party are taking 2 hot-food containers for the purpose.

Thanking you in anticipation,
I am, yours faithfully,
(Illegible),
O/C B Co.,
1/8 (Undesirable).

Torpid trio are busy men once more. Not enough cocoa ready-made for ninety; fresh brew under way in fewer seconds than it takes to state the fact. Third person already anchored beside open packing-case, enormous sand-bag gaping between his knees, little sealed packets flying through his hands from box to bag in twins and triplets. By now it is Christmas morning; cakes and cigarettes are forthwith added to statutory biscuits, and a sack is what is wanted. Third person makes shift with second sandbag, which having filled, he leaves his colleagues working like benevolent fiends in the steam of fragrant cauldrons, and joins the group outside among the shell-holes.

They are consuming interim dividends of the nightly fare, as they stand about in steely silhouette against the shrouded moonlight. The scene is not quite so picturesque as it was last night, when no star of heaven could live in the light of the frosty moon and every helmet was a shining halo; tonight the only twinkle to be seen is under a helmet's rim.

'Merry Christmas, sir, an' many of 'em,' says a Tyneside voice, getting in the first shot of a severe bombardment. The third person retaliates with appropriate spirit; the interchange could not have been franker or heartier in the days of actual peace on earth and apparent good-will among men. But here they both are for a little space this Christmas morning. Cannon may drum it in with thunderous irony, and some corner-man behind a machine-gun oblige with what sounds exactly like a solo on the bones, but here in the midst of those familiar alarms the Spirit of Christmas is abroad on the battlefield. He may be frightened away – or become a casualty – at any moment. One lucky flourish with the bones, one more addition to these sharp-edged shell-holes, and how many of the party would have a groan left in him? One of them groans in spirit as he thinks, never so vividly, of countless groups as full of gay vitality as this one, blown out of existence in a blinding flash. But his hardy friends are above such morbid imaginings; the cold appears to be their only trouble, and of it they make light enough as they stamp their feet. Some are sea-booted in sand-bags, and what with their jerkins and low, round helmets, look more like a watch in oilskins and sou'-westers than a party of infantry.

'We nevaw died o' wintaw yet,' says the Tynesider. 'It takes a lot to kill an old soljaw.' But he owns he was a shipyard hand before the war; and not one of them was in the Army.

All hope it is the last Christmas of the war, but the Tyneside prognostication of 'anothaw ten yeaws' is received with perfect equanimity. There is general agreement, too, when the same oracle dismisses the latest peace offer as 'blooff.' But it must be confessed that articulate ardour is slightly damped until somebody starts a subject a great deal nearer home.

'Who'd have thought that we should live to see a Y.M. in the support line!'

Flattering echoes from entire group.

'Do you remember that chap who kept us all awake in barracks, talking of it?'

'I nevaw believed him. I thought it was a myth, sir. And nothing to pay an' all! It must be costing the Y.M. a canny bit o' money, sir?'

The third person – who has been hovering on the verge of the inveterate first – only commits himself to the statement that he helped to give away 785 cups of cocoa and packets of biscuits the night before. Rapid calculations ensue.

'Why, that must be nearly ten pounds a night, sir?'

'Something like that.'

'Heaw that, Corporal! An' now it's cigarettes an' cakes an' all!'

But the containers are ready, lids screwed down upon their steaming contents. Strong arms hoist them upon stronger backs; the plethoric sand-bags are shouldered with still less ado, and off go the party into the slate-coloured night, off through the communication trenches into the firing-line they are to hold for England until the twelve hundred and thirty-ninth daybreak of the war.

Peering after them with wistful glasses, the third person relapses altogether into the first. Take away the odd two hundred, and for a thousand days and nights my heart has been where their muffled feet will be treading in another minute. Yes; a round thousand must be almost the exact length of days since I first came out here in the spirit, and to stay. But never till this year did I seriously dream of following in the flesh, or till this moment feel the front line like a ball at my feet.

Even the day before yesterday the arrangement was not so definite as it is today; it was not the Colonel himself who was to have taken us round by special favour and appointment. Yet how easily, had the Strafe happened half-an-hour later than it did, might we not have come in for it, perhaps at the very place where the parapet was blown down! It would have been a wonderful experience, especially as there were no casualties. Will anything of the kind happen today? I have a feeling that something may; but then I have had that feeling every sentient moment up the Line. And nothing that can come can come amiss; that is another of my feelings here, if not the strongest of them all. This Christmas morning it rings almost like a carol in the heart, almost like a peal of Christmas bells – jangled indeed by the heart's own bitter flaws, and yet piercing sweet as Life itself.

But for all my elderly civilian excitement, before a risk too tiny to enter a young fighting head at all, sleep does not fail me on a new couch of my own construction. The sand-bagged lair was none too dry in the late hard frost; in the unseasonable thaw that seems to be setting in, it is no place for crabbed age. Youth is welcome to the two beds with the water now standing on their India rubber sheets, and youth seems quite honestly to prefer them; so I make mine on the biscuit-boxes in the shed, turn my toes to the still glowing coke in the boiler fire, press my soles to the hot-water bottle which has distinguished itself by freezing during the day, and huddle down as usual in all the indoor and outdoor garments I have with me, under my share of the blankets, which I have been drying assiduously every evening. The Romance of War performs its nightly unromantic office ... and I have had many a worse night upon a spring-mattress.

1918 – and After

Futility
Wilfred Owen

Move him into the sun –
Gently its touch awoke him once,
At home, whispering of fields unsown.
Always it awoke him, even in France,
Until this morning and this snow.
If anything might rouse him now
The kind old sun will know.

Think how it wakes the seeds –
Woke, once, the clays of a cold star.
Are limbs so dear-achieved, are sides
Full-nerved – still warm – too hard to stir?
Was it for this the clay grew tall?
– O what made fatuous sunbeams toil
To break earth's sleep at all?

The Bright Side
From *Tatterdemalion*, John Galsworthy

A little Englishwoman, married to a German, had dwelt with him eighteen years in humble happiness and the district of Putney, where her husband worked in the finer kinds of leather. He was a harmless, busy little man with the gift for turning his hand to anything which is bred into the peasants of the Black Forest, who on their upland farms make all the necessaries of daily life – their coarse linen from home-grown flax, their leather gear from the hides of their beasts, their clothes from the wool thereof, their furniture from the pine logs of the Forest, their bread from home-grown flour milled in simple fashion and baked in the home-made ovens, their cheese from the milk of their own goats. Why he had come to England he probably did not remember – it was so long ago; but he would still know why he had married Dora, the daughter of the Putney carpenter, she being, as it were, salt of the earth: one of those Cockney women, deeply sensitive beneath a well-nigh impermeable mask of humour and philosophy, who quite unselfconsciously are always doing things for others. In their little grey Putney house they had dwelt those eighteen years, without perhaps ever having had time to move, though they had often had the intention of doing so for the sake of the children, of whom they had three, a boy and two girls. Mrs Gerhardt – she shall be called, for her husband had a very German name, and there is more in a name than Shakespeare dreamed of – Mrs Gerhardt was a little woman with large hazel eyes and dark crinkled hair in which there were already a few threads of grey when the war broke out. Her boy David, the eldest, was fourteen at that date, and her girls, Minnie and Violet, were eight and five, rather pretty children, especially the little one. Gerhardt, perhaps because he was so handy, had never risen. His firm regarded him as indispensable and paid him fair wages, but he had no 'push,' having the craftsman's temperament, and employing his spare time in little neat jobs for his house and his neighbours, which brought him no return. They made their way, therefore, without that provision for the future which necessitates the employment of one's time for one's own ends. But they were happy, and had no enemies; and each year saw some mild improvements in their studiously clean house and tiny back garden. Mrs Gerhardt, who was cook, seamstress, washerwoman, besides being wife and mother, was almost notorious in that street of semi-detached houses for being at the disposal of any one in sickness or trouble. She was not strong in body, for things had gone wrong when she bore her first, but her spirit had that peculiar power of seeing things as they were, and yet refusing to be dismayed, which so embarrasses Fate. She saw her husband's defects clearly, and his good qualities no less distinctly – they never quarrelled. She gauged her children's characters too, with an admirable precision, which left, however, loopholes of wonder as to what they would become.

The outbreak of the war found them on the point of going to Margate for Bank Holiday, an almost unparalleled event; so that the importance of the world catastrophe was brought home to them with a vividness which would otherwise have been absent from folks so simple, domestic, and far-removed from that atmosphere in which the egg of war is hatched.

Over the origin and merits of the struggle, beyond saying to each other several times that it was a dreadful thing, Mr and Mrs Gerhardt held but one little conversation, lying in their iron bed with an immortal brown eiderdown patterned with red wriggles over them. They agreed that it was a cruel, wicked thing to invade 'that little Belgium,' and there left a matter which seemed to them a mysterious and insane perversion of all they had hitherto been accustomed to think of as life. Reading their papers – a daily and a weekly, in which they had as much implicit faith as a million other readers – they were soon duly horrified by the reports therein of 'Hun' atrocities; so horrified that they would express their condemnation of the Kaiser and his militarism as freely as if they had been British subjects. It was therefore with an uneasy surprise that they began to find these papers talking of 'the Huns at large in our midst,' of 'spies,' and the national danger of 'nourishing such vipers.' They were deeply conscious of not being 'vipers,' and such sayings began to awaken in both their breasts a humble sense of injustice as it were. This was more acute in the breast of little Mrs Gerhardt, because, of course, the shafts were directed not at her but at her husband. She knew her husband so well, knew him incapable of anything but homely, kindly busyness, and that he should be lumped into the category of 'Huns' and 'spies' and tarred with the brush of mass hatred amazed and stirred her indignation, or would have, if her Cockney temperament had allowed her to take it very seriously. As for Gerhardt, he became extremely silent, so that it was ever more and more difficult to tell what he was feeling. The patriotism of the newspapers took a considerable time to affect the charity of the citizens of Putney, and so long as no neighbour showed signs of thinking that little Gerhardt was a monster and a spy it was fairly easy for Mrs Gerhardt to sleep at night, and to read her papers with the feeling that the remarks in them were not really intended for Gerhardt and herself. But she noticed that her man had given up reading them, and would push them away from his eyes if, in the tiny sitting-room with the heavily-flowered walls, they happened to rest beside him. He had perhaps a closer sense of impending Fate than she. The boy, David, went to his first work, and the girls to their school, and so things dragged on through that first long war winter and spring. Mrs Gerhardt, in the intervals of doing everything, knitted socks for 'our poor cold boys in the trenches,' but Gerhardt no longer sought out little jobs to do in the houses of his neighbours. Mrs Gerhardt thought that he 'fancied' they would not like it. It was early in that spring that she took a deaf aunt to live with them, the wife of her mother's brother, no blood-relation, but the poor woman had nowhere else to go; so David was put to sleep on the horsehair sofa in the sitting-room because she 'couldn't refuse the poor thing.' And then, of an April afternoon, while she was washing the household sheets, her neighbour, Mrs Clirehugh, a little spare woman all eyes, cheekbones, hair, and decision, came in breathless and burst out:

'Oh! Mrs Gerhardt, 'ave you 'eard? They've sunk the Loositania! Has I said to Will: Isn't it horful?'

Mrs Gerhardt, with her round arms dripping soap-suds, answered: 'What a dreadful thing! The poor drowning people! Dear! Oh dear!'

'Oh! Those Huns! I'd shoot the lot, I would!'

'They are wicked!' Mrs Gerhardt echoed: 'That was a dreadful thing to do!'

But it was not till Gerhardt came in at five o'clock, white as a sheet, that she perceived how this dreadful catastrophe affected them.

'I have been called a German,' were the first words he uttered; 'Dollee, I have been called a German.'

'Well, so you are, my dear,' said Mrs Gerhardt.

'You do not see,' he answered, with a heat and agitation which surprised her. 'I tell you this *Lusitania* will finish our business. They will have me. They will take me away from you all. Already the papers have: "Intern all the Huns." He sat down at the kitchen table and buried his face in hands still grimy from his leather work. Mrs Gerhardt stood beside him, her eyes unnaturally big.

'But Max,' she said, 'what has it to do with you? You couldn't help it. Max!'

Gerhardt looked up, his white face, broad in the brow and tapering to a thin chin, seemed all distraught.

'What do they care for that? Is my name Max Gerhardt? What do they care if I hate the war? I am a German. That's enough. You will see.'

'Oh!' murmured Mrs Gerhardt, 'they won't be so unjust.'

Gerhardt reached up and caught her chin in his hand, and for a moment those two pairs of eyes gazed, straining, into each other. Then he said:

'I don't want to be taken, Dollee. What shall I do away from you and the children? I don't want to be taken, Dollee.'

Mrs Gerhardt, with a feeling of terror and a cheerful smile, answered:

'You mustn't go fancyin' things, Max. I'll make you a nice cup of tea. Cheer up, old man! Look on the bright side!'

But Gerhardt lapsed into the silence which of late she had begun to dread.

That night some shop windows were broken, some German names effaced. The Gerhardts had no shop, no name painted up, and they escaped. In Press and Parliament the cry against 'the Huns in our midst' rose with a fresh fury; but for the Gerhardts the face of Fate was withdrawn. Gerhardt went to his work as usual, and their laborious and quiet existence remained undisturbed; nor could Mrs Gerhardt tell whether her man's ever-deepening silence was due to his 'fancying things' or to the demeanour of his neighbours and fellow workmen. One would have said that he, like the derelict aunt, was deaf, so difficult to converse with had he become. His length of sojourn in England and his value to his employers, for he had real skill, had saved him for the time being; but, behind the screen, Fate twitched her grinning chaps.

Not till the howl which followed some air raids in 1916 did they take off Gerhardt, with a variety of other elderly men, whose crime it was to have been born in Germany. They did it suddenly, and perhaps it was as well, for a prolonged sight of his silent misery must have upset his family till they would have been unable to look on that bright side of things which Mrs Gerhardt had, as it were, always up her sleeve. When, in charge of a big and sympathetic constable, he was gone, taking all she could hurriedly get together for him, she hastened to the police station. They were friendly to her there: She must cheer up, Missis, 'e'd be all right, she needn't worry. Ah! she could go down to the 'Ome Office, if she liked, and see what could be done. But they 'eld out no 'ope! Mrs Gerhardt waited till the morrow, having the little Violet in bed with her, and crying quietly into her pillow; then, putting on her Sunday best she went down to a building in Whitehall, larger than any she had ever entered. Two hours she waited, sitting unobtrusive, with big anxious eyes, and a line between her brows. At intervals of half an hour she would get up and ask the messenger cheerfully:

'I 'ope they haven't forgotten me, sir. Perhaps you'd see to it.' And because she was cheerful the messenger took her under his protection, and answered:

'All right, Missis. They're very busy, but I'll wangle you in some 'ow.'

When at length she was wangled into the presence of a grave gentleman in eye-glasses, realisation of the utter importance of this moment overcame her so that she could not speak. 'Oh! dear' – she thought, while her heart fluttered like a bird – 'he'll never understand; I'll never be able to make him.' She saw her husband buried under the leaves of despair; she saw her children getting too little food, the deaf aunt, now bedridden, neglected in the new pressure of work that must fall on the only breadwinner left. And, choking a little, she said:

'I'm sure I'm very sorry to take up your time, sir; but my 'usband's been taken to the Palace; and we've been married over twenty years, and he's been in England twenty-five; and he's a very good man and a good workman; and I thought perhaps they didn't understand that; and we've got three children and a relation that's bedridden. And of course, we understand that the Germans have been very wicked; Gerhardt always said that himself. And it isn't as if he was a spy; so I thought if you could do something for us, sir, I being English myself.'

The gentleman, looking past her at the wall, answered wearily:

'Gerhardt – I'll look into it. We have to do very hard things, Mrs Gerhardt.'

Little Mrs Gerhardt, with big eyes almost starting out of her head, for she was no fool, and perceived that this was the end, said eagerly:

'Of course I know that there's a big outcry, and the papers are askin' for it; but the people in our street don't mind 'im, sir. He's always done little things for them; so I thought perhaps you might make an exception in his case.'

She noticed that the gentleman's lips tightened at the word outcry, and that he was looking at her now.

'His case was before the Committee no doubt; but I'll inquire. Good-morning.'

Mrs Gerhardt, accustomed to not being troublesome, rose; a tear rolled down her cheek and was arrested by her smile.

'Thank you, sir, I'm sure. Good-morning, sir.'

And she went out. Meeting the messenger in the corridor, and hearing his 'Well, Missis?' she answered:

'I don't know. I must look on the bright side. Good-bye, and thank you for your trouble.' And she turned away feeling as if she had been beaten all over.

The bright side on which she looked did not include the return to her of little Gerhardt, who was duly detained for the safety of the country. Obedient to economy, and with a dim sense that her favourite papers were in some way responsible for this, she ceased to take them in, and took in sewing instead. It had become necessary to do so, for the allowance she received from the government was about a quarter of Gerhardt's weekly earnings. In spite of its inadequacy it was something, and she felt she must be grateful. But, curiously enough, she could not forget that she was English, and it seemed strange to her that, in addition to the grief caused by separation from her husband from whom she had never been parted not even for a night, she should now be compelled to work twice as hard and eat half as much because that husband had paid her country the compliment of preferring it to his own. But, after all, many other people had much worse trouble to grieve over, so she looked on the bright side of all this, especially on those days once a week when alone, or accompanied by the little Violet, she visited that Palace where she had read in her favourite journals to her great comfort that her husband was treated like a prince. Since he had no money he was in what they called 'the battalion,' and their meetings were held in the bazaar, where things which 'the princes' made were exposed for sale.

Here Mr and Mrs Gerhardt would stand in front of some doll, some blotting-book, calendar, or walking-stick, which had been fashioned by one of 'the princes.' There they would hold each other's hands and try to imagine themselves unsurrounded by other men and wives, while the little Violet would stray and return to embrace her father's leg spasmodically. Standing there, Mrs Gerhardt would look on the bright side, and explain to Gerhardt how well everything was going, and he mustn't fret about them, and how kind the police were, and how auntie asked after him, and Minnie would get a prize; and how he oughtn't to mope, but eat his food, and look on the bright side. And Gerhardt would smile the smile which went into her heart just like a sword, and say:

'All right, Dollee. I'm getting on fine.' Then, when the whistle blew and he had kissed little Violet, they would be quite silent, looking at each other. And she would say in a voice so matter-of-fact that it could have deceived no one:

'Well, I must go now. Good-bye, old man!'

And he would say:

'Good-bye, Dollee. Kiss me.'

They would kiss, and holding little Violet's hand very hard she would hurry away in the crowd, taking care not to look back for fear she might suddenly lose sight of the bright side. But as the months went on, became a year, eighteen months, two years, and still she went weekly to see her 'prince' in his Palace, that visit became for her the hardest experience of all her hard week's doings. For she was a realist, as well as a heroine, and she could see the lines of despair not only in her man's heart but in his face. For a long time he had not said: 'I'm getting on fine, Dollee.' His face had a beaten look, his figure had wasted, he complained of his head.

'It's so noisy,' he would say constantly; 'oh! it's so noisy – never a quiet moment – never alone – never–never–never–never. And not enough to eat; it's all reduced now, Dollee.'

She learned to smuggle food into his hands, but it was very little, for they had not enough at home either, with the price of living ever going up and her depleted income ever stationary. They had – her 'man' told her – made a fuss in the papers about their being fed like turkeycocks, while the 'Huns' were sinking the ships. Gerhardt, always a spare little man, had lost eighteen pounds. She, naturally well covered, was getting thin herself, but that she did not notice, too busy all day long, and too occupied in thinking of her 'man.' To watch him week by week, more hopeless, as the months dragged on, was an acute torture, to disguise which was torture even more acute. She had long seen that there was no bright side, but if she admitted that she knew she would go down; so she did not. And she carefully kept from Gerhardt such matters as David's overgrowing his strength, because she could not feed him properly; the completely bedridden nature of auntie; and worse than these, the growing coldness and unkindness of her neighbours. Perhaps they did not mean to be unkind, perhaps they did, for it was not in their nature to withstand the pressure of mass sentiment, the continual personal discomfort of having to stand in queues, the fear of air raids, the cumulative indignation caused by stories of atrocities true and untrue.

In spite of her record of kindliness towards them she became tarred with the brush at last, for her nerves had given way once or twice, and she had said it was a shame to keep her man like that, gettin' iller and iller, who had never done a thing. Even her reasonableness – and she was very reasonable – succumbed to the strain of that weekly sight of him, till she could no longer allow for the difficulties which Mrs Clirehugh assured her the Government had to deal with. Then one day she used the words 'fair play,' and at once it became current that she had 'German sympathies.' From that time on she was somewhat doomed. Those who had received kindnesses from her were foremost in showing her coldness, being wounded in their self-esteem. To have received little benefits, such as being nursed when they were sick, from one who had 'German sympathies' was too much for the pride which is in every human being, however humble an inhabitant of Putney. Mrs Gerhardt's Cockney spirit could support this for herself, but she could not bear it for her children. David came home with a black eye, and would not say why he had got it. Minnie missed her prize at school, though she had clearly won it. That was just after the last German offensive began; but Mrs Gerhardt refused to see that this was any reason. Little Violet twice put the heart-rending question to her: 'Aren't I English, Mummy?'

She was answered: 'Yes, my dear, of course.'

But the child obviously remained unconvinced in her troubled mind.

And then they took David for the British army. It was that which so upset the applecart in Mrs Gerhardt that she broke out to her last friend, Mrs Clirehugh:

'I do think it's hard, Eliza. They take his father and keep him there for a dangerous Hun year after year like that; and then they take his boy for the army to fight against him. And how I'm to get on without him I don't know.'

Little Mrs Clirehugh, who was Scotch, with a Gloucestershire accent, replied:

'Well, we've got to beat them. They're such a wicked lot. I daresay it's 'ard on you, but we've got to beat them.'

'But we never did nothing,' cried Mrs Gerhardt; 'it isn't us that's wicked. We never wanted the war; it's nothing but ruin to him. They did ought to let me have my man, or my boy, one or the other.'

'You should 'ave some feeling for the Government, Dora; they 'ave to do things.'

Mrs Gerhardt, with a quivering face, had looked at her friend.

'I have,' she said at last in a tone which implanted in Mrs Clirehugh's heart the feeling that Dora was 'bitter.'

She could not forget it; and she would flaunt her head at any mention of her former friend. It was a blow to Mrs Gerhardt, who had now no friends, except the deaf and bedridden aunt, to whom all things were the same, war or no war, Germans or no Germans, so long as she was fed.

About then it was that the tide turned, and the Germans began to know defeat. Even Mrs Gerhardt, who read the papers no longer, learned it daily, and her heart relaxed; that bright side began to reappear a little. She felt they could not feel so hardly towards her 'man' now as when they were all in fear; and perhaps the war would be over before her boy went out. But Gerhardt puzzled her. He did not brighten up. The iron seemed to have entered his soul too deeply. And one day, in the bazaar, passing an open doorway, Mrs Gerhardt had a glimpse of why. There, stretching before her astonished eyes, was a great, as it were, encampment of brown blankets, slung and looped up anyhow, dividing from each other countless sordid beds, which were almost touching, and a whiff of huddled humanity came out to her keen nostrils, and a hum of sound to her ears. So that was where her man had dwelt these thirty months, in that dirty, crowded, noisy place, with dirty-looking men, such as those she could see lying on the beds, or crouching by the side of them, over their work. He had kept neat somehow, at least on the days when she came to see him – but that was where he lived! Alone again (for she no longer brought the little Violet to see her German father), she grieved all the way home. Whatever happened to him now, even if she got him back, she knew he would never quite get over it.

And then came the morning when she came out of her door like the other inhabitants of Putney, at sound of the maroons, thinking it was an air raid; and, catching the smile on the toothless mouth of one of her old neighbours, hearing the cheers of the boys in the school round the corner, knew that it was Peace. Her heart overflowed then, and, withdrawing hastily, she sat down on a shiny chair in her little empty parlour. Her face crumpled suddenly, the tears came welling forth; she cried and cried, alone in the little cold room. She cried from relief and utter thankfulness. It was over – over at last! The long waiting – the long misery – the yearning for her 'man' – the grieving for all those poor boys in the mud, and the dreadful shell holes, and the fighting, the growing terror of anxiety for her own boy – over, all over! Now they would let Max out, now David would come back from the army; and people would not be unkind and spiteful to her and the children anymore!

For all she was a Cockney, hers was a simple soul, associating Peace with Good-will. Drying her tears, she stood up, and in the little cheap mirror above the empty grate looked at her face. It was lined, and she was grey; for more than two years her man had not seen her without her hat. What ever would he say? And she rubbed and rubbed her cheeks, trying to smooth them out. Then her conscience smote her, and she ran upstairs to the back bedroom, where the deaf aunt lay. Taking up the little amateur ear trumpet which Gerhardt himself had made for 'auntie,' before he was taken away, she bawled into it:

'Peace, Auntie; it's Peace! Think of that. It's Peace!'

'What's that?' answered the deaf woman.

'It's Peace, Auntie, Peace.'

The deaf lady roused herself a little, and some meaning came into the lack-lustre black eyes of her long, leathery face.

'You don't say,' she said in her wooden voice, 'I'm so hungry, Dolly, isn't it time for my dinner?'

'I was just goin' to get it, dearie,' replied Mrs Gerhardt, and hurried back downstairs with her brain teeming, to make the deaf woman's bowl of bread, pepper, salt, and onions.

All that day and the next and the next she saw the bright side of things with almost dazzling clearness, waiting to visit her 'prince' in his Palace. She found him in a strange and pitiful state of nerves. The news had produced too intense and varied emotions among those crowded thousands of men buried away from normal life so long. She spent all her hour and a half trying desperately to make him see the bright side, but he was too full of fears and doubts, and she went away smiling, but utterly exhausted.

Slowly in the weeks which followed she learned that nothing was changed. In the fond hope that Gerhardt might be home now any day, she was taking care that his slippers and some clothes of David's were ready for him, and the hip bath handy for him to have a lovely hot wash. She had even bought a bottle of beer and some of his favourite pickle, saving the price out of her own food, and was taking in the paper again, letting bygones be bygones. But he did not come. And soon the paper informed her that the English prisoners were returning – many in wretched state, poor things, so that her heart bled for them, and made her fiercely angry with the cruel men who had treated them so; but it informed her too, that if the paper had its way no 'Huns' would be tolerated in this country for the future. 'Send them all back!' were the words it used. She did not realise at first that this applied to Gerhardt; but when she did, she dropped the journal as if it had been a living coal of fire. Not let him come back to his home, and family, not let him stay, after all they'd done to him, and he never did anything to them! Not let him stay, but send him out to that dreadful country, which he had almost forgotten in these thirty years, and he with an English wife and children! In this new terror of utter dislocation the bright side so slipped from her that she was obliged to go out into the back garden in the dark, where a sou'-westerly wind was driving the rain. There, lifting her eyes to the evening sky she uttered a little moan. It couldn't be true; and yet what they said in her paper had always turned out true, like the taking of Gerhardt away, and the reduction of his food. And the face of the gentleman in the building at Whitehall came before her out of the long past, with his lips tightening, and his words: 'We have to do very hard things, Mrs Gerhardt.' Why had they to do them? Her man had never done no harm to no one! A flood, bitter as sea water, surged in her, and seemed to choke her very being. Those gentlemen in the papers – why should they go on like that? Had they no hearts, no eyes to see the misery they brought to humble folk? 'I wish them nothing worse than what they've brought to him and me,' she thought wildly: 'nothing worse!'

The rain beat on her face, wetted her grey hair, cooled her eyeballs. 'I mustn't be spiteful,' she thought; and bending down in the dark she touched the glass of the tiny conservatory built against the warm kitchen wall, and heated by the cunning little hot-water pipe her man had put there in his old handy days. Under it were one little monthly rose, which still had blossoms, and some straggly small chrysanthemums. She had been keeping them for the feast when he came home; but if he wasn't to come, what should she do? She raised herself. Above the wet roofs sky-rack was passing wild and dark, but in a little cleared space one or two stars shone the brighter for the blackness below. 'I must look on the bright side,' she thought, 'or I can't bear myself.' And she went in to cook the porridge for the evening meal.

The winter passed for her in the most dreadful anxiety. 'Repatriate the Huns!' That cry continued to spurt up in her paper like a terrible face seen in some recurrent nightmare; and each week that she went to visit Gerhardt brought solid confirmation to her terror. He was taking it hard, so that sometimes she was afraid that 'something' was happening in him. This was the utmost she went towards defining what doctors might have diagnosed as incipient softening of the brain. He seemed to dread the prospect of being sent to his native country.

'I couldn't stick it, Dollee,' he would say. 'What should I do – whatever should I do? I haven't a friend. I haven't a spot to go to. I should be lost. I'm afraid, Dollee. How could you come out there, you and the children? I couldn't make a living for you. I couldn't make one for myself now.'

And she would say: 'Cheer up, old man. Look on the bright side. Think of the others.' For, though those others were not precisely the bright side, the mental picture of their sufferings, all those poor 'princes' and their families, somehow helped her to bear her own. But he shook his head:

'No; I should never see you again.'

'I'd follow you,' she answered. 'Never fear, Max, we'd work in the fields – me and the children. We'd get on somehow. Bear up, my dearie. It'll soon be over now. I'll stick to you, Max, never you fear. But they won't send you, they never will.'

And then, like a lump of ice pressed on her breast, came the thought:

'But if they do! Auntie! My boy! My girls! However shall I manage if they do?'

Then long lists began to appear, and in great batches men were shovelled wholesale back to the country whose speech some of them had well-nigh forgotten. Little Gerhardt's name had not appeared yet. The lists were hung up the day after Mrs Gerhardt's weekly visit, but she urged him if his name did appear to appeal against repatriation. It was with the greatest difficulty that she roused in him the energy to promise.

'Look on the bright side, Max,' she implored him. 'You've got a son in the British army; they'll never send you. They wouldn't be so cruel. Never say die, old man.'

His name appeared but was taken out, and the matter hung again in awful suspense, while the evil face of the recurrent nightmare confronted Mrs Gerhardt out of her favourite journal. She read that journal again, because, so far as in her gentle spirit lay, she hated it. It was slowly killing her man, and all her chance of future happiness; she hated it, and read it every morning. To the monthly rose and straggly little brown-red chrysanthemums in the tiny hothouse there had succeeded spring flowers – a few hardy January snowdrops, and one by one blue scillas, and the little pale daffodils called 'angels' tears.'

Peace tarried, but the flowers came up long before their time in their tiny hothouse against the kitchen flue. And then one wonderful day there came to Mrs Gerhardt a strange letter, announcing that Gerhardt was coming home. He would not be sent to Germany – he was coming home!

Today, that very day – any moment he might be with her. When she received it, who had long received no letters save the weekly letters of her boy still in the army, she was spreading margarine on auntie's bread for breakfast, and, moved beyond all control, she spread it thick, wickedly, wastefully thick, then dropped the knife, sobbed, laughed, clasped her hands on her breast, and without rhyme or reason, began singing: 'Hark! the herald angels sing.' The girls had gone to school already, auntie in the room above could not hear her, no one heard her, nor saw her drop suddenly into the wooden chair, and, with her bare arms stretched out one on either side of the plate of bread and margarine, cry her heart out against the clean white table. Coming home, coming home, coming home! The bright side! The little white stars!

It was a quarter of an hour before she could trust herself to answer the knocking on the floor, which meant that 'auntie' was missing her breakfast. Hastily she made the tea and went up with it and the bread and margarine. The woman's dim long face gleamed greedily when she saw how thick the margarine was spread; but little Mrs Gerhardt said no word of the reason for that feast. She just watched her only friend eating it, while a little moisture still trickled out from her big eyes on to her flushed cheeks, and the words still hummed in her brain:

'Peace on earth and mercy mild,'

'Jesus Christ a little child.'

Then, still speaking no word, she ran out and put clean sheets on her and her man's bed. She was on wires, she could not keep still, and all the morning she polished, polished. About noon she went out into her garden, and from under the glass plucked every flower that grew there – snowdrops, scillas, 'angels' tears,' quite two dozen blossoms. She brought them into the little parlour and opened its window wide. The sun was shining, and fell on the flowers strewn on the table, ready to be made into the nosegay of triumphant happiness. While she stood fingering them, delicately breaking half an inch off their stalks so that they should last the longer in water, she became conscious of someone on the pavement outside the window, and looking up saw Mrs Clirehugh. The past, the sense of having been deserted by her friends, left her, and she called out:

'Come in, Eliza; look at my flowers!'

Mrs Clirehugh came in; she was in black, her cheekbones higher, her hair looser, her eyes bigger. Mrs Gerhardt saw tears starting from those eyes, wetting those high cheekbones, and cried out:

'Why, what's the matter, dear?'

Mrs Clirehugh choked. 'My baby!' Mrs Gerhardt dropped an 'angels' tear,' and went up to her.

'Whatever's happened?' she cried.

'Dead!' replied Mrs Clirehugh. 'Dead o' the influenza. 'E's to be buried today. I can't – I can't – I can't.' Wild choking stopped her utterance. Mrs Gerhardt put an arm round her and drew her head on to her shoulder.

'I can't – I can't –' sobbed Mrs Clirehugh; 'I can't find any flowers. It's seein' yours made me cry.'

'There, there!' cried Mrs Gerhardt. 'Have them. I'm sure you're welcome, dearie. Have them – I'm so sorry!'

'I don't know,' choked Mrs Clirehugh, 'I 'aven't deserved them.' Mrs Gerhardt gathered up the flowers.

'Take them,' she said. 'I couldn't think of it. Your poor little baby. Take them! There, there, he's spared a lot of trouble. You must look on the bright side, dearie.'

Mrs Clirehugh tossed up her head.

'You're an angel, that's what you are!' she said, and grasping the flowers she hurried out, a little black figure passing the window in the sunlight.

Mrs Gerhardt stood above the emptied table, thinking: 'Poor dear – I'm glad she had the flowers. It was a mercy I didn't call out that Max was coming!' And from the floor she picked up one 'angels' tear' she had dropped, and set it in a glass of water, where the sunlight fell. She was still gazing at it, pale, slender, lonely in that coarse tumbler, when she heard a knock on the parlour door, and went to open it. There stood her man, with a large brown-paper parcel in his hand. He stood quite still, his head a little down, the face very grey. She cried out:

'Max!' but the thought flashed through her: 'He knocked on the door! It's his door – he knocked on the door!'

'Dollee?' he said, with a sort of question in his voice.

She threw her arms round him, drew him into the room, and shutting the door, looked hard into his face. Yes, it was his face, but in the eyes something wandered – lit up, went out, lit up.

'Dollee,' he said again, and clutched her hand.

She strained him to her with a sob.

'I'm not well, Dollee,' he murmured.

'No, of course not, my dearie man; but you'll soon be all right now – home again with me. Cheer up, cheer up!'

'I'm not well,' he said again.

She caught the parcel out of his hand, and taking the 'angels' tear' from the tumbler, fixed it in his coat.

'Here's a spring flower for you, Max; out of your own little hothouse. You're home again; home again, my dearie. Auntie's upstairs, and the girls'll be coming soon. And we'll have dinner.'

'I'm not well, Dollee,' he said.

Terrified by that reiteration, she drew him down on the little horsehair sofa, and sat on his knee. 'You're home, Max, kiss me. There's my man!' and she rocked him to and fro against her, yearning yet fearing to look into his face and see that 'something' wander there – light up, go out, light up. 'Look, dearie,' she said, 'I've got some beer for you. You'd like a glass of beer?'

He made a motion of his lips, a sound that was like the ghost of a smack. It terrified her, so little life was there in it.

He clutched her close, and repeated feebly:

'Yes, all right in a day or two. They let me come – I'm not well, Dollee.' He touched his head.

Straining him to her, rocking him, she murmured over and over again, like a cat purring to its kitten:

'It's all right, my dearie – soon be well – soon be well! We must look on the bright side – My man!'

Britain's Daughters
Colin Mitchell

They talk about the Tommy and the brave things he has done,
The brave things he is just about to do.
'Tis mountains high the homage and the praise that he has won;
The world acclaims him; he deserves it too.
But what about our women, Britain's daughters, passing fair;
The finest race of women on the Earth?
Have they been praised unsparingly? Have they received their share
Of honour that should advertise their worth?

We see them in the canteens where they toil so laughingly,
And feed the hungry soldier every day.
We see them on the 'buses where they tender chaffingly
The humble fares along the jolting way.
We find them donning breeches, milking cows and making cheese;
How charming is the agricultural maid!
She lets the men go fighting, and she tries so hard to please,
And hides her fear whene'er she feels afraid.

The chauffeuse is the neatest and the sweetest little girl,
Bedecked in livery of olive green.
She manages a motor-van or makes your senses whirl
When taking out a pullman-limousine.
The girl of no vocation's fining all her good by stealth;
It drains her purse alarmingly 'tis true;

But be she poor or be she rich she's thinking of the health
Of Tommy – and that everlasting stew!

Impossible it is for me to mention all the work
That our beloved women find to do.
Suffice it then to say that they are never known to shirk,
Though novelty has flown, and romance too.
But of the valiant daughters of this dear old troubled land
The nurses 'tis a Tommy ne'er forgets.
God bless you and reward you, sisters of the Healing Hand;
A life of honour, yours, with no regrets.

After the Armistice
From *A History of the Irish Guards*, Rudyard Kipling

And, thus dispersed, after a little shelling of Assevant during the night, the Irish Guards received word that 'an Armistice was declared at 11 a.m. this morning, November 11'.

Men took the news according to their natures. Indurated pessimists, after proving that it was a lie, said it would be but an interlude. Others retired into themselves as though they had been shot, or went stiffly off about the meticulous execution of some trumpery detail of kit-cleaning. Some turned round and fell asleep then and there; and a few lost all holds for a while. It was the appalling new silence of things that soothed and unsettled them in turn. They did not realise till all sounds of their trade ceased, and the stillness stung in their ears as soda-water stings on the palate, how entirely these had been part of their strained bodies and souls. ('It felt like falling through into nothing, ye'll understand. Listening for what wasn't there, and tryin' not to shout when you remembered for why.') Men coming up from Details Camp, across old 'unwholesome' areas, heard nothing but the roar of the lorries on which they had stolen their lift, and rejoiced with a childish mixture of fear as they topped every unscreened rise that was now mere scenery such as tourists would use later. To raise the head, without thought of precaution against what might be in front or on either flank, into free, still air was the first pleasure of that great release. To lie down that night in a big barn beside unscreened braziers, with one's smiling companions who talked till sleep overtook them, and, when the last happy babbler had dropped off, to hear the long-forgotten sound of a horse's feet trotting evenly on a hard road under a full moon, crowned all that had gone before. Each man had but one thought in those miraculous first hours: 'I – even I myself, here – have come through the War!' To scorn the shelter of sunken roads, hedges, walls or lines of trees, and to extend in unmartial crowds across the whole width of a *pavé*, were exercises in freedom that he arrived at later. 'We cannot realise it at all'... 'So mad with joy we don't feel yet what it all means.' The home letters were all in this strain.

The Battalion was relieved on the 12th November by the 2nd Grenadiers and billeted in the Faubourg de Mons. All Maubeuge was hysterical with its emotions of release, and well provided with wines which, here as elsewhere, had somehow missed the German nose. The city lived in her streets, and kissed everybody in khaki, that none should complain. But the Battalion was not in walking-out order, and so had to be inspected rigorously. Morning-drill outside billets next day was in the nature of a public demonstration – to the scandal of the grave sergeants!

On the 14th a great thanksgiving service was held in the Cathedral for all the world, the Battalion providing the Guard of Honour at the Altar, and lining the Place d'Armes at the presentation of a flag by the Mayor of Maubeuge to the Major-General. The massed drums of the Division played in the square in the afternoon, an event to be remembered as long as the Battalion dinner of the evening. They were all route-marched next morning for an hour and a half to steady them, and on the 16th, after dinner, set off in freezing weather for the first stage of their journey to Cologne. It ran via Bettignies and then to Villers-Sire-Nicole, a matter of five and a half miles.

On the 17th they crossed the Belgian frontier at Givet and reached Binche through a countryside already crowded with returning

English, French, Italian, and Belgian prisoners. One diary notes them like migrating birds, 'all hopping along the road, going due west.' Binche mobbed the drums as one man and woman when they played in the town at Retreat, but it was worse at Charleroi on the 19th, where they could hardly force their way through the welcoming crowds. The place was lit from end to end, and the whole populace shouted for joy at deliverance.

Now that they had returned as a body to civilisation, it was needful they should be dressed, and they were paraded for an important inspection of great-coats, and, above all, gloves. That last, and the fact that belts, when walking out, were worn over the great-coats were sure signs that war was done, and His Majesty's Foot Guards had come into their own. But they found time at Charleroi, among more pleasant duties, to arrest three German soldiers disguised as civilians.

On the 23rd they left, for Sart-St-Laurent, whose Mayor, beneath a vast Belgian flag, met and escorted them into the town. The country changed as they moved on from flat coal-districts to untouched hills and woods. On the 24th they picked up a dump of eighty-four guns of all calibres, handed over according to the terms of the Armistice; passed through a tract of heavily wired country, which was 'evidently intended for the Meuse Line that the Germans were to have fallen back on'; and a little later crossed (being the first of the Division to do so) the steeply banked, swiftly running Meuse by a pontoon bridge. Next their road climbed into Nanine, one of the loveliest villages, they thought, they had ever seen. But their hearts were soft in those days, and all that world of peace seemed good. They dared not halt at Sorinne-la-Longue the next day, as the place was infected with influenza ('Spanish fever'), so pushed on to Lesves, and on the 26th November to Sorée, where was another wayside dump of thirty or forty Hun guns. It is noteworthy that the discarded tools of their trade frankly bored them. Where a Hun, under like circumstances, would have re-triumphed and called on his servile Gods, these islanders (of whom almost a half were now English) were afflicted with a curious restlessness and strong desire to get done with the work in hand. All their world was under the same reaction. They had to wait at Sorée for three days, as supplies were coming up badly. Indeed, on the 28th November, the diary notes bitterly that 'for the first time in the war the supplies failed to arrive. The Quartermaster managed to improvise breakfasts for the Battalion.' It was not all the fault of bad roads or the dispersion of the troops. The instant the strain was taken off, there was a perceptible slackening everywhere, most marked in the back-areas, on the clerical and forwarding sides. Everyone wanted to get home at once, and worked with but half a mind; which, also, is human nature.

They were on the road again by December 5 with the rest of their brigade, and reached Méan in the afternoon over muddy roads. By the 6th they were at Villers-St-Gertrude hill-marching through beautiful scenery, which did not amuse them, because, owing to the state of communications, supplies were delayed again. So, on the 8th December at Lierneux, fifteen miles from Villers-St-Gertrude, another halt was called for another three days, while company officers, homesick as their men, drilled them in the winter dirt. On the 11th they crossed the German frontier line at Recht, and the drums played the Battalion over to the 'Regimental March.' ('But, ye'll understand, we was all wet the most of that time and fighting with the mud an' our boots. 'Twas Jerry's own weather the minute we set foot in his country, and we none of us felt like conquerors. We was just drippin' Micks.') At Vielsalm, almost the last village outside Germany, they picked up a draft of sixty men to share with them the horrors of peace ahead, and a supply-system gone to bits behind them.

Their road wound through small and inconspicuous hamlets among wooded hills, by stretches of six or seven hours' marching a day. The people they had to deal with seemed meek and visibly oppressed with the fear of rough treatment. That removed from their minds, they stepped aside and looked wonderingly at the incomprehensible enemy that tramped through their streets, leaving neither ruin nor rape behind. By the 18th December the advance had reached Lovenich, and, after two days' rest there, they entered

Cologne on the 23rd December with an absence of display that might or might not have been understood by the natives. They had covered more than two hundred miles over bad roads in bad boots that could not be repaired nor thrown away, and but one man had fallen out. The drums played 'Brian Boru' when they entered the Hohenzollern Ring; their Major-General beheld that last march, and they were duly photographed in the wet; while the world that saw such photographs in the weekly illustrated papers was honestly convinced that the Great War and all war was at an end for evermore.

Then really serious trouble overtook them, which was, in some sort, a forecast of the days to come. Their billets at Nippes, in the suburbs of Cologne, were excellent and clean, though, of course, in need of the usual 'improvements' which every battalion of the Brigade is bound to make; but on Christmas Day, owing to transport difficulties, the men's Christmas dinner did not arrive! This thing had never happened in the whole history of the war! Pressure of work in the front line had delayed that dinner, as on the Somme; enemy attentions had caused it to be eaten in haste, a sort of Passover, as in the dread Salient, but complete breakdown was unheard of. The Battalion, rightly, held it mortal sin, and spoke their minds about the transport which was fighting mud and distance across the hills as loyally as ever. It was the back-areas that had been caught unprepared by the peace. But, on Christmas night (superb and unscrupulous staff-work went to secure it), a faithful lorry ploughed in from Paris with what was wanted, and on Boxing Day the full and complete Christmas dinner was served, and for the fifth and last time their Commanding Officer performed the sacred ritual of 'going round the dinners.'

They sat them down, twenty-two officers and six hundred and twenty-eight other ranks, and none will know till Judgment Day how many ghosts were also present. For the first time since August, '14, the monthly returns showed no officer or man killed, wounded, or missing. The two battalions had lost in all two thousand three hundred and forty-nine dead, including one hundred and fifteen officers. Their total of wounded was five thousand seven hundred and thirty-nine. Of both these the 1st Battalion, by virtue of thirteen months longer in the field, could reckon more than a generous half.

They were too near and too deeply steeped in the war that year's end to realise their losses. Their early dead, as men talked over the past in Cologne, seemed to belong to immensely remote ages. Even those of that very spring, of whom friends could still say, 'If So-and-so had only lived to see this!' stood as far removed as the shadowy great ones of the pre-bomb, pre-duckboard twilight; and, in some inexpressible fashion, they themselves appeared to themselves the only living people in an uncaring world. Yet Cologne was alive with soldiery; roads were roaring full, as communications were restored; men stood guard over visible gun- and ammunition-dumps; the Battalion joined in marches to the bridge-heads, attended football matches, saw hosts of new faces belonging to new troops of all breeds; and watched about them, in the wet, grey weather, the muddy-faced Hun-folk, methodically as usual, trying to find out just how far it was expedient to go with the heralds of the alleged new order.

'But ye'll understand, when everything was said and done, there was nothing real to it at all, except when we got to talking and passing round the names of them we wished was with us. We was lonely in those days. The half of us was Church of England by then, too. But we were lonely, ye'll understand, as units. And our billets, mind ye, magnificent, with walls and lockers and doors and all. The same for the officers! And there was Mr _____ that I'd known well any time these last two winters, freezing and swearing alongside of me in any shell-hole we could find, and glad to be out of the wind – and now, him cursin' in his quarters because he had not the Jerry-talk for the German for: 'Turn off that dam' steam-heat!' And that's war also.

'But ye might tell that we was lonely, most of all. Before God, we Micks was lonely!'

Jem Blythe Comes Home
L. M. Montgomery

One spring day, when the daffodils were blowing on the Ingleside
lawn, and the banks of the brook in Rainbow Valley were sweet with
white and purple violets, the little, lazy afternoon accommodation
train pulled into the Glen station. It was very seldom that passengers
for the Glen came by that train, so nobody was there to meet it except
the new station agent and a small black-and-yellow dog, who for
four and a half years had met every train that had steamed into Glen
St. Mary. Thousands of trains had Dog Monday met and never had
the boy he waited and watched for returned. Yet still Dog Monday
watched on with eyes that never quite lost hope. Perhaps his dog-
heart failed him at times; he was growing old and rheumatic; when
he walked back to his kennel after each train had gone his gait was
very sober now – he never trotted but went slowly with a drooping
head and a depressed tail that had quite lost its old saucy uplift.

One passenger stepped off the train – a tall fellow in a faded
lieutenant's uniform, who walked with a barely perceptible limp. He
had a bronzed face and there were some grey hairs in the ruddy curls
that clustered around his forehead. The new station agent looked at
him anxiously. He was used to seeing the khaki-clad figures come
off the train, some met by a tumultuous crowd, others, who had sent
no word of their coming, stepping off quietly like this one. But there
was a certain distinction of bearing and features in this soldier that
caught his attention and made him wonder a little more interestedly
who he was.

A black-and-yellow streak shot past the station agent. Dog
Monday stiff? Dog Monday rheumatic? Dog Monday old? Never
believe it. Dog Monday was a young pup, gone clean mad with
rejuvenating joy.

He flung himself against the tall soldier, with a bark that choked
in his throat from sheer rapture. He flung himself on the ground and
writhed in a frenzy of welcome. He tried to climb the soldier's khaki
legs and slipped down and grovelled in an ecstasy that seemed as if

it must tear his little body in pieces. He licked his boots and when the lieutenant had, with laughter on his lips and tears in his eyes, succeeded in gathering the little creature up in his arms, Dog Monday laid his head on the khaki shoulder and licked the sunburned neck, making queer sounds between barks and sobs.

The station agent had heard the story of Dog Monday. He knew now who the returned soldier was. Dog Monday's long vigil was ended. Jem Blythe had come home.

The Boy Who Came Back
From *Echoes of the War*, Stephen Leacock

The war is over. The soldiers are coming home. On all sides we are assured that the problem of the returned soldier is the gravest of our national concerns.

So I may say it without fear of contradiction – since everybody else has seen it – that, up to the present time, the returned soldier is a disappointment. He is not turning out as he ought. According to all the professors of psychology he was to come back bloodthirsty and brutalised, soaked in militarism and talking only of slaughter. In fact, a widespread movement had sprung up, warmly supported by the businessmen of the cities, to put him on the land. It was thought that central Nevada or northern Idaho would do nicely for him. At the same time an agitation had been started among the farmers, with the slogan 'Back to the city,' the idea being that farm life was so rough that it was not fair to ask the returned soldier to share it.

All these anticipations turn out to be quite groundless.

The first returned soldier of whom I had direct knowledge was my nephew Tom. When he came back, after two years in the trenches, we asked him to dine with us. 'Now, remember,' I said to my wife, 'Tom will be a very different being from what he was when he went away. He left us as little more than a school boy, only in his first year at college; in fact, a mere child. You remember how he used to bore us with baseball talk and that sort of thing. And how shy he was!

You recall his awful fear of Professor Razzler, who used to teach him mathematics. All that, of course, will be changed now. Tom will have come back a man. We must ask the old professor to meet him. It will amuse Tom to see him again. Just think of the things he must have seen! But we must be a little careful at dinner not to let him horrify the other people with brutal details of the war.'

Tom came. I had expected him to arrive in uniform with his pocket full of bombs. Instead of this he wore ordinary evening dress with a dinner jacket. I realised as I helped him to take off his overcoat in the hall that he was very proud of his dinner jacket. He had never had one before. He said he wished the 'boys' could see him in it. I asked him why he had put off his lieutenant's uniform so quickly. He explained that he was entitled not to wear it as soon as he had his discharge papers signed; some of the fellows, he said, kicked them off as soon as they left the ship, but the rule was, he told me, that you had to wear the thing till your papers were signed.

Then his eye caught a glimpse sideways of Professor Razzler standing on the hearth rug in the drawing room.

'Say,' he said, 'is that the professor?' I could see that Tom was scared. All the signs of physical fear were written on his face. When I tried to lead him into the drawing room I realised that he was as shy as ever. Three of the women began talking to him all at once. Tom answered, yes or no – with his eyes down. I liked the way he stood, though, so unconsciously erect and steady. The other men who came in afterwards, with easy greetings and noisy talk, somehow seemed loud-voiced and self-assertive.

Tom, to my surprise, refused a cocktail. It seems, as he explained, that he 'got into the way of taking nothing over there.' I noticed that my friend Quiller, who is a war correspondent, or, I should say, a war editorial writer, took three cocktails and talked all the more brilliantly for it through the opening courses of the dinner, about the story of the smashing of the Hindenburg line. He decided, after his second Burgundy, that it had been simply a case of sticking it out. I say 'Burgundy' because we had substituted Burgundy, the sparkling kind, for champagne at our dinners as one of our little war economies.

Tom had nothing to say about the Hindenburg line. In fact, for the first half of the dinner he hardly spoke. I think he was worried about his left hand. There is a deep furrow across the back of it where a piece of shrapnel went through and there are two fingers that will hardly move at all. I could see that he was ashamed of its clumsiness and afraid that someone might notice it. So he kept silent. Professor Razzler did indeed ask him straight across the table what he thought about the final breaking of the Hindenburg line. But he asked it with that same fierce look from under his bushy eyebrows with which he used to ask Tom to define the path of a tangent, and Tom was rattled at once. He answered something about being afraid that he was not well posted, owing to there being so little chance over there to read the papers.

After that Professor Razzler and Mr Quiller discussed for us, most energetically, the strategy of the Lorraine sector (Tom served there six months, but he never said so) and high explosives and the possibilities of aerial bombs (Tom was 'buried' by an aerial bomb but, of course, he didn't break in and mention it).

But we did get him talking of the war at last, towards the end of the dinner; or rather, the girl sitting next to him did, and presently the rest of us found ourselves listening. The strange thing was that the girl was a mere slip of a thing, hardly as old as Tom himself. In fact, my wife was almost afraid she might be too young to ask to dinner: girls of that age, my wife tells me, have hardly sense enough to talk to men, and fail to interest them. This is a proposition which I think it better not to dispute.

But at any rate we presently realised that Tom was talking about his war experiences and the other talk about the table was gradually hushed into listening.

This, as nearly as I can set it down, is what he told us: That the French fellows picked up baseball in a way that is absolutely amazing; they were not much good, it seems, at the bat, at any rate not at first, but at running bases they were perfect marvels; some of the French made good pitchers, too; Tom knew a *poilu* who had lost his right arm who could pitch as good a ball with his left as any man on the American side; at the port where Tom first landed and where they trained for a month they had a dandy ball ground, a regular peach, a former parade ground of the French barracks. On being asked WHICH port it was, Tom said he couldn't remember; he thought it was either Boulogne or Bordeaux or Brest – at any rate, it was one of those places on the English Channel. The ball ground they had behind the trenches was not so good; it was too much cut up by long range shells. But the ball ground at the base hospital (where Tom was sent for his second wound) was an A1 ground. The French doctors, it appears, were perfectly rotten at baseball, not a bit like the soldiers. Tom wonders that they kept them. Tom says that baseball had been tried among the German prisoners, but they are perfect duDs. He doubts whether the Germans will ever be able to play ball. They lack the national spirit. On the other hand, Tom thinks that the English will play a great game when they really get into it. He had two weeks' leave in London and went to see the game that King George was at, and says that the King, if they will let him, will make the greatest rooter of the whole bunch.

Such was Tom's war talk.

It grieved me to note that as the men sat smoking their cigars and drinking liqueur whiskey (we have cut out port at our house till the final peace is signed) Tom seemed to have subsided into being only a boy again, a first-year college boy among his seniors. They spoke to him in quite a patronising way, and even asked him two or three direct questions about fighting in the trenches, and wounds and the dead men in No Man's Land and the other horrors that the civilian mind hankers to hear about. Perhaps they thought, from the boy's talk, that he had seen nothing. If so, they were mistaken. For about three minutes, not more, Tom gave them what was coming to them. He told them, for example, why he trained his 'fellows' to drive the bayonet through the stomach and not through the head, that the bayonet driven through the face or skull sticks and – but there is no need to recite it here. Any of the boys like Tom can tell it all to you, only they don't want to and don't care to.

They've got past it.

But I noticed that as the boy talked – quietly and reluctantly enough – the older men fell silent and looked into his face with the realisation that behind his simple talk and quiet manner lay an inward vision of grim and awful realities that no words could picture.

I think that they were glad when we joined the ladies again and when Tom talked of the amateur vaudeville show that his company had got up behind the trenches.

Later on, when the other guests were telephoning for their motors and calling up taxis, Tom said he'd walk to his hotel; it was only a mile and the light rain that was falling would do him, he said, no harm at all. So he trudged off, refusing a lift.

Oh, no, I don't think we need to worry about the returned soldier. Only let him return, that's all. When he does, he's a better man than we are, Gunga Dinn.

That Exploit of Yours
Ford Madox Ford

I meet with two soldiers sometimes here in Hell.
The one, with a tear on the seat of his red pantaloons
Was stuck by a pitchfork,
Climbing a wall to steal apples.

The second has a seeming silver helmet,
Having died from a fall from his horse on some tram-lines
In Dortmund.

These two,
Meeting in the vaulted and vaporous caverns of Hell
Exclaim always in identical tones:
'I at least have done my duty to Society and the Fatherland!'
It is strange how the cliché prevails...
For I will bet my hat that you who sent me here to Hell
Are saying the selfsame words at this very moment
Concerning that exploit of yours.

The Peace Conference
From *An Onlooker in France*, Sir William Orpen

I now got a reminder that I was due in Paris to paint the Peace Conference. The whole thing had gone from my mind. I afterwards found the letter, which I apparently had received and read, dated December, telling me to go to Paris, but I was so sick I did not realise what it was about. I realised now right enough, so I packed my bag and breezed away to Paris, and found that great family gathering, the Peace Conference, and the life of the 'Astoria' and the 'Majestic' commenced for me.

For the most part, my life consisted now of painting portraits at the Astoria, or attending the Conference at the Quai d'Orsay. During these I did little drawings of the delegates. For a seat I was usually perched up on a window-sill. It was very amusing to sit there and listen to Clemenceau – 'Le Tigre' – putting the fear of death into the delegates of the smaller nations if they talked too long. Apparently, the smaller the nation he represented, the more the delegate felt it incumbent on himself to talk, but after a while, Clemenceau, with the grey gloves whirling about, would shout him down.

President Wilson occasionally rose and spoke of love and forgiveness. Lloyd George just went on working, his secretaries constantly rushing up to him, whispering and departing, only to return for more whispers. Mr Balfour, whose personality made all the other delegates look common, would quietly sleep. The Marquis Siongi was the only other man who could hold his own at all with Mr Balfour in dignity of appearance.

As a whole there was just a little mass of black frock-coated figures – 'frocks' as we called them – sitting and moving about under the vast decoration of Le Salon de l'Horloge. Some of the little people seemed excited, but for the most part they looked profoundly bored, yet they were changing the face of the map, slices were being cut off one country and dumped on to another. It was all very wonderful, but I admit that all these little 'frocks' seemed to me very small personalities, in comparison with the fighting men I had come in contact with during the war.

They appeared to think so much – too much – of their own personal importance, searching all the time for popularity, each little one for himself – strange little things. President Wilson made a great hit in the Press with his smile. He was pleased at that, and after this he never failed to let you see all his back teeth. Lloyd George grew hair down his back, I presume from Mr Asquith's lead. Paderewski – well, he was always a made-up job. In short, from my window-seat it was easy to see how self-important the majority of all these little black 'frocks' thought themselves. It was all like an *opéra bouffe*, after the people I had seen, known and painted during the war; and these, as the days went by, seemed to be gradually becoming more and more forgotten. It seemed impossible, but it was true. The fighting man, alive, and those who fought and died – all the people who made the Peace Conference possible, were being forgotten, the 'frocks' reigned supreme. One was almost forced to think that the 'frocks' won the war. 'I did this,' 'I did that,' they all screamed, but the silent soldier man never said a word, yet he must have thought a lot.

I remember when the Peace Terms were handed to the Germans at the Trianon Palace, I tried my hardest to get a card to enable me to see it, but failed. This may not seem strange, but it really was, considering that about half the people who were present were there out of curiosity alone. They were just friends of the 'frocks.' This ceremony took place at 2.30 p.m. on that particular day. I happened to leave my room and go into the hall of the Astoria for something about 3 p.m. There I met Field-Marshal Sir Henry Wilson. I said: 'How did you get back so soon, sir?' He said: 'Back from where?' I said: 'From the handing over of the Peace Terms.' 'Oh,' he said, 'I haven't been there. They wouldn't give me a pass, the little 'frocks' wouldn't give me one.' 'I've been trying for days, sir,' I said. 'They expect me to paint them, but they won't let me see them.' 'Look here, little man,' he said. 'I've been thinking as I was walking back here, and I'll give you a little piece of advice: "Laugh at those who cry, and cry at those who laugh." Just go back to your little room and think that over and you will feel better.'

When I painted Sir Henry, he gave me his views on the brains and merits of many of the delegates, views full of wit and brilliant criticism, but when I had finished painting him I came under his kindly lash. He called me 'a nasty little wasp,' and he kept a 'black book' for any of his lady friends who said the sketch was like him. In it their names were inscribed, and they were never to be spoken to again. With all his fun, Sir Henry was a deep thinker, and towered over the majority of the 'frocks' by his personality, big outlook and clear vision.

General Botha was big, large and great in body and brain – elephantine! Everything on an immense scale, even to his sense of humour. He had no sign of pose, like most of the 'frocks.' He never seemed to try to impress anyone. One could notice no change in his method or mode of conversation according to whom he was speaking. The great mind just went on and uttered what it thought, regardless of whom it uttered it to. In Mrs Botha he had the ideal wife. Together they were like two school-children. 'Louis' and 'Mother,' how well they knew each other, and how they loved their family and home! They were always talking of 'home' and longing to get back to it. Alas! Louis only got back there for a very short time, and now 'home' will never be the same for 'Mother.'

What arguments they used to have – fierce arguments which always ended the same way! 'Louis' would make some remark which would absolutely pulverise 'Mother's' side of the question, and as she was stammering to reply, he would say very gently: 'It's all right, Mother, it's all right, you've won.' And she would flash out with: 'Don't you dare to say that to me, Louis! You always say that when you get the best of the argument.'

She used to complain to me how terrible the General's love for bridge was, and how she used to be kept up so late. He would laugh and say: 'But, Mother, you didn't get up till nine this morning. I was walking in the Bois at half-past six.'

I remember one afternoon they came to my room and Mrs Botha said: 'Well, Louis, what kind of a morning had you?' He replied: 'Not very good, Mother, not very good. You see, Mother, Clemenceau got very irritated with President Wilson, and Lloyd George the same with Orlando. No, it wasn't a very pleasant morning. Nearly everyone was irritable.'

Then 'Mother' said: 'I think it disgusting, Louis, that these men, settling the peace of the world, should allow their own little petty irritabilities to interfere with the great work.' And Botha replied: 'Ah! Mother, you must make allowances. Men are only human.' 'I don't make allowances,' jerked in 'Mother,' 'I think it's disgusting.' 'Don't say that, Mother,' he replied. 'I remember one time, long ago, when we made our little peace, you used to get very irritable at times, and I had to make a lot of allowances for you. You must try and make the same for these poor people now.' 'Mother' never even replied to this, but jumped from her chair and left the room, and the big man's face broadened into a smile. Yes, Botha was big – a giant among men.

I wrote and asked President Wilson to sit, and got a reply saying that as his time was fully occupied with the Peace Conference work, he regretted that he was unable to give any sittings.

I also wrote to Mr Lansing and Colonel House, asking them. The Colonel rang up the same afternoon and said, 'Certainly,' would I name my day and hour? Which I did; and along he came, a charming man, very calm, very sure of himself, yet modest. During the sitting he asked me if I had painted the President. I replied: 'No.' He then asked me if I was going to do so, and I replied: 'No,' that the President had refused to sit. He said: 'Refused?' I said: 'Yes; he hasn't got the time.' 'What damned rot!' said the Colonel, 'he's got a damned sight more time than I have. What day would you like him to come to sit?' I named a day, and the Colonel said: 'Right! I'll see that he's here,' and he did. Mr Lansing was also very good about giving sittings, and we had a good time, as he loves paintings, and knows all the art galleries in Europe. He also paints himself in his spare time, and all through the Conference at the Quai d'Orsay he drew caricatures of the different delegates. President Wilson told me he had a large collection of these.

The Emir Feisul sat. He had a nice, calm, thoughtful face. Of course, his make-up in garments made one think of Ruth, or, rather, Boaz. He could not let me work for one minute without coming round to see what I was doing. This made the sittings a bit jerky. I was going to paint another portrait of him for his home, but we never hit off times when we were both free.

I asked Mr Balfour to sit, and he asked me to lunch to arrange it. I remember he came to my room about 12.15 p.m. He was sound asleep by 12.35 p.m., but woke up sharp at 1p.m., and left for lunch. What a head! It put all other heads out of the running. So refined, so calm, so strong, a fitting head for such a great personality.

Dr E. J. Dillon very kindly asked me to dinner to meet Venezelos, and he arranged for him to sit, which he did at the Mercèdes Hotel. He had a beautiful head, with far-seeing blue eyes, which had a distinctly Jewish look. It was difficult to paint him, as he had no idea of sitting at all. It was a pity, as he had a wonderful head to paint. His flesh was fresh and rosy like a young boy's.

Da Costa, of Portugal, came along: a bright little man, full of health and energy; and after him that quiet, thoughtful friendly person, Sir Robert Borden, of Canada; even then he looked rather tired and overworked.

The day arrived when President Wilson was to sit. He was to come at 2 p.m., so I went back to the Astoria about 1.30 p.m. When I got to the door I found a large strange man ordering all the English motors to go one hundred yards down the Rue Vernet. No British car was allowed to stop closer. When I entered the Astoria, one of the Security Officers told me that an American detective had been inquiring the direct route the President was to take to my room. I went on into another little room I had, where I kept my paints and things; and there I found two large men sitting in the only two chairs. They took no notice of me, and were quite silent, so I proceeded to get ready. Taking off my belt and tunic, and putting on my painting coat, I started to squeeze out colours, when suddenly in marched an enormous man.

He looked all round the room and said in a deep voice: 'Is Sir William Orpen here?' 'Yes, I'm here,' I said. He walked up to me and, towering over me, looked down and said in grave doubt: 'Are you Sir William Orpen?' 'Yep,' I replied, in my best American accent. 'Well,' he said, 'be pleased to dress yourself and proceed to the door and prepare to receive the President of the United States of America.' That finished me – I had been worked up to desperate action. So I looked up as fully as I could in his face, and uttered one short, thoroughly English word, but one which has a lot to it. Immediately the two large men and the enormous one left the room in utter silence.

Shortly afterwards the President arrived, smiling as usual; but he was a good sort, and he laughed hard when I told him the story of the detectives. He was very genial and sat well, but even then he was very nervous and twitchy. He told endless stories, mostly harmless, and some witty. I only remember one. A king was informed that all the men in his State were obeying their wives; so he ordered them all before him on a certain day and spoke to them, saying he had heard the fact about their obeying their wives, and he wished to ascertain if it was so. So he commanded, 'All men who obey their wives go to my left!'

They all went to his left except one miserable little man, who remained where he was, alone. The king turned, and said to him: 'Are you the only man in my State who does not obey his wife?' 'No, sire,' said the little man, 'I obey my wife, sire.' 'Then why do you not go to my left as I commanded?' 'Because, sire,' said the little man, 'my wife told me always to avoid a crush.' It's a mild story, but it's the only one I remember. The only other thing I recollect about President Wilson is that he had a great admiration for Lord Robert Cecil.

George Adam gave a great dinner one night out at some little country place near Paris. Mr Massey, of New Zealand, and Admiral Heaton Ellis were the two chief people present. Massey was a most pleasant big man, with kind, blue eyes – a simple, honest, straightforward person, large in body and big enough in brain to laugh at himself. He made me feel I was back painting the honest people in the war. He had none of the affectations of the 'frocks.'

I painted the Marquis Siongi in his flat in the Rue Bassano. There one worked in the calm of the East. People entered the room, people left, but I never heard a sound. The Marquis sat – never for one second did his expression give an inkling of what his brain was thinking about. He never moved; his eyelids never fluttered, and beside me all the time I worked, curled up on a sofa, was his daughter – surely one of the most beautiful women I have ever seen, soft and gentle, with her lovely little white feet. I loved it all. When I left that flat I could not help feeling I was going downstairs to a lower and more common world, a world where passions and desires were thrust upon one's eyes and ears, leaving no room for imagination or wonder. I never pass down the Rue Bassano now that I do not think of the Marquis and those lovely little white feet, the gentle manners and the calm of the East which pervaded those apartments.

General Smuts sat, a strong personality with great love for his own country, and a fearless blue eye. I would not like to be up against him, yet in certain ways he was a dreamer and poet in thought. He loved the people and hated the 'frocks.' He and I had a great night once at the servants' dance down in the ballroom of the Majestic. I found him down there during the evening, and he said: 'You've got sense, Orpen. There is life down here, but upstairs it's just death.

Waste
G. A. Studdert Kennedy

Waste of Muscle, waste of Brain,
Waste of Patience, waste of Pain
Waste of Manhood, waste of Health
Waste of Beauty, waste of Wealth
Waste of Blood, and waste of Tears
Waste of Youth's most precious years,
Waste of ways the Saints have trod,
Waste of Glory, waste of God – War!

The Signing of the Peace
From *An Onlooker in France*, Sir William Orpen

The great day of the signing of the Peace was drawing near, and I worked hard to get the centre window in the Hall of Mirrors reserved for the artists. In the end, the French authorities sanctioned this. They also promised to do a lot more things which would have made the ceremony much more imposing, but these they did not do. It is a strange thought, but surely true, that the French as a nation seem to take, at present, little interest in pomp and ceremony. The meetings of the delegates at the Quai d'Orsay, the handing over of the Peace Terms to our late enemies, were all rather rough-and-tumble affairs, and, in the end, the great signing of the Treaty had not as much dignity as a sale at Christie's. How different must the performance have been in 1870! One man, at least, was there who knew the difference – Lord Dunraven, who attended both ceremonies.

I drove out in the morning to Versailles with George Mair and Adam, and we all had lunch at the Hôtel des Reservoirs. When we started to go to the Palace I found they had yellow Press tickets, by which they were admitted by the side gate nearest the hotel; but I had a white ticket, and had to enter by the main front gate. When I went round towards this gate I found that all the way down the square, and further along the road as far as the eye could see, the route was lined with people, about one hundred deep, with two rows of French cavalry in front. These people had all taken their places, and they would not let me through. I thought for sure I was going to miss the show, and the sweat of nerves broke out on me. By great luck I met a French Captain, to whom I, in my very broken French, explained my plight. He was most kind, took my card, made a way through the crowd, explained and showed my card to the military horsemen, and I was let through. Then the sweat began to run. I found myself about three-quarters of a mile away from the entrance to the Palace, all by myself in this human-sided avenue – thousands of people staring at me. I expected every minute to be arrested. Naturally, no one else entered on foot. They all drove up in their cars. Guards at the gates scanned my dripping face, but not a word was uttered to me, no pass was asked for – nothing!

The marble staircase was most imposing, lined on each side by Municipal Guards, but the Hall of Mirrors was pandemonium, a mass of little humans, all trying to get to different places. In the end I got to the centre window. It was empty. I was the first artist to arrive, and very satisfied I was to have got there safely. Suddenly, up walked a French Colonel, who told me to get out. I showed him my card and told him this was the window reserved for artists. He explained that this had been changed, and that the next window was reserved for them, and led me off there. There I found all the French and American artists huddled together. As soon as the Colonel left, I crept back to the centre window. I was turned back again. This creeping to the centre window and being turned back continued till I spoke to M. Arnavon, who advised me to stop in the artists' window till just before the show started, and then to go to the middle window. Just before the beginning there was great excitement. A stream of secretaries came up the Hall, two carrying chairs, and with them two grubby-looking old men. The chairs were placed in the centre window, and the old chaps sat themselves down. They were country friends of Clemenceau's, and he had said that morning that they were to have the centre window, and that artists could go to – somewhere else. When the proceedings commenced I slipped in behind their chairs, and, except for a glare from 'Le Tigre,' I was left in peace.

Clemenceau rose and said a few words expressing a desire that the Germans would come forward and sign. Even while he was saying these few words the whole hall was in movement – nothing but little black figures rushing about and crushing each other. Then, amidst a mass of secretaries from the French Foreign Office, the two Germans, Hermann Müller and Doctor Bell, came nervously forward, signed, and were led back to their places. Some guns went off on the terrace – the windows rattled. Everyone looked rather nervous for a moment, and the show was over, except for the signatures of the

Allies. These were written without any dignity. People talked and cracked jokes to each other across tables. Lloyd George found a friend on his way up to sign his name, and as he had a story to tell him, the whole show was held up for a bit, but after all, it may have been a good story. All the 'frocks' did all their tricks to perfection. President Wilson showed his back teeth; Lloyd George waved his Asquithian mane; Clemenceau whirled his grey-gloved hands about like windmills; Lansing drew his pictures and Mr Balfour slept. It was all over. The 'frocks' had won the war. The 'frocks' had signed the Peace! The Army was forgotten. Some dead and forgotten, others maimed and forgotten, others alive and well – but equally forgotten. Yet the sun shone outside my window and the fountains played, and the German Army – what was left of it – was a long, long way from Paris.

The next great show was the triumphal march through the Arc de Triomphe. It was fine! But it must be admitted that the Americans scored. They had picked men trained for months for this march, and along they came in close formation, wearing steel helmets. It was a fine sight!

But there were great moments when Foch passed, and when Haig passed at the head of his men, and the roars that came from the Astoria must have been heard a long way off. The Astoria was the hotel reserved by the Kaiser for his friends to witness his triumphal entry into Paris, so we had a good view. He chose well.

I remember during the war, when a 'frock' visited some fighting zone, he was always very well looked after and entertained by whatever H.Q. he visited, and I was amazed on this day to find Field-Marshal Lord Haig and General Sir John Davidson lunching alone at the Majestic. Lord Allenby was also lunching at another table and General Robertson at another. To me it was ununderstandable. These representatives of the dead and the living of the British Army, on the day of its glory, being allowed to lunch alone, much as they might have wished it.

As far as I remember, Lord Derby gave a dinner in their honour that evening, but I am certain the 'frocks' did nothing. After all, why should they fuss themselves? The fighting was over. The Army was nothing – harmless! Why should they trouble about these men? Why upset themselves and their pleasures by remembering the little upturned hands on the duckboards, or the bodies lying in the water in the shell-holes, or the hell and bloody damnation of the four years and odd months of war, or the men and their commanders who pulled them through from a bloodier and worse damnation and set them up to dictate a peace for the world?

The war was over, the Germans were a long, long way from the coast or Paris. The whole thing was finished. Why worry now to honour the representatives of the dead, or the maimed, or the blind, or the living that remained? Why? In Heaven's name, why not?

I remember one day, during the Peace Conference in the Astoria, asking a great English General about the delegates and how things were getting on, and he said: 'I wish the little 'frocks' would leave it to us – those who fight know best how to make peace. We would not talk so much, but we would get things settled more quickly and better.' Surely that was the truth!

Elegy in a Country Churchyard
G. K. Chesterton

The men that worked for England
They have their graves at home:
And bees and birds of England
About the cross can roam.

But they that fought for England,
Following a falling star,
Alas, alas for England
They have their graves afar.

And they that rule in England,
In stately conclave met,
Alas, alas for England
They have no graves as yet.

Notes on Authors

The head of the War Propaganda Bureau asked twenty-five leading authors to form a secret group aimed at promoting British war interests. To disguise the Government involvement, they published relevant work through companies such as Hodder & Stoughton. Authors in this collection who were part of the group are marked with an asterisk*.

Anon. (*Diary of a Nursing Sister on the Western Front*)
The anonymous writer of this lively account of a nurse's work sailed to France from Dublin, so may have come from Ireland. She had previously had experience of nursing in South Africa. Medical services were essential, but doctors, nurses and other staff often had to work in difficult and dangerous conditions.

Anon. (Mesopotamian Alphabet, from *The B.E.F. Times*)
Of the many trench newspapers that appeared during the war, the best-known is *The Wipers Times*. However, the printing-press on which the paper was produced (found by soldiers of the Sherwood Foresters at Ypres) had to be moved every time the division changed location: each time the title of the paper changed. *The B.E.F. Times* was the last but one – two issues of *The Better Times* appeared at the end of the war. Contributions to the paper came from a variety of

sources – the 'Mesopotamian Alphabet' was an anonymous offering from someone in the Indian Army in the Middle East!

Anon. (Fighting Beyond Baghdad, from *With a Highland Regiment in Mesopotamia*)

The security-conscious author of this account mentions only 'the 2nd battalion' – but he gives the CO's name: A. G. Wauchope, and this means the regiment can be identified as The Black Watch. The men had been stationed in India, going to France with the India corps in 1914. At the end of 1915 they were sent to Mesopotamia, and the book was actually written there in 1917.

Aumonier, Stacy

For some reason, Stacy Aumonier's work is little known today, though he was much admired in his lifetime. His wit and his ear for dialogue are evident in his short stories, which writers such as John Galsworthy described as 'among the best ever written'. As well as writing, he performed his own sketches on stage. In the war, he served in the Army Pay Corps, then as a draughtsman in the Ministry of National Service.

Barbusse, Henri

Before the war, Henri Barbusse had been a neo-Symbolist poet and a neo-Naturalist novelist, but it was the book he wrote as a result of his service in the trenches that made him famous. *Le Feu* (published in English as *Under Fire*) won the Prix Goncourt, the most prestigious French literary award. Barbusse was a volunteer in 1914, and *Under Fire* shows in graphic detail the lives of the *poilus*, the ordinary soldiers, in the trenches. Some criticized the book for being too realistic! Like other writers who had experienced such horrors Barbusse became a pacifist.

Barrie, J. M.

The Princess Elizabeth Gift Book was published to raise funds for The Princess Elizabeth of York Hospital for Children, located at Banstead

Wood: it became an emergency Military Hospital in World War II, was later amalgamated with the Queen Elizabeth Hospital for Children, and closed in 1998. As was usual with fund-raising gift books, many well-known authors and artists contributed. J. M. Barrie – who knew the princess and her sister Margaret – produced a serious contribution, but entirely appropriate in view of the cause it was for.

Bedford, Madeline Ida

The supply of munitions in World War I was critical. The Shell Crisis of 1915 resulted in the Munitions of War Act of 1915: the production of munitions was to be tightly controlled by a new Ministry of Munitions. Many women – some working for the first time – were employed as men joined up: the conditions were dangerous and they were mostly paid less than half the wage of male workers, though the pay was far better than domestic service. By 1918, there were around a million women working in the industry. Madeline Ida Bedford – referred to only as 'a middle class woman' – published one book of poems, *The Young Captain*, in 1917.

Bennett, Arnold*

Before the war, Arnold Bennett had lived in France for eight years. Back in Britain, he spent the war years as Director of Propaganda for France at the Ministry of Information. Bennett had visited the Western Front, and was so horrified by what he saw he was ill for weeks. *Over There: War Scenes on the Western Front* was a pamphlet Bennett wrote to encourage men to enlist in the army: he tried hard not to let his own feelings appear in it.

Binyon, Laurence

Laurence Binyon was an academic and art historian who – before and after the war – worked at the British Museum. His most famous work, the poem 'For the Fallen' is regularly read at Remembrance Day and Anzac Day services in Britain, Canada, Australia and New Zealand. During the war he volunteered as a hospital orderly, working in France and in Britain.

Boelcke, Oswald

One of the greatest aviators of the First World War, Oswald Boelcke is often described as the father of aerial combat. He worked out many of the techniques and tactics used by fighter squadrons, and for his achievements he was awarded the highest German honour, the Pour le Mérite (the Blue Max). He chose Manfred von Richthofen for his squadron, and was his mentor. After the death in 1916 of Max Immelmann, another air ace, Boelcke was forced to take leave. He visited Eastern Europe and Turkey, including a trip to Gallipoli – perhaps a very early example of battlefield tourism. Boelcke died in October 1916 when his plane collided with another in his squadron during a dog-fight over the Somme. At the time of his death he had scored 40 'kills', the highest number yet achieved.

Bridges, Robert

Robert Bridges had originally been a doctor, but turned to writing, especially poetry, when illness prevented him from practising medicine. Appointed Poet Laureate in 1913, he had the challenging task of writing a tribute to Lord Kitchener. A military hero, Kitchener became Secretary of State for War on its outbreak in 1914. He organised the largest volunteer army the world had ever seen, and warned that the war could be a long one. His death in 1916, when a torpedo hit HMS *Hampshire*, the warship carrying him to talks in Russia, shocked the nation.

Buchan, John

Combining writing with work as a diplomat and for the government, John Buchan was asked by the War Propaganda Bureau to oversee a history of the war, to be published as a monthly magazine. He also worked in France as a war correspondent for *The Times*. Buchan eventually became head of the Department of Information, 'the toughest job I ever took on'. His pamphlet, *The Battle of the Somme*, did not give a realistic picture of what had actually happened. There were, for example, no figures for British losses, which were enormous.

Cable, Boyd

Boyd Cable was the pen name of Ernest Andrew Ewart, who was born in India and served in the Boer War before moving to Australia, where he led a wandering life. He worked as a journalist in the First World War, and wrote many short stories based on his experiences on the front line 'within sound of the German guns and for the most part within shell and rifle range'.

Campbell, R. W.

R. W. Campbell was a Scottish journalist who lived and worked in Australia and New Zealand before the war, coming to have a great respect and admiration for the people he met in those countries. He served in the war, achieving the rank of captain, and wrote books about it, including *Private Spud Tamson*, set on the Western Front, and *The Kangaroo Marines*, set in the Middle East, particularly the Gallipoli Campaign.

Cather, Willa

Willa Cather was acclaimed for her novels of frontier life, set on the Great Plains of the United States. *One of Ours* won the Pulitzer Prize in 1922. The hero, Claude Wheeler, feels very restricted by his life on a Nebraska farm. His wife has gone to China to look after her missionary sister, so when America joins the war he takes the opportunity to join up. Claude and his adventures are based on Willa Cather's cousin Grosvenor. She did not intend the book to be classed as a war story, and was unhappy that it was.

Chesterton, G. K.*

G. K. Chesterton was a writer, poet, dramatist, art critic and lay theologian. He objected to socialism and capitalism, preferring to stand up for the common man and common sense. This aspect of his work can be seen in the subtly vicious last verse of his poem 'Elegy in a Country Churchyard'.

Childers, Erskine

Erskine Childers wrote *The Riddle of the Sands* as a result of several sailing expeditions to the Frisian Islands and the Baltic coasts. At the time the book came out, public opinion was against spending money on armaments, but the story, which was enormously popular, helped change this: Churchill gave Childers credit for persuading the country to pay for defences against the naval threat from Germany.

Conan Doyle, Sir Arthur*

Sir Arthur Conan Doyle originally thought that Germany's militarism was just 'a sort of boyish exuberance on the part of a robust young nation which had a fancy to clank about the world in jackboots.' However, he read Freidrich von Bernhardi's book *Germany and the Next War*, which proposed ruthless aggression and disregard of treaties – and changed his mind. Eventually he was asked to help with propaganda for the British government. When the Italian Government asked for someone from Britain to go out and see what they were doing against the Austrians, Conan Doyle went, but on condition that he could see what the British and French were doing too.

Coulson, Leslie

A poet and journalist before the war, Leslie Coulson volunteered in 1914. He sailed for Malta on Christmas Eve, 1914, serving at Gallipoli and then on the Western Front. He never came home: Coulson was killed during the Somme Offensive in 1916.

Ford, Ford Madox*

Although over age, Ford Madox Ford volunteered in 1915, and was sent to France, which ended his association with the War Propaganda Bureau. He served in the transport division, not the trenches, and was gassed and shell-shocked during the battle of the Somme. Seeing the casualties and the incompetence of military leaders made him question his previous propaganda role. His experiences eventually formed the basis of his tetralogy *Parade's End*. Ford Madox Ford's long poem 'Antwerp' was described by T. S. Eliot as 'the only good poem I have met with on the subject of war'.

Foxcroft, Charles T.

Capt. Charles Foxcroft became the MP for Bath in October 1918, at a by-election caused by the death in action of the previous MP. *The Night Sister, and other poems*, was published in 1918. The reference to Agincourt alludes to a popular story of the day, in which the soldiers retreating from Mons had the supernatural help of ghostly soldiers from Agincourt. Although the author, Arthur Machen, repeatedly explained that the tale was an invention, the idea fired people's imaginations: eventually the ancient soldiers turned into the Angel of Mons – and an urban myth was born!

Flecker, James Elroy

When war broke out, James Elroy Flecker was already seriously ill with the tuberculosis from which he died. He told a friend in November 1914, 'I have exhausted myself writing heroic Great War poems.' He worked on 'The Burial in England' as long as he could, helped by his wife. James Elroy Flecker died aged 30 in the first week of January 1915.

Galsworthy, John*

John Galsworthy was forty-seven – too old to fight when the war broke out – but he worked in France at the Benevole Hospital for disabled soldiers, and allowed his English home to be used as a rest home for wounded British soldiers. As a writer, he was a progressive, interested in ideas of social justice, and this can be seen in many of his short stories with a war setting. He worked for the War Propaganda Bureau, but would not encourage people to hate the enemy.

Girling, T. A.

Theodore Girling served in the Canadian Army Vetinary Corps, dying on active service in 1919. His book *The Salient and Other Poems* was published in 1918. His poem, 'Dumb Horses', remembers the horses, mules and donkeys used extensively during the war. As well as providing mounts for the cavalry, they hauled heavy loads and could go where motor transport couldn't. They could cope with the physical conditions – in Mesopotamia, for example, motor transport simply didn't work on sand.

Graves, Dr Karl Armgaard

Dr Armgaard Graves – who may have been the Berlin-born Max Meincke – wrote a very entertaining account of his work as a spy for Germany. However embroidered his tale may be, he was certainly arrested for spying in the Glasgow shipyards, and was eventually 'turned', to work as a spy for Britain. He was only one of many spies working in the country before and during the war.

Hardy, Thomas*

Although well into his seventies when war broke out, novelist, short story writer and poet Thomas Hardy produced a number of poems using the war and patriotism as themes.

Holtby, Winifred

Winifred Holtby was for a short time a member of the Women's Army Auxilliary Corps (W.A.A.C.), but soon after she reached France the war ended. She was a writer and journalist, with a special interest in the place of women in society. *The Crowded Street* traces the lives of five women, starting before the war and ending after it: in this extract, just as the war breaks out Mrs Hammond, aware that her two daughters are doing nothing for the war effort, takes one to stay with an aunt and uncle. The incident described resulted in 137 deaths, and nearly 600 wounded.

Hornung, E. W.

E. W. Hornung – Sir Arthur Conan Doyle's brother-in-law – was famous for his stories about Raffles, a gentleman thief, and perhaps the first anti-hero. After E. W. Hornung's son and only child was killed at Ypres in 1915, he joined the Y.M.C.A., looking after soldiers on leave. Towards the end of 1917 he was accepted as a volunteer in France, where, amongst other activities, the Y.M.C.A. ran many canteens close to the front line, in which soldiers could get a cup of tea, relax, or buy small necessities such as matches or writing paper. As well as his canteen work, the Y.M.C.A. asked E. W. Hornung to set up a library for soldiers, near Arras.

Studdert Kennedy, G. A.

Geoffrey Studdert Kennedy was an Anglican clergyman who volunteered as an army chaplain at the outbreak of war. He worked in the trenches with ordinary soldiers, who were very appreciative of the cigarettes he gave them, and nicknamed him 'Woodbine Willie'. Studdert Kennedy won the Military Cross at Messines Ridge in 1917, after going into No Man's Land to help the wounded. He wrote several books of poetry based on his war experiences – and after the Armistiice he became a vocal pacifist.

Kipling, Rudyard*

Rudyard Kipling had warned the country about German ambition, and when war came he was asked to help with propaganda. He did so, but in private he was extremely critical of the way the war was being fought: he thought the huge death rate on the Western Front was because politicians had failed to learn the lessons of the Boer War. Kipling's son, John, who joined the Irish Guards, died at Loos, aged eighteen. Later, the Irish Guards asked him to write their regimental history. It is brilliant and original. Kipling said, 'This will be my great work, it is done with agony and bloody sweat.'

Lawrence, D. H.

Although he wasn't a conscientious objector, Lawrence scorned militarism and did not want to be involved in the war. His health was poor, so he escaped being called up – but the authorities were suspicious of his opinions, and of his German wife Frieda (she was

Manfred von Richthofen's cousin). When they lived in Cornwall they were harassed: they were frequently asked for their papers, their house was searched, they were accused of spying and of signalling to German submarines. This extract is part of two extraordinary chapters in his novel, *Kangaroo*, in which the character Rupert Somers relives Lawrence's wartime experiences.

Lawrence, T. E.

Known in his lifetime as 'Lawrence of Arabia' because of his exploits in the Middle East, T. E. Lawrence was a scholar and archaeologist before the war. When war broke out, he was posted to Intelligence as an expert on Arabia. Joining the forces of sheik Faisal al Husayn in 1916, he led a successful guerrilla campaign against the Turks, taking the port of Aqaba in 1917, and distracting the Turks from the British invasion of Palestine.

Lawson, Henry

Considered by many to be Australia's best short story writer, Lawson was also a highly-esteemed poet. H suffered from poverty, depression, and alcoholism, even having a spell in prison (for non-payment of child maintenance), but when he died in 1922 he was given a state funeral.

Leacock, Stephen

The Canadian academic and political scientist Stephen Leacock was also renowned for his humour – for some years he was the best-known humourist in the English-speaking world. He wrote several short stories with a war background. *The Boy Who Came Back* uses the fact that many who had been through the war didn't want to talk about it, while those who hadn't experienced it talked of nothing else.

Levey, Sivori

During the war Sivori Levey served as a lieutenant in the 13th West Yorkshire Regiment. He was a poet, dramatist, pianist and composer, with a number of popular songs to his credit. He arranged musical recitals and plays, and published commentaries on Shakespeare and Browning.

Lewis, R.

When war broke out, R. Lewis was second mate on a small boat sailing between St John's, Newfoundland, and various ports on the coast of Labrador. He joined the 94th Argyle and Sutherland Highlanders, part of the 25th Battalion. Reaching France via England, he became a Lewis gunner, and rose from private to lieutenant. Wounded at Arleux (just after Vimy Ridge, and part of the Battle of Arras), he was eventually shipped home to Canada.

Lindsay, Vachel

Vachel Lindsay liked to perform his poetry – he regarded himself as a modern version of a mediaeval troubadour, and acted, sang, chanted, whispered or shouted his work as appropriate. On several occasions he walked from city to city in America, trading recitations for food and lodgings. 'The Jazz Bird', written in 1918, celebrated the achievements of black Americans in the American army. 'I have the utmost respect for Jazz in the young people, and I feel that without it there would be no American armies in Europe today. I do not claim that the Jazz Bird is a poem. It is a humoresque, of course. But it is the Jazz in these youngsters that will win this war. It is the same thing that Yankee Doodle was in the days of Washington.'

Manning, Frederic

Australian by birth, Frederic Manning came to England as a young man. When the war broke out, he was a very minor figure in Edwardian literary society. Joining up in 1915, he failed officer training and fought in the trenches during the Battle of the Somme. Manning's publisher suggested he wrote something about his wartime experiences: *The Middle Part of Fortune*, which used the language of the ordinary soldiers, came out in 1929 as a limited edition. An expurgated edition for general circulation – *Her Privates*

We – made Manning's name. 'There are no English novels that came out of the Great War with a similar status.'

Mansfield, Katherine
New Zealand-born Katherine Mansfield started writing short stories at school. As a young woman, she moved to London, where she led a Bohemian life, making friends with writers such as D. H. Lawrence and Virginia Woolf. She continued writing, and also travelled in Europe, in fact living in southern France for part of the war. Several of her short stories have wartime settings.

McConnell, James R.
James McConnell had learned to fly as a student. In 1915, along with a number of other young Americans, he went to France to serve with the American Ambulance Corps – he won the Croix de Guerre for his bravery. He was convinced that America should be doing more in the war against Germany, and joined a group of American aviators in the Lafayette Escadrille, flying Nieuport biplanes. At first these men had to fly the planes with one hand, and fire machine guns with the other. They only got planes fitted with mounted machine guns after Verdun. McConnell died in aerial combat over the Somme in March 1917.

Mercier, Cardinal Désiré
Cardinal Désiré Mercier, Archbishop of Malines (Mechelin) was a teacher, theologian and scholar. An expert on St. Thomas Aquinas, he was also a student of philosophy, psychology and metaphysics. Following the German invasion, King Albert and his government had to leave Belgium, and this somewhat unlikely character became the leader of the Belgian resistance. He published a series of open letters – read by the Allies and neutral countries, as well as by the Belgians – in which with passion he rallied the people and set out the horrors Belgians had to endure. He was well known, and very popular amongst German Catholics, so the military authorities did not dare to do more to him than keep

him under house arrest. He managed to stop the deportations of Belgian labourers to work in Germany.

Mitchell, Colin

Colin Mitchell volunteered for the army, and was sent to France. He was killed on 22 March 1918, during the German spring assault. His body was never found.

Montgomery, L. M.

L. M. Montgomery's novel *Anne of Green Gables* was an instant success when it was published in 1908, and over the years she wrote further novels about the character and her family. *Rilla of Ingleside* tells what happens to Anne, her family and their community during the First World War, in which Rilla's three brothers, and many friends, go off with the Canadian Expeditionary Force. It is darker in tone than the other 'Anne' books, and is the only contemporary Canadian novel about the First World War written by a woman.

Newbolt, Sir Henry*

As a poet, Sir Henry Newbolt wrote of war in terms of sportsmanship – a view held by many at the outset of the conflict. When it became apparent that this war was not a game, his poems fell out of favour in Britain. Newbolt – also a novelist, dramatist and lawyer – was appointed controller of telecommunications at the Foreign Office during the war. He also wrote two official naval histories.

Orpen, Sir Willliam

The Irish painter William Orpen was one of several artists recruited in 1917 by the War Propaganda Bureau to paint pictures of the Western Front. He spent four years doing this – his work carried on to include the peace negotiations – and his sketches and paintings are a vivid and haunting record of life in and out of the trenches. He admired the ordinary soldiers enormously, and detested the 'frocks', the politicians he felt had betrayed the soldiers. He was outspoken and controversial: perhaps the best of all the war artists. He left almost all the work he did at this time to the nation.

Owen, Wilfred

Wilfred Owen came from a very modest background, and although intellectually gifted, he struggled to get the university education he wanted because of the cost. He was working in France when war broke out, and thought of joining the French army. In fact he enlisted with the Artists' Rifles Officers' Training Corps, achieving a commission, which he would not have had in the peacetime army. His poetry exposed the squalor and horror of the trenches and the use of gas, shocking readers who still thought war might be glamorous. He was shot and killed a few days before the Armistice. The news reached his home on Armistice Day.

Rosenberg, Isaac

The son of a Jewish couple who had migrated from Lithuania, Isaac Rosenberg was brought up in the East End of London. He trained as an artist, writing poetry as well. Although he hated the idea of war and killing, he joined up in October 1915, because he found his mother would get an allowance if he did. He continued to write poems in the trenches, using any scraps of paper that he could find. Rosenberg was killed in April 1918, but his remains, together with ten other soldiers from his regiment, were not found until 1926. They could not be individually identified, so all eleven were buried together. He is regarded as one of the greatest of the war poets.

Reed, John

John Reed was an American journalist, who made his name as a war correspondent when he reported on the Mexican Revolution. He travelled to Eastern Europe in 1915 with the Canadian artist Boardman Robinson (they were arrested on more than one occasion as suspect spies), journeying through Greece, Serbia, Roumania, Bulgaria, Russia and Turkey. What he saw in his travels made him wholly opposed to war, and he became a pacifist. Serbia was attacked by Austria after a Serbian student, Gavrilo Princip, assassinated the Archduke Franz Ferdinand of Austria. Many take this as the trigger that started the war.

Saki (H. H. Munro)

Saki (the pen name of Hector Hugh Munro) saw that Germany was a danger to Britain: his warning was in the form of a novel set in a future in which Germany had successfully invaded the country. Saki looked at the way this affected various groups with the wit and satire that marked his short stories. He loved natural history – in many cases he felt animals were superior to humans – and his article about birds, published in the *Westminster Gazette*, was the last thing he wrote. Saki was over age but joined up as an ordinary soldier, although he could have had a commission.

Thomas, Edward

Edward Thomas worked as a biographer and critic until the outbreak of war. It was at that point he turned to writing poetry. He enlisted in1915, and produced 140 poems in the two years until his death in 1917. His work combines his intense love of the British countryside with his military experiences.

von Richthofen, Manfred

Manfred von Richthofen was the most famous of all the fighter pilots of World War I, not least because he scored the highest number of 'kills' (80). Wounded in 1917, he wrote his memoires, *Der Rote Kampfflieger*, while he recuperated. The account was heavily edited for German propaganda purposes. Later, he said the book was 'too arrogant' and that he was 'no longer that kind of person'. He was shot down over the Somme in 1918.

Wharton, Edith

Edith Wharton was a highly-esteemed American novelist, who won the Pulitzer Prize and was nominated three times for the Nobel Prize for Literature. In 1911, she moved to France to live. When war broke out, she was one of the few foreigners allowed to visit the front line, and throughout the war she worked hard for many charitable causes, including helping refugees. She was awarded the Legion of Honour in 1916.